CENSUS OF INDIA 1911

Census of India 1871-1951, 9 Sets In 384 Bindings (9788121258876) Rs. 700000

Census of India 1911, 23 Vols. In 41 Bindings (9788121271271) Rs. 69000

1. India - Report (9788121275071) Rs. 2475 (Vol. I, Pt. 1)
2. India - Tables (9788121275057) Rs. 2225 (Vol. I, Pt. 2)
3. Andaman and Nicobar Islands - Report & Tables (9788121275033) Rs. 900 (Vol. II, Pt. 1 & 2)
4. Assam - Report (9788121275019) Rs. 1000 (Vol. III, Pt. 1)
5. Assam - Tables (9788121274999) Rs. 1300 (Vol. III, Pt. 2)
6. Baluchistan - Report & Tables (9788121274975) Rs. 950 (Vol. IV, Pt. 1 & 2)
7. Bengal, Bihar And Orissa And Sikkim - Report (9788121274951) Rs. 3100 (Vol. V, Pt. 1)
8. Bengal - Tables (9788121274937) Rs. 2250 (Vol. V, Pt. 2)
9. Bihar And Orissa - Tables and Bengal And Sikkim - Chapter I of Administrative Volume (9788121274913) Rs. 1800 (Vol. V, Pt. 3 & 4)
10. City of Calcutta - Report and Tables and Administrative (9788121274876) Rs. 1300 (Vol. VI, Pt. 1 & 2 & 3)
11. Bombay - Report (9788121274814) Rs. 1950 (Vol. VII, Pt. 1)
12. Bombay - Imperial Tables and Administrative Report (9788121274791) Rs. 3300 (Vol. VII, Pt. 2 & 3)
13. Bombay (Town And Island) - Report And Tables (9788121274753) Rs. 1250 (Vol. VIII, Pt. 1 & 2)
14. Burma - Report (9788121274739) Rs. 2250 (Vol. IX, Pt. 1)
15. Burma - Tables (9788121274715) Rs. 1480 (Vol. IX, Pt. 2)
16. Central Provinces And Berar - Report (9788121274692) Rs. 1475 (Vol. X, Pt. 1)
17. Central Provinces And Berar - Tables (9788121274678) Rs. 1900 (Vol. X, Pt. 2)
18. Coorg - Report And Tables Madras - Report (9788121274630) Rs. 1740 (Vol. XI & Vol. XII, Pt. 1)
19. Madras - Imperial And Provincial Tables (9788121274616) Rs. 1500 (Vol. XII, Pt. 2)
20. Madras - Administrative Report and city of Madras (9788121274593) Rs. 630 (Vol. XII, Pt. 3 & 4)
21. North - West Frontier Province - Report & Tables (9788121274579) Rs. 2150 (Vol. XIII, Pt. 1 & 2)
22. Punjab - Report (9788121274555) Rs. 3000 (Vol. XIV, Pt. 1)
23. Punjab - Tables (9788121274531) Rs. 2200 (Vol. XIV, Pt. 2)
24. Punjab - Appendices To The - Imperial Tables (9788121274517) Rs. 950 (Vol. XIV, Pt. 3)
25. United Provinces of Agra And Oudh - Report (9788121274494) Rs. 2225 (Vol. XV, Pt. 1)
26. United Provinces of Agra And Oudh - Tables (9788121274470) Rs. 4000 (Vol. XV, Pt. 2)
27. United Provinces of Agra And Oudh - Provincial Tables And Appendices (9788121274456) Rs. 570 (Vol. XV, Pt. 3)
28. Baroda - Report (9788121274432) Rs. 2000 (Vol. XVI, Pt. 1)
29. Baroda State - The Imperial Tables (9788121274418) Rs. 850 (Vol. XVI, Pt. 2)
30. Central India Agency - Report And Tables (9788121274395) Rs. 1470 (Vol. XVII)
31. Cochin - Report And Imperial Tables (9788121274371) Rs. 1150 (Vol. XVIII, Pt. 1 & 2)
32. Hyderabad State - Report (9788121274357) Rs. 890 (Vol. XIX, Pt. 1)
33. Hyderabad State - Imperial And Provincial Tables (9788121274333) Rs. 1750 (Vol. XIX, Pt. 2)
34. Kashmir - Report (9788121274319) Rs. 950 (Vol. XX, Pt. 1)
35. Kashmir - Tables (9788121274296) Rs. 1170 (Vol. XX, Pt. 2)
36. Mysore - Report (9788121274272) Rs. 1200 (Vol. XXI, Pt. 1)
37. Mysore - Tables (9788121274258) Rs. 1500 (Vol. XXI, Pt. 2)
38. Rajputana And Ajmer-Merwara - Report (9788121274234) Rs. 1470 (Vol. XXII, Pt. 1)
39. Rajputana And Ajmer-Merwara - Tables (9788121274210) Rs. 1700 (Vol. XXII, Pt. 2)
40. Travancore - Report (9788121274197) Rs. 1870 (Vol. XXIII, Pt. 1)
41. Travancore - Imperial Tables (9788121274173) Rs. 870 (Vol. XXIII, Pt. 2)

Owing to the antiquity and rarity of this book, certain pages are regrettably absent, and readability is compromised due to the blurring of the original text. If you possess any insights regarding the availability of these missing sections, kindly inform us. Your assistance is crucial in ensuring the completion of this significant work for the benefit of future generations.

CENSUS OF INDIA, 1911

VOLUME - XIX

HYDERABAD STATE

PART I - REPORT

MAHOMED ABDUL MAJID

GYAN

Published by

GYAN

Gyan Publishing House
5, Ansari Road
Daryaganj, New Delhi-110002
Phone: 011-47034999, 9811692060
E-mail: books@gyanbooks.com

Distribution Network
gyanbooks.com
India, USA, Canada, UK, Australia

ISBN: 978-81-212-7127-1 (Set) 23 Vols. In 41 Bindings

ISBN: 978-81-212-7435-7 (PB) Vol. XIX, Pt. I

First Published, 1913

2nd Impression 2024

Printed at: Gyan Press, Delhi.

CENSUS OF INDIA 1911

CENSUS OF INDIA, 1911.

VOLUME XIX.

HYDERABAD STATE.

PART I.

REPORT.

MAHOMED ABDUL MAJID, H. C. S.,
CENSUS SUPERINTENDENT.

Bombay:
PRINTED AT THE TIMES PRESS.
1913.

PREFACE.

His Highness the Nizam's Government desire to preface this Report with an expression of their extreme regret at the recent death of Mr. Abdul Majid, Census Superintendent of the Hyderabad State. Mr. Abdul Majid was an officer of twenty years standing when he was appointed Superintendent. The actual enumeration was carried out entirely under his directions : the statistical tables were compiled under his supervision. It only remained to complete the present volume at the time of his death. His Highness' Government now wish to place on record their high appreciation of the unflagging industry, zeal and patience with which Mr. Abdul Majid performed his duties. His death has deprived the Service of an officer of the highest character and ability.

2. The material for the present volume was provided by Mr. Abdul Majid, and it was arranged in accordance with his wishes that the volume should be written in collaboration with Mr. K. Natarajan, Editor, the Indian Social Reformer, Bombay, whose services were temporarily engaged by Government for this purpose. Owing to Mr. Abdul Majid's death the volume has been completed by Mr. Natarajan alone, and the descriptive chapters are almost entirely the work of his pen. His Highness' Government take this opportunity of making a full acknowledgment of Mr. Natarajan's authorship and of expressing their high appreciation of his work.

R. I. R. GLANCY, I.C.S.,
Assistant Minister, Finance.

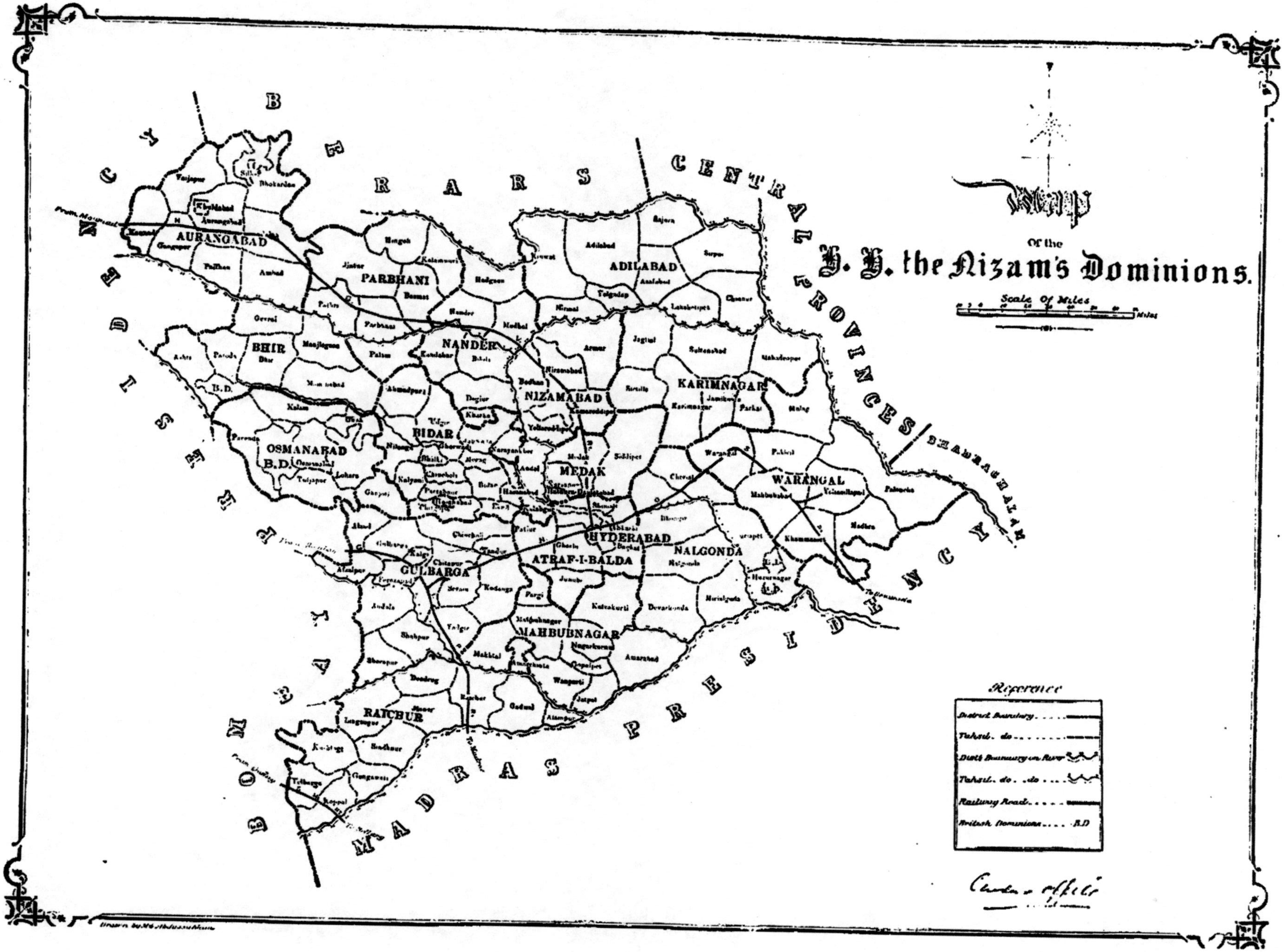

Map
of the
H. H. the Nizam's Dominions.
Scale of Miles
BERARS
CENTRAL PROVINCES
MADRAS PRESIDENCY
BOMBAY PRESIDENCY
AURANGABAD
PARBHANI
ADILABAD
BHIR
NANDER
NIZAMABAD
KARIMNAGAR
WARANGAL
OSMANABAD
B.D.
BIDAR
MEDAK
HYDERABAD
ATRAF-I-BALDA
NALGONDA
GULBARGA
MAHBUBNAGAR
RAICHUR
Reference
District Boundary
Tahsil. do
Distt Boundary on River
Tahsil. do. do
Railway Road
British Dominions .... B.D

REPORT

ON THE

CENSUS OF HIS HIGHNESS THE NIZAM'S DOMINIONS, 1911.

Chapter I.

DISTRIBUTION OF THE POPULATION.

1. The territories of His Highness the Nizam have remained unchanged both as regards their area and boundaries since the last Census. The description given of them in the Census Report for 1891, therefore, needs no modification. They lie between 15° 10′ and 21° 40′ North Latitude, and 74° 4′ and 81° 35′ East Longitude. They occupy a polygonal tract, 82,698 square miles in area, in the central portion of the table-land of the Deccan. They are bounded on the north by Khandesh (a district in the Bombay Presidency), the Berars and the Central Provinces; on the south by the rivers Tungabhadra and Krishna, which divide them from the Bellary, Kurnul and Krishna Districts of the Madras Presidency; on the east by the Wardha and the Godavari; and on the west by the Bombay Districts of Dharwar, Sholapur and Ahmednagar. The Deccan table-land is one of the twenty Natural Divisions into which, on the basis mainly of similarity of meteorological conditions, the Indian continent has been divided. It is one of the largest Natural Divisions from the point of area, covering 155,177 square miles, or 9·1 per cent. of the total area of the Indian Empire. Its mean annual rainfall was calculated to be 29·7 inches. The population of this area in 1901 was 23,441,579 representing 8 per cent. of the total population of India and a mean density of 151·1 persons per square mile. The Nizam's Dominions, occupying as they do 53·2 per cent. of the area of this table-land at its heart and centre, reproduce in an exaggerated form all that is typical of this great Natural Division. The total population of this State in 1901 was 11,141,142 or 47·5 of the population of the Deccan plateau. The density of population for the State was in the same year 134·72 per square mile as against 151·1 per square mile for the whole table-land. The normal annual rainfall for the State is between 30 and 32 inches, which is slightly higher than the mean annual average for the Deccan plateau. While the area has remained as at the previous Census, the population of the Nizam's Dominions has increased at the present Census to 13,374,676, raising the density to 162 persons per square mile. The corresponding figures for the Bombay and the Madras Deccan Districts are 172 and 145 per square mile respectively. The Nizam's Dominions enjoy an advantage over the Deccan Districts of Bombay and Madras, in that they are better endowed in respect of natural water facilities. The hill ranges which encompass the State are the watershed of the two great river systems, the Godavari and the Krishna, which

with their tributaries, the Purna and the Pranhita and the Manjra, and the Tungabhadra, the Bhima and the Musi, go to increase the productive capacity of the soil.

2. Principal events affecting the condition of the people during the decade.

The soils, the seasons and the climate of the State have been described in previous Census Reports. Information regarding the mineral and other natural resources, the principal industries, the irrigation works and roads and railways, has been brought up to a very recent date in the accounts of the Nizam's Dominions, its divisions, districts and towns in the recent Edition of the Imperial Gazetteer published in 1908. It is, therefore, only necessary here to allude briefly to events which have occurred during the decade bearing on the condition of the people. The opening of the Mahbubnagar Canal, so named after His Highness the late Nizam, in 1904, is such an event of the first importance. The canal takes off from the Manjra river, is 27 miles long, and is estimated to irrigate about 10,000 acres of land in the Medak District. Its total cost of construction was 13 lakhs of rupees. The reorganisation of the Irrigation Department and the increased attention paid to the repair and maintenance of existing works during the decade, are also administrative measures of great utility. During the period covered by the Census, the Barsi Light Railway was extended to Tadwala in 1906 and to Latur in 1911. The Purna-Hingoli line, though opened to traffic in the year after the Census, may also be mentioned here. The line, it is worthy of note, was built out of current revenue. A comprehensive scheme of railway extension has been adopted for execution in the next few years. The subject of roads has also engaged the serious attention of His Highness's Government. The coal mining and cotton mill industries in the State have shown marked progress. A Company has been working since 1901 with prospects of success for gold in the Raichur District. Schemes for the diffusion of general and technical education are under consideration.

3. Administrative Divisions.

For administrative purposes the State is divided into four divisions (Subahs) each under a Revenue Commissioner called "Subahdar." These are again sub-divided into districts each under a Magistrate and Collector called 1st Talukdar. Each district is composed of a number of minor sub-divisions called talukas or tahsils each under a Tahsildar. Two or three talukas are placed under a Sub-Divisional Officer called 2nd or 3rd Talukdar according to grade in the service. Including the Sarf-i-khas (Crown lands) district of Atraf-i-balda, which is under a Talukdar, subject to the direct control and supervision of the Sarf-i-khas Secretary, the total number of districts is 16. The average area of a district is 5,166 square miles, whilst the average population is 804,628. The largest district is Warangal with an area of 7,943 square miles and the smallest Atraf-i-balda with an area of 2,561 square miles. The district which has the largest population is Gulbarga with a population of 1,150,983 persons and Atraf-i-balda, with a population of 520,159 persons, is the least populous of any district.

A general reconstitution of divisions and districts was effected during the decade under review. The district of Lingsugar was abolished, its four Khalsa and three Jagir talukas being transferred to the Raichur District and two Khalsa talukas to the Gulbarga District. The small district of Sirpur-Tandur was raised to the standard of other districts by the addition of two talukas from the Nizamabad (Indur) District and two talukas from the Karimnagar (Elgandal) District. The district of Nalgonda was transferred from Warangal to Medak Division and the districts of Sirpur-Tandur and Bidar from Medak Division to Warangal and Gulbarga divisions respectively. The old districts of Sirpur-Tandur, Elgandal and Indur were renamed Adilabad, Karimnagar and Nizamabad. Several talukas were also transferred from one district to another. Eighteen talukas were abolished altogether and their villages distributed amongst the adjoining talukas. The accompanying map of the Nizam's Dominions shows the density of population in the several districts.

Map of Hyderabad showing density of population per square mile in the several districts.

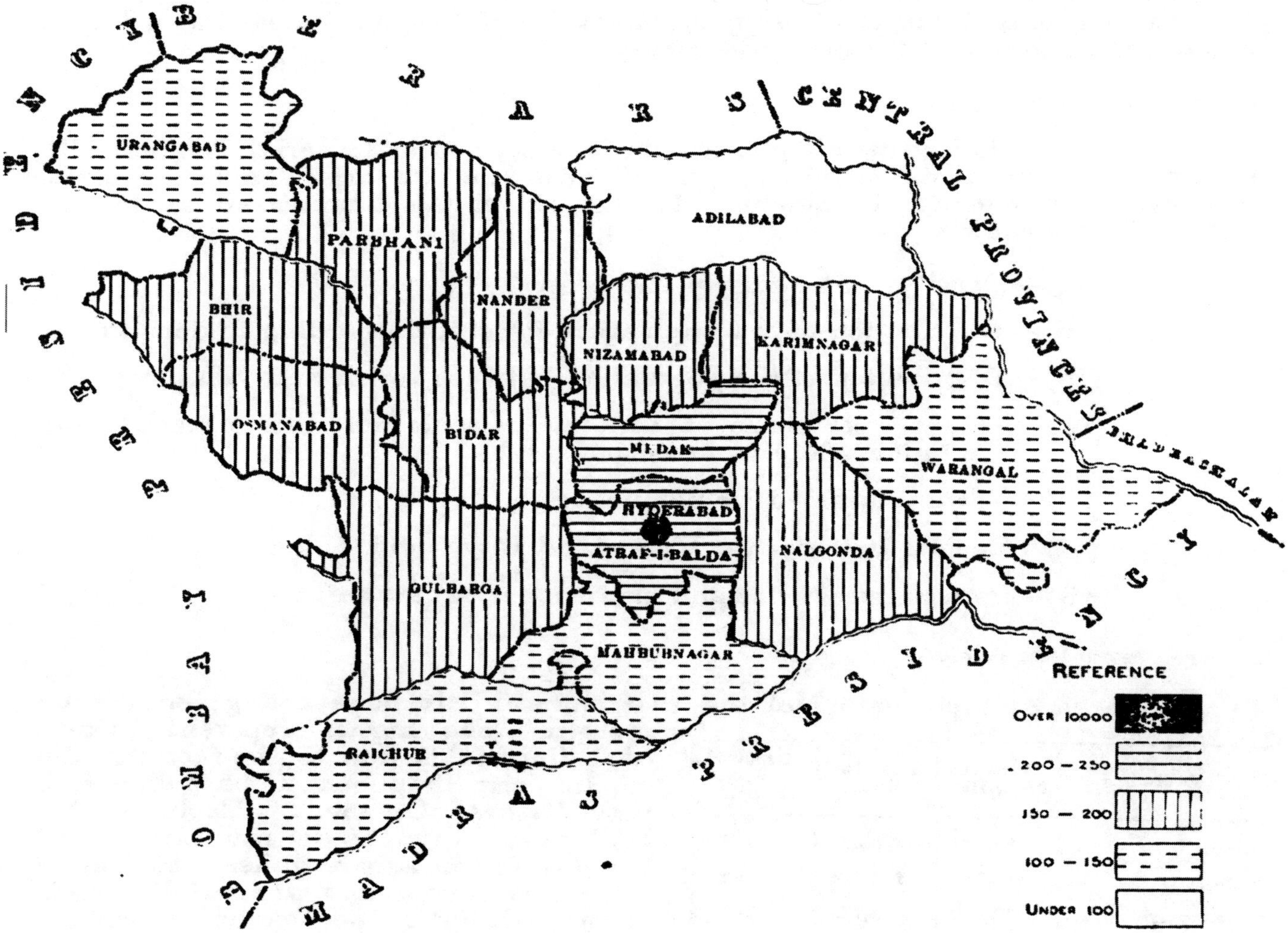

4. Natural Divisions.

While, in relation to those of the Indian continent, the geological and meteorological characters of the Deccan plateau are sufficiently uniform and distinctive to constitute it a single Natural Division, taken by itself they fall naturally into two groups dividing the area into two Natural Divisions. "The north-west portion, forming nearly half of the Natural Division, is covered with basaltic lava flows (Deccan trap); the remainder is composed of granites, gneisses and schists with a basin of paleozoic limestones, quartzites and igneous rocks in the Cuddapah area. The dry season extends from December to May. The rainfall of the wet season is chiefly due to the West Coast humid current from June to August, but occasionally in September and almost entirely in October and November it accompanies the course of storms coming up from the Bay of Bengal. The wet season is hence considerably longer than in the Konkan and usually lasts until the middle of November. As the rainfall in the large area of the West Deccan is less than 30 inches, the dry zone of the division is very liable to drought and famine." * These observations which relate to the Deccan plateau describe exactly the geological and meteorological differences between the western and eastern halves of the Nizam's Dominions. Further, "the

* Report of the Census of India, 1901, para. 27, p. 9.

trappean or black cotton soil country is a land of wheat and cotton; while Telingana or the granitic region is a land of rice and tanks." * These differences of physical nature are associated with social, economic and linguistic differences in the two Natural Divisions of the State, which are designated as Marathwara and Telingana, owing to Marathi and Telugu being the principal languages spoken in these two tracts respectively.

5. Statistical Tables.

The materials for this chapter are those contained in Imperial Tables I, III, IV and V. Provincial Table I, printed after the Imperial Tables, contains information in respect of Talukas. At the end of this Chapter are seven subsidiary Tables showing :—

(i)—Density, water supply and crops ;

(ii)—Distribution of the population classified according to density ;

(iii)—Distribution of the population between towns and villages ;

(iv)—Number per mille of the total population and of each main religion who live in towns ;

(v)—Towns classified by population ;

(vi)—Special statistics for Hyderabad City ; and

(vii)—Persons per house and houses per square mile.

6. Area and Population.

The area and population of the two Natural Divisions are given in the margin. The higher apparent density of Telingana is due to the fact that the capital city happens to be situated in that Natural Division. Exclusive of Hyderabad City, the density falls to 150 persons to the square mile. As Telingana has a mean annual rainfall, which is so essential in the Deccan, exceeding that of Marathwara, its lower density demands explanation. This is provided by the fact that Telingana contains the largest proportion of forest area in the State, no less than four out of its six Forest Divisions being situated in it. Of a total forest area of nearly 18,000 square miles, no less than 16,000 are in Telingana. If this forest area is thrown out of the calculation the mean density of the non-forest area of Telingana mounts up to 290 persons to the square mile. A more accurate comparison of the densities of the two Natural Divisions will be possible if we take only the cultivable area in each of the Divisions. Subsidiary Table 1 gives 50·5 and 69·5 as the percentages of cultivable area in Telingana and Marathwara respectively. The density for cultivable area worked out on this basis, is 322·7 persons per square mile for Telingana and 234·3 for Marathwara. If we take the cultivated area alone into consideration, the proportion will be much higher for Telingana, where only 38·8 per cent. of the total area, that is, about 12 per cent. less than the cultivable area, is cultivated, than for Marathwara where the cultivated area is 68·6 per cent. or nearly the whole of the cultivable area. The density then would be 420·1 and 234·7 per square mile in Telingana and Marathwara respectively. It is evident that, as between Telingana and Marathwara, it is not the extent or proportion of cultivated area, but the character of the cultivation, which determines their different densities. A map of Telingana is printed on the next page, showing the density of population by talukas.

Division.	Area in Sq. miles.	Population.	Density per Sq. mile.
State	82,698	13,374,676	162
Telingana ...	41,320	6,724,964	163
Marathwara ...	41,378	6,649,712	161

* Imperial Gazetteer, Vol. XIII, p. 227.

MAP OF TELINGANA.

Showing Density of Population per square mile in the several Talukas.

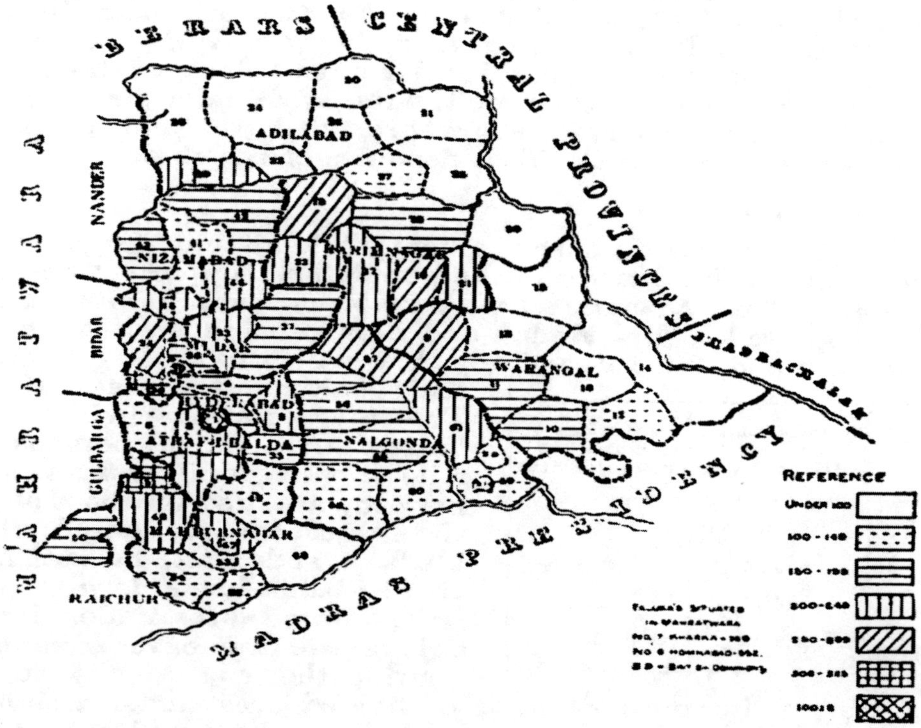

REFERENCE.

1. Hyderabad City
2. Sharki.
3. Gharbi.
4. Shumali.
5. Junubi.
6. Patlur
9. Warangal
10. Khammam
11. Mahbobabad.
12. Madhira.
13. Pakhal.
14. Paloancha.
15. Mulag.
16. Ellandapad.
17. Karimnagar.
18. Jagtial.
19. Jamiconta.
20. Mahadeopur.
21. Parkal.
22. Sersilla.
23. Sultanabad.
24. Adilabad.
25. Chinnur.
26. Asafabad.
27. Lukshatipet.
28. Kinwat.
29. Nirmal.
30. Rajura.
31. Sirpur.
32. Yelgadap.
33. Medak.
34. Andol.
35. Baghat
36. Kalabgur.
37. Siddipet.
38. Narsapur.
39. Hatnura.
40. Doulatabad.
41. Nizamabad.
42. Armur.
43. Bodhan.
44. Kamareddipet.
45. Yellareddipet.
46. Mahboobnagar.
47. Nagarkarnul.
48. Amrabad.
49. Kalvakurti.
50. Makhtal.
51. Pargi.
52. Jatpol.
53. Gopalpet.
54. Wanpart.
55. Nalgonda.
56. Bhongir.
57. Cherial.
58. Devarkonda.
59. Huzurnagar.
60. Miryalguda.
61. Suriapet.

7. Rice Cultivation and High Density.

Subsidiary table I gives the percentage of the cultivated area under rice, wheat, pulses, and "other crops" in each of the Natural Divisions and Districts. Telingana's percentage of cultivated area under every head except that of rice is less than Marathwara's. In respect of rice only, does Telingana exhibit a considerably higher percentage of cultivated area than Marathwara. It follows that, so far as the population of each of the Divisions is dependent on the agricultural industry, the higher density per cultivated area in Telingana is due to the more extensive cultivation of rice therein. This conclusion is borne out by the district figures. A glance at columns 2 and 7 of Sub-table I, shows that Adilabad has the lowest density in Telingana and the State, namely, 85 persons to the square mile, as well as the lowest percentage of cultivated area under rice, namely, 5·1 in Telingana. Its cultivated area, however, is but a small fraction, 22·1 per cent. of its total area, and the density of population calculated on that area is 384·6 per square mile. There are only two districts in Marathwara with higher densities per square mile of cultivated area, though all of them have larger percentages of their cultivated areas under every othor crop but rice. 5·1 per cent. of the cultivated area of Adilabad is under rice and it is the lowest percentage in Telingana ; the highest percentage of rice-land amongst Marathwara districts is much less, *viz.*, 2·3 in Gulbarga. Take Warangal which has the next lowest density, 114. It has 10·2 of its cultivated area under rice. It is, in fact, the fourth most considerable rice-growing district in these territories. But Warangal has one of the largest forest areas in the State and, if we have regard in our calculation to its cultivated area alone, the density jumps up to 347·5 per square mile, which, again, is exceeded only by two districts in Marathwara. Even among Marathwara districts where there is very little rice cultivation as compared with Telingana, the four highest densities belong to the districts which have the largest proportion of their cultivated area under rice. These facts go to confirm, what has been observed elsewhere, that the cultivation of rice is generally associated with relatively high densities of population.

8. Influence of Irrigation.

As amongst the rice districts, the extent of available irrigation determines to a considerable extent the density of the population supported per square mile of cultivated area. Thus, Nizamabad with 20·5 per cent. of its cultivated area under rice is superseded by Medak and Atraf-i-balda, whose corresponding percentages are 18·6 and 9·6 respectively, but which have larger proportions of their cultivated areas under irrigation. The four districts which support the largest number of persons per square mile of cultivated area, as shown in the margin, are also the districts which have the largest proportion of irrigated land. Medak stands first, notwithstanding that Atraf-i-balda has a larger proportion of its cultivated area under irrigation and enjoys the immense advantage of harbouring the capital city in its bosom, because, no doubt, of its proportion of cultivated area under rice being nearly double that of Atraf-i-balda. Medak has all her rice land under irrigation, and if Atraf-i-balda has more irrigated than rice land, it cannot affect Medak's superior capacity to support human life. Moreover, Atraf-i-balda is really water-logged and liable to malarial epidemics, which no doubt somewhat lowers its density. Irrigation yields its best effects when applied to rice cultivation. Atraf-i-balda has only a small proportion of its irrigated land under rice, while Nizamabad's percentage of irrigated area falls short of its area under rice. Karimnagar like Atraf-i-balda has a proportion of irrigated land exceeding that of its rice lands. We may conclude that, other things being equal, the proportion of the area under rice, taken along with the proportion of the area under irrigation, gives a good indication of the numerical strength of the population per cultivated square mile which a district in Telingana may be expected to support.

Districts.	Density per sq. mile of cultivated area	Percentage of irrigated to cultivated area
Medak	566·18	19·9
Atraf-i-balda... ...	550·13	27·2
Nizamabad	466·48	18·2
Karimnagar	456·02	16·5

The other four districts of Telingana present some puzzling features. Adilabad has the lowest percentage of its cultivated area under rice as also under irrigation in the whole of Telingana. Yet it comes first among these four districts in respect of the population which its cultivation supports. The only reason that can be thought of to account for the low place of Nalgonda and Mahbubnagar in our table notwithstanding that they have larger percentages of cultivated area under rice and under irrigation, is that they have the lowest rainfall, 26·4 and 26·1 inches respectively, of Telingana districts.

Districts.	Density per sq. mile of area.	Percentage of irrigated to cultivated area.
Adilabad	384·6	2·7
Warangal	347·5	12·9
Nalgonda	302·11	9·1
Mahbabnagar	298·96	10·3

The full theory of density in the Telingana districts may be stated now as follows : given a rainfall of not less than 30 inches per annum, the population which a given area can support is conditioned by the extent of it under rice and under irrigation.

9. Marathwara.

When we turn to Marathwara, we encounter a very different set of conditions. The subjoined map of Marathwara shows the density of population in its several talukas.

MAP OF MARATHWARA.

Showing Density of Population per square mile in the several Talukas.

REFERENCE.

1. Aurangabad.
2. Ambarh.
3. Bhokardan.
4. Gangapur.
5. Jalna.
6. Kannad.
7. Paithan.
8. Vaijapur.
9. Khuldabad.
10. Sillod.
11. Bhir.
12. Mominabad.
13. Ashti.
14. Gevrai.
15. Manjlegaon.
16. Patoda.
17. Nander.
18. Biloli.
19. Deglur.
20. Hadgaon.
21. Kandahar.
22. Mudhol.
23. Parbhani,
24. Basmat.
25. Hingoli.
26. Jintur.
27. Kalamnuri.
28. Pathri
29. Palam.
20. Gulbarga.
31. Chincholi.
32. Kodangal.
33. Seram.
34. Yadgir.
35. Andola
36. Shahpur.
37. Shorapur.
38. Kalgi (Jagir).
39. Afzalpur (do.)
40. Chitapur (do.)
41. Aland (do.)
42. Firozabad (do.)
43. Tandur (do)
44. Osmanabad.
45. Kalam.
46. Parenda.
47. Owsa.
48. Tuljapur.
49. Lohara(Jagir).
50. Ganjoti (do.)
51. Raichur.
52. Alampur.
53. Deodrug.
54. Gangawati.
55. Kushtagi.
56. Lingsugur.
57. Manvi.
58. Sindhnur,
59, Koppal (Jagir.)
60. Yelbarga (do.)
61. Gadwal (do.)
62. Amarchinta(do.)
63. Bidar.
64. Nilanga
65. Ahmadpur.
66. Udgir.
67. Janwada.
68. Hasanabad (Jagir).
69 Bhalki (do.
70. Partabpur (do.)
71. Chincholi.
72. Narayankher.
73. Chitgopa (Jagir).
74. Ghorwadi (do.)
75. Ekeli (do.)
76 Kalyani (do.)
77. Murag (do.)

69·5 per cent. of the area of the Division is cultivable as against 50·5 in Telingana. The cultivated area is 68·6 per cent. so that less than 1 per cent. of the cultivable area is uncultivated as against 12 per cent. in Telingana. But the density of population per square mile of cultivated area in Marathwara is only 234·7 while in Telingana it is 420·1. In seeking for the causes of this disparity, the first thing which strikes one is that the principal cereal crop of Marathwara is not rice but wheat. The irrigated area is inconsiderable and the rainfall is almost everywhere less than in the Telingana Division. On the other hand, the soil of Marathwara is retentive of moisture, and does not need as much water as that of Telingana. The Marathwara ryot is, if anything, more painstaking, as he has need to be, than his Telingana counterpart. All these considerations go to show that the crops raised in Marathwara do not sustain as high densities of population as those of Telingana. In Subsidiary Table I, the percentage of cultivated area in the Natural Divisions and districts is given under four heads of crops, rice, wheat, pulses and "other crops." Marathwara's percentages under all heads except rice are higher than that of Telingana. Of its total cultivated area only 1·1 per cent. is under rice, whereas Telingana's proportion is 10·3. Notwithstanding this, the four districts which have the largest densities in Marathwara are, as already stated, the four which have the largest percentages of their cultivated area under rice. These are Gulbarga, Nander, Bidar and Osmanabad. Parbhani, Nander, Aurangabad and Bhir have the largest percentages of wheat area, but they occupy lower places than the rice-growing districts. Nander has 8·8 per cent. of its cultivated area under wheat as against 11·1 per cent. for Parbhani; nevertheless its density per cultivated square mile is higher than that of the latter, because, probably, of its larger rice area. The density per square mile of cultivated area and the proportion of the cultivated to the total area for the Marathwara districts is given in the marginal table. It is curious that the first in this list is the district which has the lowest percentage of cultivated area, while the last is that which has the largest percentage. The explanation is that most of the soil of Osmanabad consists of the fertile regar or black cotton soil, and besides *jowar*, wheat, rice and *bajra*, cotton is grown in all the talukas. Raichur has the lowest rainfall in the Nizam's Dominions and the soil in a large part of the district is a poor one. Gulbarga which has the second highest density in Marathwara, has also the second lowest percentage of its area under cultivation. This district partakes of the character partly of the Marathwara and partly of Telingana in regard to its climate and soil. It is noteworthy that, though neither Osmanabad nor Gulbarga, has any forest area worth mentioning, their percentages of cultivable area are the lowest in Marathwara.

Districts.	Density per square mile of cultivated area.	Percentage of cultivated to total area.
Osmanabad	438·02	41·8
Gulbarga	394·9	43·8
Bidar	242·71	72·1
Nander	230·19	80·8
Parbhani	202·39	75·1
Aurangabad	198·02	70·7
Bhir	196·1	77·0
Raichur	170·58	86·2

10. Pulses and Other Crops.

Rice and wheat, however, occupy but a small portion of the area under cultivation in the Nizam's Dominions though they, especially rice, occupy in the agricultural industry a position of importance unapproached by any other crops. The strategic importance, so to speak, of rice in the agricultural economy, is well brought out by the fact that Atraf-i-balda which has a larger proportion of its cultivated area under wheat, pulses and "other crops" as well as under irrigation, supports a smaller number of persons to the square mile than Medak which has a larger proportion of rice area. Pulses are cultivated over a larger area than either of the cereals, the percentages to the total cultivated area being, rice 4·4, wheat 3·7, pulses 7·4. Atraf-i-balda and Medak in Telingana, and Aurangabad,

Bhir, Nander and Bidar in Marathwara have areas ranging from 21 to 11 per cent. of their total cultivated areas under pulses. But the largest proportion of the cultivated area in these territories is under "other crops." Three crops, namely, *jowar*, cotton and *bajra* are cultivated to a larger extent than any others. Rice, *til* and wheat come next below them in the order of acreage. There has been a considerable expansion of cotton cultivation during the decade as the marginal figures show.

Period.	Area under Cotton cultivation in acres.	Percentages of total cultivated area.
1902	1,083,000	5·2
1905	2,536,610	13·8
1907	3,480,143	18·3
1908	3,100,084	15·9
1909	2,901,942	14·7
1910	3,401,042	17·0

II. Areas and Population according to Density.

Subsidiary Table II gives some interesting details relating to the distribution of territory and population according to density. Over 60 per cent. of His Highness's subjects live in areas where the density of population is from 150 to 300 persons per square mile. These areas comprise 41,913 square miles or slightly over 50 per cent. of these territories. The highest densities in this category are met with in the Jagir taluk of Chitgopa in the Bidar District (299), Jamikunta taluk in the Karimnagar District (275), Gulburga taluka (274), Jagtial taluka also in the Karimnagar District (273), Amarchinta taluka in the Raichur District (269) and Warangal taluka (268). The districts noted in the margin have 75 per cent. and more of their areas and population in this class. Bhir has 82·4 per cent. of its population living in areas of this density, though the area itself is only 69·9 per cent. of its total. Less than one-third of the population of these Dominions live in densities of under 150 per square mile, the area so occupied being 39,813 square miles or about 48 per cent. of the State. Over 93 per cent. of the area of the Adilabad District is of this class, and the other districts which have high proportions of this low-density area are Raichur 79·3, Aurangabad 73·3, and Warangal 67·2. In Adilabad, Raichur and Warangal the population on this area is 84·5, 27·3 and 39·5 per cent. respectively of their totals while in Aurangabad 67·2 of the population dwell on it. The first three districts have large forest areas with scattered populations, but Aurangabad's presence in this list is a grim reminder of its losses owing to famine and plague. Some of the talukas in this category have extremely meagre densities such as 25 (Mulug), 48 (Paloncha), 75 (Yellandlapad), 81 (Pakhal) all in the Warangal District, 70 (Mahadeopur) in Karimnagar, 70 (Adilabad), 48 (Rajura), 62 (Asafabad), 77 (Kinwat and Yelgadap), 85 (Chinnur), 89 (Sirpur) all in the Adilabad District and 36 (Amrabad in Mahbubnagar).

Densities of between 150-300.

Districts.	Percentage of	
	Area.	Population.
Medak	85·2	80·0
Nander	81·5	87·1
Karimnagar	80·7	93·2
Osmanabad	79·1	84·7
Nizamabad...	75·9	80·3
Atrafibalda	75·0	75·2

There are a few instances of densities lower than 100 per square mile in Marathwara. These are Patoda (81) and Ashti (93), both in Bhir, Jintur (89) in Parbhani, and Chincholi (94) and Afzalpur (98) both in Gulbarga. More than 6 per cent. of the population of the State live in densities exceeding three hundred persons per square mile. There are three talukas which have a density of between 300 and 450, one taluka with a density from 450-600, and one City, the Capital, with a density exceeding 10,012 persons to the square mile. Kharka in Atraf-i-balda has 368 persons to the square mile, Kalabgur in Medak, 325, and Pargi in Mahbubnagar 308. The areas of these three talukas are 132 and 390 and 377 square miles respectively. Homnabad in Atraf-i-balda has a density of 552 persons per square mile. It is noteworthy that all these exceptional densities occur in Telingana. Hyderabad City covers an area of 50 square miles and has a density of 10,012 persons to the square mile. The City proper, consisting of City *Anderun* and City *Berun*, has an area of 11·46 square miles and the density here is 18,112 per square mile. The City *Anderun*, area 2 square miles, has a population of 131,335, or the enormous number of 65,668 per square mile. In Ward IV of this area the density per square mile rises to 94,548 persons.

12. Towns.

Subsidiary Table III is compiled for the purpose of showing the distribution of the population between Towns and Villages. For Census purposes the word "Town" was held to include every Municipality, every cantonment, all civil lines not included within Municipal limits and every other continuous collection of houses inhabited by about 5,000 persons and possessing urban characteristics. This definition is the same as that adopted at the last Census. The total number of towns in the State, thus defined, is 85 as against 78 in 1901 and 77 in 1891. Of these 65 belong to Khalsa, 3 to Sarf-i-khas and 17 to Jagirs. 53 of these towns are centres of trade and industry, and the remaining 32 are either headquarters of districts and tahsils, or places of pilgrimage. The last two classes of towns are not capable of rapid or indefinite increase whether as regards number or population. The essential condition of the growth of towns of the first class, is development of means of communication. Unlike places of pilgrimage, whose sanctity is often in proportion to their inaccessibility, centres of trade and industry can only exist where there are abundant facilities of communication in the shape of good roads, railways, or waterways. There are no navigable rivers or canals in the State, and there has not been any progress worth mentioning in respect of roads, during the decade. Of the total number of towns 44 are Municipalities, and two are both Municipalities and Cantonments. In 1901 there were 6 Municipalities and Cantonments, and 16 Municipalities. The large increase in the number of Municipalities during the decade is a noteworthy feature. But, of course, the success of Municipal Government is entirely dependent on the presence of a considerable, intelligent and educated population. The increase of 7 towns during the last decade is due to the rise of 9 places to urban rank and the lapse of two towns into rural areas. The two towns which have ceased to be towns are Hasanparthi in Warangal and Sagar in Raichur. The former has had but a brief enjoyment of the honour of township, as it became a town for the first time only at the 1901 Census. A religious fair is held annually in the place in honour of a Hindu deity, and the sudden rise and fall of the population would suggest that the 1901 Census was taken at about the time of the fair. Sagar has been a town with a population just above the qualifying line of 5,000 persons at the two preceding Censuses and its disappearance from the category of towns is not a matter requiring special notice.

Districts.	Towns.
Warangal	Khammamet. Urus-Karimabad. Warangal Fort.
Karimnagar	Peddapalli. Dharmapuri.
Atraf-i-balda	Mahammadnagar.
Medak	Sangareddipet.
Gulbarga	Chitapur.
Bidar	Ekeli.

The 9 new towns are those mentioned in the margin. Only one of these, Khammamet, is a Municipality, and all have attained the rank of towns by the growth of population. One of them Mahammadnagar (Fort Golconda) has a population of less than 1,500 souls. But its real population is obscured by the fact of the troops stationed there, about 5,000 in number, being included in the population of Hyderabad City. Of the remaining 8 new towns, three namely, Sangareddipet, Ekeli, Warangal Fort, and Dharmapuri have just passed their 5,000. Urus-Karimabad has a population of 7,173 and had one of 5,784 at the last Census, so that in its case the recognition due to its growth has been tardy. Peddapalli, which has now a population of 7,260, had only 2,783 at the 1901 Census, though it had 5,993 in 1891. It was a town in 1891 ceased to be one in 1901, and had become one again in 1911. It will belie its tradition if it remains a town at the next Census. It is generally places of pilgrimages which emerge out of and lapse again into rural areas in this whimsical fashion. It is not clear why Khammamet in Warangal (9,117) and Chitapur (9,355) in Gulbarga were not included long before among towns, seeing that they had populations exceeding 8,000 at the two preceding Censuses; nor why Khammamet with a slightly smaller population should be a Municipality while Chitapur is denied the honour. It is inconceivable that places with populations of over 8,000 and 9,000 persons should not have developed the "urban characteristics" which were found sufficient in the case of places like Hasanprathi and Peddapalli which cross and re-cross the border line between town and village at every Census.

13. Variations in Urban population.

The net addition to the urban population owing to the variation in the number of towns is 46,162. The total urban population at the present Census is 1,295,305 and at the last it was 1,126,948. The difference between these two figures is 168,357 representing an increase of 14·8 per cent. The addition to the population of the old towns during the decade was 122,195. 54·9 per cent. of the increase is accounted for by two towns—Hyderabad City and Hanamkonda town—which had additions of 52,157 and 14,966 respectively during the decade. The population of the following towns increased by over 2,500 persons during the same period: Nizamabad, 4,482; Nander, 3,441; Gulbarga, 3,209; Yellandlapad, 3,537; Manvat, 3,607; Karimnagar, 2,595; Vemalwada, 2,703; Peddapalli, 4,477; and Raichur, 2,869. The case of Hyderabad City is treated separately. The remarkable growth of Hanamkonda is largely due to its being the official headquarters of the important Revenue Division of Warangal. The same remark applies to Nizamabad which, besides, is an industrial centre of importance. It has a rice husking factory and cotton-ginning and pressing factories. It is also an important station on the Hyderabad Godavari Valley Railway. Nander is also an important station on the same Railway, and besides, being the headquarters of the district and taluk of that name, is a flourishing centre of trade and industry. The place is held in veneration by the Sikhs as the scene of the labours of Guru Govind in his last days. The steady growth of Gulbarga during the last forty years is a proof of the vitality of some of the ancient cities of India under modern conditions. It is also a large centre of trade and has of late years become a most prosperous town and a rival of Sholapur in the Bombay Presidency. A new era of prosperity commenced since it was made the headquarters of a division in 1874. Besides all the features appertaining to its official character it has cotton-spinning and weaving mills. It is on the Great Indian Peninsula Railway. Yellandlapad in Warangal has grown into importance as a town during the last twenty years. It was first recognised as one at the 1901 Census. It is the centre of the coal mining industry. The town of Manvat in the Parbhani District is a busy centre of the grain trade. It experienced a set-back owing to famine at the last Census, but it has more than made up for it at the present one. Karimnagar is a centre of the tanning industry in the Nizam's Dominions.

14. Decadent Towns.

Relatively, the number of towns that show a decrease of population are fewer than those which show increases. Most of the former are to be found at the end of Imperial Table IV, among towns which hover on the margin of townhood. A few hundred persons this side or that, would raise them to the giddy glory of township or plunge them into the dismal abyss of villagedom. There are, however, a few other towns the decreases in whose case call for notice. Prominent of these is Latur in Osmanabad. At the last Census it had a population of 10,479. Its record previous to that was one of steady growth. At the present Census, however, its enumerated population is only 7,560. It is a great centre of the cotton and grain trade and the Barsi Railway was extended to it during the decade. The decreases in Latur and other towns in the Osmanabad District are attributed to plague which was raging virulently in them at the time of the Census. Plague is also partly responsible for the decreases in the towns in the Aurangabad District, and in several towns in Marathwara generally. Out of 25 towns which show decreases in population at the present Census, 21 are Marathwara towns. All the five towns in the Aurangabad District, three out of four towns in the Bhir District, two out of five in Bedar, two out of ten in Gulbarga, four out of six in Osmanabad, three out of nine in Raichur and two out of seven in Parbhani, have smaller populations than at the last Census. All these districts, with the exception of Gulbarga, showed a decrease of population at the last Census as the result of the famine of 1900. Plague too has wrought much havoc in several of these districts. Of the four Telingana towns which show decreases, the case of Fort Golconda has already been explained. The decline of Armur in the Nizamabad District is apparently due to the decline of its silk industry. Homnabad in Atraf-i-balda has continued to decline in prosperity since the opening of the Nizam's State Railway, which has diverted its trade. Balkonda has declined because it has lain far out of the influences which make for progress.

15. Proportion of Urban and Rural population.

The number of persons per mille of the total population residing in towns is 97, the corresponding figure at the last Census being 101. In Telingana the proportion is 115 per 1,000 persons, while in Marathwara it is only 79. If the City of Hyderabad be excluded, a larger proportion of the population of Marathwara live in towns than of Telingana, but famine and, especially, plague have done much to check the increase of the urban population in the former Division. Hindus have only 71 persons per mille living in towns in the whole State, while the corresponding proportions are, for Musalmans, 318; Christians, 383; Parsis, 778; and Jains 182. Warangal, amongst the Districts, has the highest proportion of urban Hindus, while Atraf-i-balda has the lowest proportion of urban Musalmans. This distribution marks out the Hindu as the mainstay of the agricultural industry, while all other classes have larger proportions of town-dwellers and, as such, depend on trade and handicrafts to a much larger extent. Subsidiary Table V classifies the towns according to population. There is one town, Hyderabad City, with a population exceeding 100,000, four with populations exceeding 20,000 but under 40,000, eighteen with populations between 10,000 and 20,000, fifty-eight between 5,000, and 10,000, and four below 5,000. 38·7 per cent. of the total urban population live in Hyderabad City, and 31·8 per cent. in towns of the 5th class (populations between 5,000 and 10,000). The largest increase, however, has been in the populations of towns of the 4th class (10,000 to 20,000). It is interesting to note that in the two last classes of towns, comprising 33 per cent. of the urban population of the State, the proportions of females to 1,000 males, are 1,004 and 1,070 respectively, while in all other towns they are considerably less than those of males. It would seem that the crowded life of large towns is as unfavourable to female life as the monotonous drudgery of the village. Small towns, which combine the advantages of rural life with the healthier interests of towns, seem to be most congenial to female vitality. The urban population of the State has increased by 41·8 per cent. since 1881, while the general population has increased during the same period by only 35·8 per cent.

16. Villages.

For Census purposes the village was taken to mean the revenue Mouza (Survey unit), that is, a collection of houses situated generally in the centre of a definite area having well marked boundaries and constituting a unit for administrative purposes. It often contains two or more residential villages and sometimes it is uninhabited, but as it is a definite enclave not liable to change, its adoption as a Census village enables comparison to be made between the population at different periods. The number of villages at the present Census is 20,151 as against 20,011 in 1901. Villages are classed in groups according to population in the Imperial Tables. In the first and largest group, with populations under 500, there are 1,607 villages less than in 1901. This represents a decrease of 13·7 per cent. But this is only apparent as all the other groups show increases showing that the tendency is towards larger and larger aggregates. This points to the gradual settling down of the Animistic and Nomadic tribes who inhabit most of the small hamlets with populations of under 500. In the second group of villages, having populations varying from 500 to 1,000, there are 5,220 as against 4,344 at the previous Census. In the third group 1,000—2,000, the numbers at the two Censuses are 2,511 and 1,862 respectively. A deduction of one should be made from the number for Golconda Fort, with a population of less than 2,000 classed as a town. The fourth group, 2,000—5,000, consisting of over-grown villages and budding towns, numbers 730 as against 514, which was their number ten years ago. There are three full-blown towns included in this group, whereas there was none in 1901. The actual number of villages with populations from 2,000 to 5,000 is, therefore, 727. Ten villages have populations of between 5,000 and 10,000. In 1901, there were no villages in this group. Their growth is thus a phenomenon wholly of the last ten years. Their non-inclusion among towns suggests that many of them are in the nature of temporary aggregations. The average population per village, taking all the groups together is 599 for the whole State, 664 in Telingana and 548 in Marathwara. The smaller average of Marathwara villages reflects the character of their cultivation less concentrated than that of Telingana.

17. Distribution of the Rural population.

903 persons out of every 1,000 persons in these Dominions live in villages. Of every 1,000 village-dwellers, 5 live in villages scarcely distinguishable from the smaller towns in respect of size. In Medak residents of this type of village number 23 per 1,000 of the rural population; in Raichur, 12; in Atraf-i-balda, 10; in Bhir, 9; in Aurangabad and Parbhani, 8; and in Gulbarga, 6. It is noteworthy that Marathwara has a larger proportion of its rural population than Telingana in the largest and the smallest type of villages. In respect of the intervening two types, Telingana is pre-eminent. Large villages are more likely to be formed where crops have to be subjected to some mechanical process at certain seasons of the year, such as ginning, as a preliminary to their being carried, perhaps over long distances, to their market. Where the crops raised are consumed in the district, there is not likely to be much need of their being subjected to a centralized mechanical process. The larger average of Telingana villages is but a feature of their extensive rice cultivation. With the exception of Nizamabad and Warangal, every Telingana District has a higher average of rural population than any Marathwara District.

18. Village and Urban Life.

The essential difference between town and village life in India is, briefly, that while the regime of status continues to dominate the latter much as it did a hundred years ago, the principle of contract has begun to control to a larger or smaller extent the relations between man and man in towns. The first stage in the transformation is the appearance in the village of persons following callings outside those followed by the members of the village community. The money-lender is the type and symbol of this class. The cultivation of crops intended chiefly for export, that is, with a view to bringing in more money, also hastens the process of urbanisation. Both these phenomena are discernible to a greater extent in Marathwara than in Telingana. Marathwara also contains more capitals and ex-capitals of former dynasties, and the colonies of such capitals or ex-capitals. Sir Henry Maine called attention to the existence in India of great deserted cities, often in close proximity to one another, in proof of his opinion that the most famous of all Indian cities grew out of camps. Marathwara has several such ruined cities to interest the antiquarian. It has, too, its fair share of places of pilgrimage, the other great cause of the origin of Indian towns. But the chief impulse towards de-ruralisation in Marathwara in modern times proceeds from cotton and the money-lender. The uncertainty of the rainfall throws the cultivator in the hands of the money-lender. And the money-lender leads to cotton, as being the most paying crop. Telingana is the granary of the State. Marathwara's great need is facilities of communication to bring in food and to take its cotton and oil-seeds to the nearest sea-port. The evolution from the agricultural to the manufacturing stage, has already begun in Marathwara. Its cotton and wheat are the great sources of the capital which it requires to start modern industries. When a country begins to produce the raw materials of manufacture in place of food crops, it has started on the road to industrialization. The raw materials may have to be sent out for a time to fetch the best prices. But, ultimately, they will be worked up near where they are produced. The railways which take away the cotton will bring back machinery and will in the end carry the cotton goods of Hyderabad to the great distributing centres.

19. Houses.

In 1891 a Census house was defined as the dwelling place of one or more families with their dependants and servants, having a separate principal entrance from the public road, street, lane or other thoroughfare. In 1901 the same definition was repeated with only slight modifications. This definition had several disadvantages. In the first place, as the Superintendent for the year 1891 remarked, it was not correctly understood by the enumerators. Secondly, it indicated the unit to be a structural one. In European countries great importance is attached to statistics of houses as they throw light on the question of over-crowding, but in this country the question seldom arises even in large towns like Hyderabad, and the structure or building as a Census unit possesses no value at all. For these reasons the definition was abandoned for the purpose of the present Census and a house was defined as "the dwelling place of a commensal family with its resident dependants such as mother, widowed sister, younger brothers, etc., and its servants who reside in the house." The residence of a commensal family, thus adopted as the Census unit, was perfectly intelligible and so the definition was easily grasped and accurately applied by the enumerators.

20. Number of houses.

The number of occupied houses in the State is 2,713,843. Owing to the change in the definition, a comparison with the statistics of the last Census is not likely to be profitable. The definition now adopted makes it possible that what was enumerated as one house in 1901 might have been enumerated at the present Census as two or three. It is, therefore, impossible to say to what extent the increase in the number of houses, which amounted to 430,396, is due to a real increase and how much of it is due to the change in the definition. The latter cause is more likely to have affected the statistics of houses in towns than in villages, as the village house is rarely sufficient to accommodate more than one household. The number of houses in towns and villages at the present and the previous Censuses are given in the margin. As the urban population has increased since the last Census by only 14·8 per cent., the considerably larger increase in the number of houses is due largely to the change of definition.

	No. of houses.		Increase per cent.
	1901.	1911.	
Towns	239,494	291,441	+ 21·6
Villages	2,043,953	2,422,404	+ 18·5
Total ...	2,283,447	2,713,845	+ 18·8

21. Number of persons in each house.

While the number of houses per square mile has increased to 32·8 from 27·6 in 1901 and 1891, as the result no doubt partly of the changed definition, the number of persons per house does not show any decrease. On the other hand, there is a slight increase, the averages being 4·9 in 1911 as against 4·8 in 1901. The attempt to accommodate a 20 per cent. increase of population with an increased house-room of only 18 per cent. must lead to an increase in the number of persons per house, even if the increased house-room were not to some extent a matter of definition. It should be remembered too that in 1901 many houses had been robbed of their inmates owing to the ravages of famine. In Marathwara the number of persons in a house has remained stationary since 1901 at 4·7. In Telingana it has increased by ·2 per cent. Whatever the reason, whether the cradles in Telingana homes are more often full or families in Marathwara tend to separate earlier, the average per house in the former division is as a rule higher than in the latter. The fact that there are 97 houses per 100 married females aged 15 and over in Marathwara, while there are only 94 in Telingana, would seem to favour the latter conclusion. While only one out of eight districts in Marathwara, Nander has an average of five persons, only two out of the same number of districts in Telingana have less than that number per occupied house.

22. Hyderabad City.

The City of Hyderabad is the fourth largest City in India. Its area of 50 square miles comprises the City Proper, 11·46 square miles, consisting of the City *Anderun* (within the walls), which has an area of two square miles, and the City Berun (without the walls), 9·46 square miles, Chadarghat 20·84 square miles, Residency Bazars 0·53 square mile and Secunderabad including Bolarum 17·17 square miles. The number of persons per square mile for the whole City is 10,012. In the City Proper, this rises to 18,112, and in the City *Anderun* to 65,668. In Ward IV of the latter, it is 94,548, and Subsidiary Table VI shows that the population here is 22·6 per cent. less than what it was in 1901. The most important event in the history of the City during the decade was the disaster occasioned by floods in the Musi in September 1908. About 18,000 houses were washed away and there was considerable loss of life and property. The calamity, however, has not affected the growth of the population of the City which increased from 448,466 in 1901 to 500,623, an increase of 11·6 per cent. As compared with 1881, the increase is 36·3 per cent. The only effect of the floods of 1908 has been to induce people to abandon the riverside Wards and to make new homes for themselves in those more secure from the vagaries of the river. This movement can be studied in detail in the figures given in Subsidiary Table VI.

23. Population of the City according to birth-place and sex.

More than one-fifth of the population of the City have their birth-places elsewhere. This large immigrant population accounts for the low proportion of women in the City, 937 to 1,000 males. With the exception of a single Ward in Chadarghat which has 1,015 female to 1,000 male persons, the City Proper has the highest proportion of females, 970 per 1,000 males. In Ward 2 of the City *Anderun*, it is 982, and in Ward VI and VII of *Berun*, 981. The Residency Bazars and Secunderabad have less than 900 females to 1,000 males. These evidently are the chief centres of the foreign element in the City.

24. Houses.

There are 111,509 occupied houses in the city of which 45,537 are located in the City Proper. The average for the whole City is 2,230·18 houses per square mile, while for the City Proper it is 3,973·56. The average number of persons per house for the whole City is 4·4. In 1881 it was 5·4. It decreased to 4·2 in 1891, but since then it has steadily risen. In 1901 it was 4·3. The number of houses in 1901 was 102,077. The increase in it during the decade, amounting to 9·24 per cent., has not kept pace with the increase of population, 11·6 per cent.

25. Population by Religions.

The population of the City is made up of 262,131 Hindus, 219,896 Musalmans, 16,240 Christians, and other religionists numbering less than 1,000 for each religion. The Sikhs in the City number 978 ; the Parsis, 808; and the Jains, 379. At the last Census there were 243,241 Hindus and 189,152 Musalmans in the City. The Hindu population has increased by 7·7 per cent. and the Musalman by 16·2 per cent. in the decade.

I.—Density, Water Supply and Crops.

Natural Division and District.	Mean density per square mile in 1911.	Percentage of total area.		Percentage of cultivated area which is irrigated.	Normal rainfall.	Percentage of cultivated area under			
		Cultivable.	Cultivated.			Rice.	Wheat.	Pulses.	Other crops.
1	2	3	4	5	6	7	8	9	10
State	162	60·0	53·7	6·2	30·2	4·4	3·7	7·4	84·5
Telingana	163	50·5	38·8	13·0	32·7	10·3	0·4	5·5	83·8
Hyderabad City	10,012	......	......	......	29·6	......	......	......	......
Atraf-i-balda	208	49·1	36·9	27·2	29·5	9·6	2·0	21·8	67·1
Warangal	114	38·0	32·8	12·9	38·8	10·2	......	5·2	84·6
Karimnagar	197	52·5	43·2	16·5	33·7	12·3	......	3·6	84·1
Adilabad	85	33·4	22·1	2·7	37·2	5·1	0·7	4·6	89·6
Medak	214	46·1	37·8	19·9	35·4	18·6	2·4	13·1	65·9
Nizamabad	174	54·1	37·3	18·2	38·2	20·5	0·3	5·7	73·5
Mahbubnagar	145	68·9	48·5	10·3	26·1	7·6	......	2·3	90·1
Nalgonda	171	71·1	56·6	9·1	26·4	7·0	......	2·7	90·3
Marathwara	161	69·5	68·6	2·4	27·7	1·1	5·5	8·5	84·9
Aurangabad	140	70·9	70·7	3·3	25·8	0·2	6·7	11·1	82·0
Bhir	151	77·3	77·0	2·9	25·6	0·5	15·3	12·8	81·4
Nander	186	81·4	80·8	2·3	31·6	1·8	8·8	11·4	78·0
Parbhani	152	76·4	75·1	2·1	32·2	0·7	11·1	7·1	81·1
Gulbarga	171	44·2	43·3	3·7	28·1	2·3	1·7	8·2	87·8
Osmanabad	161	41·3	41·3	3·0	26·6	1·4	4·9	3·9	89·8
Raichur	147	87·5	86·2	1·3	21·6	0·9	1·7	3·2	94·2
Bidar	175	74·4	72·1	1·9	30·3	1·7	4·8	11·1	82·4

II.—Distribution of the Population Classified according to Density.

District and Natural Division.	Talukas with a population per square mile of															
	Under 150.		150-300.		300-450.		450-600.		600-750.		750-900.		900-1050.		1050 and over.	
	Area.	Population.	Area.	Population.	Area.	Population.	Area.	Population.	Area.	Population.	Area.	Population.	Area.	Population.	Area.	Population.
1	2	3	4	5	6	7	8	9	10	11	12	13	14	15	16	17
State	39,813	4,191,886	41,913	8,377,966	899	291,495	23	12,706	...	...	...	...	...	...	50	500,623
	48·14	31·34	50·68	62·64	1·09	2·18	·03	·10							·06	3·74
Telingana	20,036	1,726,200	20,312	4,193,940	899	291,495	23	12,706	...	...	...	...	...	...	50	500,623
	48·49	25·67	49·16	62·36	2·18	4·34	·05	·19							·12	7·44
Hyderabad City ...	...	...	...	...	...	...	...	...	...	...	...	...	...	...	50	500,632
															100·0	100·0
Atraf-i-balda	486	67,681	1,920	391,200	182	48,572	23	12,706	...	...	...	...	...	...	...	...
	19·0	13·0	75·0	75·2	5·1	9·3	0·9	2·5								
Warangal	5,337	357,768	2,606	547,646	...	...	...	...	...	...	...	...	...	...	...	...
	67·2	39·5	32·8	60·5												
Karimnagar	1,106	77,241	4,627	1,054,396	...	...	...	...	...	...	...	...	...	...	...	...
	19·3	6·8	80·7	93·2												
Adilabad	6,814	524,428	480	95,998	...	...	...	...	...	...	...	...	...	...	...	...
	93·4	84·5	6·6	15·5												
Medak...	85	10,802	2,740	549,418	390	126,917	...	...	...	...	...	...	...	...	...	...
	2·7	1·6	85·2	80·0	12·1	18·4										
Nizamabad	789	111,842	2,424	456,167	...	...	...	...	...	...	...	...	...	...	...	...
	24·1	19·7	75·9	80·3												
Mahbubnagar ...	3,062	267,139	1,708	364,033	377	116,006	...	...	...	...	...	...	...	...	...	...
	59·5	35·8	33·2	48·7	7·3	15·5										
Nalgonda	2,357	309,299	3,747	735,082	...	...	...	...	...	...	...	...	...	...	...	...
	38·6	29·6	61·4	70·4												
Marathwara ...	19,777	2,465,686	21,601	4,184,026	...	...	...	...	...	...	...	...	...	...	...	...
	47·8	37·1	52·2	62·9												
Aurangabad	4,553	584,778	1,659	285,009	..	...	...	...	...	...	...	...	...	...	...	...
	73·3	67·2	26·7	32·8												
Bhir	1,243	109,503	2,889	513,028	...	...	...	...	...	...	...	...	...	...	...	...
	30·1	17·6	69·9	82·4												
Nander	704	90,976	3,093	613,578	...	...	...	...	...	...	...	...	...	...	...	...
	18·5	12·9	81·5	87·1												
Parbhani	2,773	316,411	2,354	463,263	...	...	...	...	...	...	...	...	...	...	...	...
	54·1	40·6	45·9	59·4												
Gultarga	2,413	266,397	4,306	884·586	...	..	...	...	...	...	...	...	...	...	...	...
	35·9	23·1	64·1	76·9												
Osmanabad	734	97,533	2,783	538,444	...	...	...	...	...	...	...	...	...	...	...	...
	20·9	15·3	79·1	84·7												
Raichur	5,383	724,446	1,408	272,238	...	...	...	...	...	...	...	...	...	...	...	...
	79·3	27·3	20·7	72·7												
Bidar	1,974	275,642	3,109	613,885	...	...	...	...	...	...	...	...	...	...	...	...
	38·8	31·0	61·2	69·0												

Note:—The figures below the absolute ones represent the proportion per cent. which the area and population of each density group bear to the total area and population of the State, natural division and district.

III.—DISTRIBUTION OF THE POPULATION BETWEEN TOWNS AND VILLAGES.

Natural Division and District.	Average population per		Number per mille residing in		Number per mille of urban population residing in towns with a population of				Number per mille of rural population residing in villages with a population of			
	Town.	Village.	Towns.	Villages.	20,000 and over.	10,000 to 20,000.	5,000 to 10,000.	Under 5,000.	5,000 and over.	2,000 to 5,000.	500 to 2,000.	Under 500.
1	2	3	4	5	6	7	8	9	10	11	12	13
State	15,239	599	97	903	485	185	318	12	5	164	587	244
Telingana	24,899	664	115	885	695	74	223	8	3	177	631	189
Hyderabad City ...	500,628	...	1,000	...	1,000	...	...	...	...	...	...	...
Atraf-i-balda ...	4,140	590	16	984	...	...	821	179	10	187	607	246
Warangal	14,675	669	81	919	486	217	297	...	...	163	681	156
Karimnagar ...	7,774	949	48	952	...	215	785	...	...	244	654	102
Adilabad	8,046	367	39	961	...	...	1,000	...	...	42	558	400
Medak	8,320	683	48	952	...	...	1,000	...	23	164	619	194
Nizamabad	8,359	691	73	927	...	415	472	113	...	210	577	213
Mahbubnagar ...	10,550	614	28	972	...	590	410	...	...	135	644	221
Nalgonda	7,437	860	14	986	...	...	1,000	...	...	288	645	117
Marathwara ...	9,693	548	79	921	176	348	457	19	6	152	545	297
Aurangabad ...	15,312	434	88	912	456	382	162	...	8	86	510	396
Bhir	10,050	572	65	935	...	674	326	...	9	178	520	293
Nander	9,058	499	77	923	...	324	676	...	...	127	524	349
Parbhani	9,547	471	86	914	...	585	415	...	8	105	509	378
Gulbarga	10,556	660	92	908	307	218	429	46	6	216	553	225
Osmanabad	7,132	683	67	933	...	239	761	...	...	179	613	208
Raichur	9,137	553	83	917	304	147	490	59	12	163	529	296
Bidar	7,844	592	62	938	...	483	567	...	...	144	608	253

IV.—Number per Mille of the Total Population and of each Main Religion who live in Towns.

Natural Division and District.	Number per mille who live in towns.					
	Total population.	Hindu.	Musalman.	Christian.	Jain.	Parsi.
1	2	3	4	5	6	7
State ...	97	71	318	383	182	778
Telingana ...	115	82	439	417	613	856
Hyderabad City ...	1,000	1,000	1,000	1,000	1,000	1,000
Atraf-i-balda ...	16	12	47	26	436	......
Warangal ...	81	80	281	77	409	646
Karimnagar ...	48	43	164	319	906	......
Adilabad ...	39	37	159	393	16	......
Medak ...	48	41	117	205	142	200
Nizamabad ...	74	62	213	111	389	1,000
Mahbubnagar ...	28	25	72	406	......	......
Nalgonda ...	14	10	89	24	......	769
Marathwara ...	79	60	218	238	163	615
Aurangabad ...	88	65	287	203	68	849
Bhir ...	65	51	205	1,000	134	200
Nander ...	77	57	244	290	182	725
Parbhani ...	86	68	246	230	169	250
Gulbarga ...	92	68	225	236	471	440
Osmanabad ...	67	57	159	87	153	646
Raichur ...	83	66	234	385	332	341
Bidar ...	62	42	181	266	169	......

V.—Towns Classified by Population.

Class of Town	Number of towns of each class in 1911.	Proportion to total urban population.	Number of females per 1,000 males.	Increase per cent. in the population of towns as classed at previous census.			Increase per cent. in urban population of each class from 1881 to 1911	
				1901 to 1911.	1891 to 1901.	1881 to 1891.	(a) in towns as classed in 1881.	(b) in the total of each class in 1911 as compared with the corresponding total in 1881.
1	2	3	4	5	6	7	8	9
Total	85	100	960	+ 9·9	+ 2·2	+ 11·5	+ 25·7	+ 41·8
I—100,000 and over	1	38·7	937	+ 11·6	+ 8·0	+ 13·0	+ 36·3	+ 36·3
II— 50,000—100,000	...	...	...	...	...	...	...	....
III— 20,000— 50,000	4	9·9	944	+ 2·6	— 1·0	+ 17·0	+ 26·9	+ 74·5
IV— 10,000— 20,000	18	18·4	936	+ 12·3	— 4·9	+ 9·3	+ 11·4	+ 43·2
V— 5,000— 10,000	58	31·8	1,004	+ 8·7	+ 0·4	+ 10·2	+ 16·9	+ 40·2
VI—Under 5,000	4	1·2	1,070	...	...	...	...	....

VI.—Hyderabad City.

CITY.	Population in 1911.	Number of persons per square mile.	Number of females to 1,000 males.	Proportion of foreign born per mille.	Percentage of variation.			
					1901 to 1911.	1891 to 1901.	1881 to 1891.	Total 1881 to 1911.
1	2	3	4	5	6	7	8	9
Hyderabad City	500,623	10,012	937	227	+ 11·6	+ 8·1	+ 13·0	+ 36·3
(1) *The City Municipality*	*207,562*	*18,112*	*970*		+ *7·6*			
Anderun	*131,335*	*65,668*	*967*		+ *2·5*			
Ward I	34,369	61,373	955		+ 10·8			
Ward II	34,880	69,760	982		+ 9·5			
Ward III	34,667	53,834	972		+ 16·6			
Ward IV	27,419	94,548	959		— 22·6			
Berun	*76,227*	*8,058*	*975*		+ *17·6*			
Ward V	36,806	16,961	969	Figures by Wards are not available.	+ 11·6	Figures by Wards are not available.	Figures by Wards are not available.	Figures by Wards are not available.
Ward VI	25,151	5,229	981		+ 10·6			
Ward VII	14,270	5,754	981		+ 56·1			
(2) *Chadarghat Municipality* ...	*161,600*	*7,754*	*950*		+ *13·5*			
Ward A—VIII	24,906	5,944	974		+ 19·8			
Ward B— IX	38,628	6,281	909		+ 40·2			
Ward C— X	31,193	70,893	941		— 14·7			
Ward D— XI	24,672	41,817	965		+ 0·9			
Ward E— XII	20,153	5,038	1,015		+ 26·2			
Troops	*22,048*	*4,031*	*939*		+ *30·1*			
(3) *The Residency Bazars*	*17,971*	*33,908*	*891*		+ *6·3*	+ *14·9*		1891-1911 + *22·1*
(4) *Secunderabad including Bolaram.*	*113,490*	*6,610*	*868*		+ *3·3*	+ *3·9*		+ *7·4*

N. B.—" Foreign-born " in the heading of column 5 has been taken to mean " born outside the city. "

VII—PERSONS PER HOUSE AND HOUSES PER SQUARE MILE.

Natural Division and District.	Average number of persons per house.				Average number of houses per square mile.			
	1911	1901	1891	1881	1911	1901	1891	1881
1	2	3	4	5	6	7	8	9
State	**4·9**	**4·8**	**5·0**	**5·2**	**32·8**	**27·6**	**27·6**	**22·4**
Telingana	**5·1**	**4·9**	**5·2**	**5·3**	**31·7**	**26·3**	**23·9**	**20·0**
Hyderabad City	4·4	4·3	4·2	5·4	2,330·1	2,105·0	1,992·5	1,392·7
Atraf-i-balda	4·9	4·7	5·1	4·3	40·8	35·5	30·7	33·7
Warangal	5·2	5·2	5·5	5·6	21·6	17·2	14·6	11·2
Karimnagar	5·3	5·0	5·5	5·6	36·6	29·1	27·4	22·9
Adilabad	5·1	5·3	5·3	5·4	16·5	12·4	11·5	10·3
Medak	5·1	4·9	5·1	5·5	41·6	33·4	32·4	26·0
Nizamabad	4·6	4·7	5·0	5·3	37·4	32·3	30·2	25·8
Mahbubnagar	5·0	4·8	5·1	4·8	28·9	24·2	21·6	18·6
Nalgonda	5·5	5·4	5·6	5·5	30·9	26·1	22·6	18·2
Marathwara	**4·7**	**4·7**	**4·9**	**5·2**	**33·8**	**28·8**	**31·2**	**24·9**
Aurangabad	4·7	4·9	5·0	5·2	29·4	28·8	26·5	32·6
Bhir	4·6	4·3	4·9	5·0	32·4	27·3	31·1	26·9
Nander	5·0	4·5	4·3	4·4	36·8	33·2	42·4	40·7
Parbhani	4·5	5·0	5·0	6·6	33·2	25·0	31·2	20·0
Gulbarga	4·8	4·8	4·8	5·1	35·4	32·2	28·9	21·5
Osmanabad	4·6	4·7	4·9	5·9	39·1	31·9	36·7	25·8
Raichur	4·7	4·9	4·9	5·1	30·7	27·9	26·5	20·0
Bidar	4·8	4·6	5·0	5·1	35·8	31·3	34·5	29·3

Chapter II.

MOVEMENT OF POPULATION.

26. By "movement of population" is here meant the movement of population in respect of number, and not movement from one place to another. The latter movement forms the subject-matter of the next Chapter under the head, Migration. Imperial Table II contains the statistical material for this Chapter. Three Subsidiary Tables supply proportional figures and the vital statistics collected during the decade under review. The variations in the population of talukas have not been computed in Provincial Table I as the wholesale redistribution of their areas has made the work extremely difficult. For the same reason Subsidiary Table IV has not been prepared.

27. The population of His Highness the Nizam's Dominions at the four Censuses taken since 1881 is given in the margin. The population at the present Census exceeds that recorded in 1901 by 2,233,534 and that recorded in 1881 by 3,529,082. The increase during the decade is thus 20 per cent. and that during the last 30 years 35·8 per cent. The increase since 1881 is the net result of the increases during 1881-1891 and 1901-1911 counteracted to some extent by the decrease during 1891-1901. The subjoined map shows the variations in the population of these Dominions.

Increase of Population.		Variation per cent.
1881	9,845,594	...
1891	11,537,040	+ 17·1
1901	11,141,142	— 3·5
1911	13,374,676	+ 20

MAP OF HYDERABAD

Showing variation in population by districts.

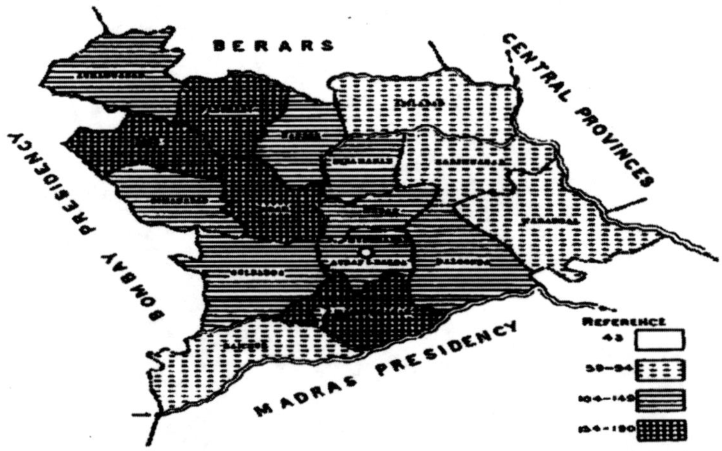

28. **Normal growth of population.**

If the increase between the Census of 1881 and 1891 be regarded as the result of the normal growth of the population of these territories, and if the intervening period had not been affected by the effects of famine and plague, the population at the present Census should be 15,817,281 instead of 13,374,676. Notwithstanding that the increase during the last decade amounts to 20 per cent. the population of this State is still poorer by 2,442,605 persons owing to the calamities of the concluding years of the last century.

29. Causes of the increase of population.

The area of the Nizam's Dominions remains what it was at the Census of 1881. No part of the increase in population is, therefore, due to territorial changes. It is probable that the enumeration at the present Census was somewhat more accurate than at previous ones. In the last Census Report of India, it was suggested that, in the case of Elgandal (the present Karimnagar) District, the recorded decrease was not sufficiently accounted for by the reason advanced, namely, a decrease of 4 square miles in area. The case of Elgandal was perhaps not exceptional in this respect, or it may be that there were other reasons not mentioned in the Hyderabad Census Report, to account for the deficiency. In any case, there is no means of ascertaining what proportion of the increased population should be assigned to improvement in enumeration and what to other causes. It will be seen, however, in the sequel, that there is no need and no room for the introduction of reasons which lie outside the statistics to account for the increase. The increase is a real increase.

30. Effect of migration.

Although the subject of migration will be considered in detail in the next Chapter, it is necessary to get rid of this element in order to understand the extent of the natural growth of population. Subsidiary Table II gives the actual numbers of Immigrants and Emigrants. The latter exceed the former by 46,280. The natural population is obtained by adding this number to the actual population. The figure thus obtained is 13,420,956 as against 11,112,236 in 1901. The increase of the natural population is slightly in excess of that of the actual population, the difference being, ·7 per cent. The difference between the actual and the natural population is so small, not more than ·3 per cent., that for all practical purposes the actual population may be regarded as the natural population. Besides, as the ages of immigrants and emigrants are not recorded, it is impossible to pursue further the present discussion on the basis of the natural population.

31. Statistics of births and deaths.

All possible adventitious causes, *viz.*, accession of new territory, improved enumeration, and the effects of migration having been disposed of, there is only one door left to knock at for an explanation of the increase of population, and that is, excess of births over deaths during the decade. The most direct and simple proof of this would be furnished by the record of vital statistics if they were reliable. But, although there is such a record, it is not worth much as the system of registration is in a rudimentary stage. Subsidiary Table III gives the totals of births and deaths as they were registered during the decade, and the net result is an excess of 104,056 deaths over births. But as the actual counting of heads has revealed an excess of 2,233,534 persons over the population of ten years ago, it is obviously impossible to place reliance on the registered number of births and deaths. Even in Hyderabad City where the registration might be expected to be carried out with more care than in any other part of the State, it shows a net loss of 6,336 souls in the decade, whereas the enumeration at the Census gives an addition of 38,302 persons to the population of 1901. This is the first occasion in which registered figures are incorporated in a Census Report of the State, and there is cause for encouragement in the thought that even in Provinces where the registration of vital statistics has been in vogue for a longer period than in the Nizam's Dominions, very nearly the same anomalies, as those noticed here, have been observed. At the same time, considering that the accurate registration of vital statistics is the first and most important condition of improved Sanitary and Public Health Administration, His Highness's Government will, no doubt, adopt effective measures to secure a fuller and more accurate registration of births and deaths in all parts of these Dominions.

32. An era of high birth-rate and low death-rate.

An attempt will be made in the next Chapter to make a rough estimate of the birth and death-rates on the basis of such materials as are available. For the present, it may be assumed that the decade preceding the present Census was one of a high birth-rate and a very low death-rate as compared with the previous decade. The weak and the worn, the very young and the very old, having been wiped off by the famines in 1891-1901, those who were left were the more virile both as regards fecundity and resistance to the influences tending to death. Owing to this cause the years following a famine show abnormal increases of population and this tendency was assisted in the Nizam's Dominions by the generally favourable seasons during the last decade. Although in two years of the decade there was a deficient rainfall, and in one year much loss was occasioned by floods due to heavy rain in September, the decade was on the whole a period of agricultural prosperity. There was a steady rise in the area under cultivation from 26,539 square miles in 1901 to 49,657 square miles in 1911. The large increase in 1911 is due to the inclusion for the first time of the figures for Jagir areas which amount to 18,925 square miles. Excluding this the figures fall to 30,732 square miles for the State, 19,317 for Marathwara and 11,415 for Telingana.

33. Progress in Irrigation.

Canal.	Present area (acres).	Estimated area (acres).
Ootkur-Marapalli... ...	1,856	6,294
Musaepet Canal	1,614	2,181
Musi Canal	4,020	28,418
Shaligowraram Canal ...	2,631	14,629
Majra Canal	4,250	7,417

The marked progress made with respect to irrigation in the State contributed also greatly to this end. The marginal statement shows in detail the area now irrigated by some of the great projects completed during the decade, and the maximum area which each is expected ultimately to command.

34. Improvement in means of communication.

The opening of the Hyderabad-Godavari Railway, in October 1900, has had an important effect in stimulating trade and industry in the districts through which it runs, namely, Medak, Nizamabad, Nandar, Parbhani and Aurangabad. The extension of the Barsi Light Railway to Tadwalla and Latur has been alluded to in the 1st Chapter. There has not been much progress made in respect of roads during the decade.

35. Industrial growth.

A large number of ginning and pressing factories, most of them along the Godavari Valley Railway, and a few rice-husking factories and oil mills have sprung up during the period under review. Many of the ginning factories, working only during the cotton season, were closed at the time the Census was taken, and were not returned in the industrial schedules.

36. Prices.

Price of food-grains fluctuated according to the seasons but, on the whole, they have remained at a higher level than before the famines of the closing years of the last century. The causes of this phenomenon are complex. The increased cultivation of non-food crops, for export, on the best lands, necessitating the relegation of food crops to the margin of cultivation, thus increasing their cost of production, is probably one of them.

37. State of public health.

Except for the prevalence of plague and cholera in some districts the state of public health has been fairly good during the decade under review. Plague claims an annual mortality of 9,880 but this average falls to 1,804 if the deaths of 1902 and the two succeeding years (a total of 68,217) be excluded. The districts that suffered most were Aurangabad, Osmanabad, Gulbarga, Bidar, Bhir, Parbhani and Raichur. Cholera prevailed in one part or another of the State during all years of the decade. It was virulent during the years 1901, 1903, 1904 and 1905, and was mild in the remaining years.

38. Movement of population in the Natural Divisions.

While the increase of population in the State during the decade amounted to 20 per cent. in the two Natural Divisions—Telingana and Marathwara—it increased by 24 and 16·4 per cent. respectively. Since 1881, the population of Telingana has increased by 52·3 per cent. while that of Marathwara has increased only by 22·4 per cent. In 1881-91 the growth of population in the two Divisions was about equal, 17·5 per cent. in Telingana and 16·8 per cent. in Marathwara. In the next decade, Telingana suffered comparatively less from famine, the only effect of which was to pull down the rate of increase of the population to 4·6 per cent. ; whereas in Marathwara the ravages of plague, superadded to those of famine, had the effect of bringing out an actual reduction of population amounting to 10 per cent. In the last decade Telingana, which had about 300,000 persons less in 1901 than Marathwara, has not only made good the deficiency but is able to show about 75,000 persons more than Marathwara. Again, while in Telingana the number of immigrants have increased by about 5,000, and that of emigrants decreased by about 28,000 persons, in Marathwara immigrants show a decrease of over 111,000 since 1901. As a set-off, there were about 14,000 emigrants less than in that year. It is a sign of the improving economic position that there were fewer emigrants from both Divisions during the decade. The stream of emigration from Marathwara is still of much greater volume than that from Telingana. The great reduction in the number of immigrants is noteworthy. This subject, however, will be treated in more detail in the next Chapter. The conclusion to be drawn from a comparison of the migration statistics of Telingana and Marathwara is clear. The former Division has been in the enjoyment of a more continuous spell of prosperity and is in a more thriving condition than the latter.

39. Effect of redistribution of Districts on Statistics.

A comparison of the Statistics of Districts and Talukas with those of previous Censuses has become difficult owing to the wholesale redistribution of them during the decade. In the case of Districts, the effects of changes on their population brought about by inter-district transfers have been calculated and the figures have been adjusted accordingly in Imperial Table II. In the case of Talukas, this has not been done. The result is that while a comparison of the district figures is possible up to a certain point, it is not at all possible in the case of Talukas. Even as regards Districts, adjustment has been possible only as regards the actual population. The effects of inter-State migration in some districts are considerable, and it has not been found possible to adjust the migratory population to the redistributed territories. Though the influence of immigration and emigration is insignificant with reference to the State as a whole, there is a good deal of internal migration, and its effect on the statistics of the districts is often very considerable. It is, therefore, of no use discussing the variations in the natural population, and it also invests any deductions about the movement of the actual population in the districts, with a considerable amount of uncertainty. The latter attempt may nevertheless have some value as an indication of tendencies.

40. Movement of population by Districts.

The movement of population in the districts are to be explained generally by the same causes that have been found to hold for the whole State. As the population has been adjusted to the reconstituted districts in the Tables, there is no need here to examine how far any variations are due to changes of area. It is likely that there was a larger degree of inaccurate enumeration in the sparsely populated forest districts and of wild and nomadic tribes, as also of the castes whose proximity is regarded as polluting and with whom the Hindu enumerators are likely to have been frugal of questions and answers. But there is no means of even approximately estimating the extent to which such inaccuracies may have affected the statistics. As regards the effects of migration on the district populations, it has been already pointed out that it has not been found possible to adjust the migratory population at the last Census to the redistributed areas. The only course left is to correlate as far as possible the variations in population in the districts to their agricultural condition, their state of public health, and any developments of trade and industry in them, during the decade. The movement of the urban population has been dealt with in the preceding Chapter. Owing to reasons connected with the wholesale redistribution of territory, it has not been possible to adjust the figures of the previous Censuses to the changed areas of the several talukas. This chapter, will, therefore, conclude with a brief notice of the salient agricultural, industrial and public health features of the decade in the several districts.

41. Variation in density.

The subjoined map shows the variations in density of population in the State and the Natural Divisions and Districts. The density for the State as a whole has increased from 119 persons to the square mile in 1881 to 162 persons to the square mile in the present Census. Of the two Natural Divisions, Telingana has had the largest increase. Starting with but 107 persons to the square mile in 1881, its density has increased in thirty years to 162, whereas Marathwara, which had a density of 131 in 1881, has now 161 persons to the square mile. This is no doubt due to the fact that while Telingana has been reclaimed from the jungle largely during the last thirty years, the conditions of Marathwara have on the whole been considerably more settled all throughout the period, except for the devastating famine at the end of the last century. It is to be expected, too, that, in the absence of any serious change in the industrial conditions of the two Divisions, the increase of population in Telingana will be larger in the immediate future than in Marathwara, owing to the fact that the proportion of cultivable area still remaining uncultivated, is larger in the former than in the latter Division. The same observations hold good for the variations in the densities of the several districts. The industrial conditions remaining the same, the increase of population and, consequently, of density in a district will be in proportion to the extent of the land available for cultivation in it. The District figures are discussed in some detail in the remaining paragraphs of this Chapter.

MAP OF HYDERABAD.

Showing variation in density by districts.

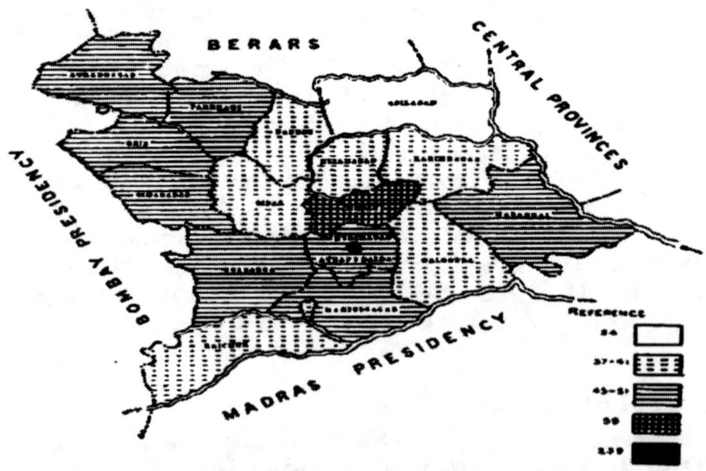

42. Increase of Population by Districts.

In seven out of the eight Telingana districts, the increase of population during the decade was either equal to or exceeded the mean for the State. In five of them, it exceeded the average for the Natural Division. Only in the case of the Nizamabad District did the ratio of increase fall below the State average. As this is the sole case of a Telingana district falling behind in the race of population, it is

State	+ 20·0
Telingana	+ 24·0
Karimnagar	+ 35·4
Medak...	+ 29·3
Adilabad	+ 28·1
Warangal	+ 26·4
Mahbubnagar	+ 24·1
Atrafibalda	+ 20·5
Nalgonda	+ 20·0

worthy of special attention. The population of this district increased only by 14·1 per cent. during the decade. In the whole State, taking the two Natural Divisions, this is the third lowest increase in the period under review. Nizamabad is the new name of a district carved out of what was known as Indur at the last Census. But as the effect of the changes on the population of districts brought about by interdistrict transfers has been calculated and adjusted in the Statistics in the Imperial and Subsidiary tables, there is no need to consider the actual figures of the old Indur District. From Subsidiary Table I, it appears that the area which is now the Nizamabad district, was one of the three Telingana districts which experienced an actual decrease of population at the Census of 1901. Between, 1881 and 1891, its population increased by 11·1 per cent., but in the next decade, it decreased by 0·7. The increase in the present decade, 14·1 per cent. is somewhat higher than that in 1881-1891. The density has increased from 138 in 1881 and 152 in 1901 to 174 per square mile. The density per square mile of cultivated area in the district is high, and, in the absence of special circumstances, the growth of population cannot be expected to rise to a sensational level.

43. Karimnagar.

This district showed the largest increase of population during the decade in the whole of these Dominions. The population enumerated at the present Census was 35·4 per cent. more than that which inhabited the area comprising the district, at the previous Census. The population showed a decrease of 4·2 per cent. in the ten years 1891-1901, but the Census Commissioner of India was of opinion that the enumeration was faulty as the reason assigned for the decrease was in his opinion not sufficient to account for it. If the population had been under-estimated in 1901 the increase at the present Census will, of course, be less abnormal. The view of the Census Commissioner of India would seem to receive support from the remarkable variations in the population of certain villages in the district which are noted in the margin. In these five villages taken together, the population, if the enumeration in 1901 was correct, must be supposed to have quadrupled itself. The increase in the population of the district is probably not so large as it appears. Still it has been considerable, and the explanation seems to be that the seasons have been favourable and that there has been no serious epidemics during the decade. The cultivated area increased from 1,426 in 1903 to 2,006 square miles in 1911 and that under irrigation from 266 to 410 square miles in the same period. The increase of population during 1881-1891 in this district was 17 per cent.

Sarf-i-Khas villages in Karimnagar Taluka.

Village.	Population.	
	1901.	1911.
1. Totapalli	197	1456
2. Jangaon	443	1642
3. Rangunda	390	971
4. Kachanpalli	215	806
5. Potapalli	483	1533
	1,628	6,408

44. Other districts in Telingana.

The districts which show the lowest and the highest increases amongst Telingana districts, have been dealt with above. It will be sufficient to indicate any special features of the decade calculated to influence the growth of population in the other districts, instead of indulging in a game of permutation and combination of the causes mentioned in connection with the two districts the statistics of which have been examined above. Next to Karimnagar, Medak has the highest percentage of increase, namely, 29·3. This district also showed a slight decrease, 0·5 per cent., of population in the previous decade. Two events of the first important to the material prosperity of the district occurred one just before and the other during the decade. The first was the advent of the Godavari Valley Railway and the second, the completion of the Mahbubnagar Canal to which reference has been made in the last chapter. The seasons have been propitious and there were no epidemics. The cultivated area increased from 504 square miles in 1903 to 741 in 1911. Adilabad shows the next highest increase 28·1. This is a very sparsely populated district, and its high rate of increase is not surprising. It has only 85 persons to the square mile. The district has large forest areas which await the plough. It is also inhabited by a prolific race, the Gonds. The conversion of it into a full district during the decade, would seem to have made it more attractive to settlers. Warangal, the other district which had an increase of population higher than the mean for Telingana, also enjoyed the positive blessings of good seasons and the negative ones of absence of epidemics. Special features of its history during the decade, are repairs to the Laknawaram tank, the largest sheet of water in these Dominions, and to another large tank known as the Ramappa, which added to the irrigation resources of the district. The splitting up of the extensive taluka of Pakhal into the Pakhal and Mulug talukas, has placed this wide jungle tract under better and more efficient administration. The Nizam's Guaranteed State Railway which traverses 6 out of 8 talukas of this district, has also contributed to its amenities. The cultivated area increased from 2,428 square miles in 1903 to 2,613 in 1911. The increase in the other three districts of Telingana are due to the generally favourable conditions of the decade.

45. Marathwara.

The population of Marathwara has not increased as rapidly as that of Telingana. Its percentage of increase during the decade is 16·4 as against 24·0 of Telingana. This seems the more remarkable as Marathwara, as the Division severely affected by famine in the previous decade, might have been expected to show a larger increase than Telingana. The occurrence of plague in some of the Marathwara districts has been a counteracting influence. Even otherwise the increase of population in Marathwara cannot cope with that of Telingana. For one thing, practically all the cultivable area in the Division has come under cultivation, and there is very little room for expansion. It has been pointed out in the first Chapter that rice cultivation, which is inconsiderable in Marathwara, has the capacity of supporting a proportionately larger population than that of any other crops. The scanty and uncertain rainfall is another feature of the conditions of Marathwara which is opposed to a rapid growth of population. It seems probable that Marathwara is already supporting a population much nearer to the maximum capacity of its agriculture than Telingana. If it develops modern industries, its possibilities will, of course, vastly increase. The case of Marathwara furnishes a good illustration of what has been offered in paragraph 37 as one probable cause of the high prices of food-grains. Nearly all the cultivable land is cultivated. The population is pressing against the margin of cultivation. Large areas and, as a rule, the more fertile ones, have been transferred to the production of non-food crops which bring higher prices. While the total cultivated areas increased by 15·1 per cent. between the years 1902 and 1910, the area under cotton increased by 21·4 per cent. during the same period. Much of this cotton land lies in Marathwara. Under these circumstances, inferior soils have to be taken up for the cultivation of food grains with the result that the cost of cultivation is constantly increasing, and has to be met by a higher level of prices.

46. Movement of population in Marathwara Districts.

It follows from what has been said in the last paragraph that a considerable expansion of the population in the Marathwara districts cannot be expected in the natural course of things, and that when such an expansion does occur, some new development in the shape either of the substitution of more paying crops or improved methods in cultivation, or of the establishment of new industries, should be looked for in explanation of it. When, however, the pressure of the land has been recently relieved by some great natural calamity or by emigration, the population will expand at a rapid rate till it encounters again the iron limits set by the lack of cultivable land to the growth of a predominantly agricultural community. The percentages of increase of population in the Marathwara districts, are precisely what the foregoing observations lead us to expect. The two lowest increases are in Gulburga (9·1) and Raichur (6·8), and these were the only two districts in the Division which showed increases of population in 1901. When all the other Marathwara districts lost in population, and some of them heavily, Gulburga had an increase of 11·9 and Raichur, 3·9. The increase of population in these two districts since 1881, has been uninterrupted. During the last 30 years Gulburga has added 53 per cent. and Raichur, 43 per cent. to their respective populations, the highest ratio amongst the other Marathwara districts being 18·5 (Aurangabad) and 18·0 (Osmanabad). In Raichur 86·2 per cent. of the total area is cultivated, the cultivable proportion being 87·5 per cent. In Gulburga, the corresponding figures are 43·3 and 44·2. These circumstances are amply sufficient to explain the low rate of increase during the decade in these two districts, and, indeed, a higher rate of growth would have been surprising. There were adventitious causes, such as the partial crop failure in 1904-5, 1907-8, and in 1909-10, and plague has been a regular annual visitant during the decade, but these may be regarded as simply incidental to the prime fact that the limits of cultivation, according to prevailing methods, have been reached. Raichur too had its seasons of partial failure of crops, and visitations of plague, but in its case as in that of Gulburga the principal reason of the low rate of increase is that the cultivable area is practically all under cultivation.

47. The increases in Marathwara during the decade occurred in Bhir (26·4), Nander (21·4), Parbhani (20·4), Aurangabad and Osmanabad (19·8) each, and Bidar (18·9). These increases are almost exactly in the same order as the decreases during the previous decade, as shown by the marginal table. That the increases are mainly due to the losses in 1901, is sufficiently plain. In Nander and Aurangabad the rebound has been proportionately greater than the loss during 1891-1901, but there are reasons for it. Nander, as was pointed out in the 1st Chapter, is one of the three districts of Marathwara which grow rice on a considerable scale, while Parbhani is not. The only other event which has, no doubt, had a beneficial effect, is the opening of the Hyderabad Godavari Valley Railway. This railway, however, runs through both Nander and Parbhani, and cannot explain the different rates at which their respective populations have responded to the more favourable conditions of the decade. The higher rate of growth of population in Aurangabad, notwithstanding that its loss during 1891-1901 was less than that of Osmanabad and Bidar, is explained by the fact that Aurangabad is one of the most important centres of modern industry in the State.

District.	Increase in 1901-1911.	Percentage Decrease in 1891-1901.
Bhir	+ 26·4	— 23·4
Nander	+ 21·4	— 17·6
Parbhani	+ 20·4	— 19·6
Osmanabad	+ 19·8	— 17·5
Aurangabad	+ 19·8	— 12·9
Bidar	+ 18·9	— 15·9

SUBSIDIARY TABLE I.—Variation in relation to density since 1881.

District and Natural Division.	Percentage of variation Increase + Decrease —			Percentage of net variation in period 1881 to 1911.	Mean density per square mile.			
	1901 to 1911.	1891 to 1901.	1881 to 1891.		1911.	1901.	1891.	1881.
1	2	3	4	5	6	7	8	9
State	+20·0	— 3·5	+17·1	+35·8	162	135	140	119
Telingana	+24·0	+ 4·6	+17·5	+52·3	163	131	126	107
Hyderabad City...	+ 8·2	+ 8·0	+12·9	+32·1	10,012	9,246	8,557	7,578
Atrafibalda	+20·5	+ 5·2	+ 9·1	+38·5	208	168	160	147
Warangal	+26·4	+11·8	+26·3	+78·7	114	90	81	64
Karimnagar	+35·4	— 4·2	+17·0	+51·8	197	146	152	130
Adilabad	+28·1	+ 7·6	+10·5	+52·4	85	66	62	56
Medak	+29·3	— 0·5	+14·2	+46·8	214	165	166	146
Nizamabad	+14·1	— 0·7	+11·1	+25·9	174	152	153	138
Mahbubnagar	+24·1	+ 4·6	+23·1	+59·9	145	117	112	91
Nalgonda	+20·0	+12·0	+26·2	+69·8	171	143	137	101
Marathwara	+16·4	—10·0	+16·8	+22·4	161	138	153	131
Aurangabad	+19·8	—12·9	+18·6	+18·5	140	117	134	118
Bhir	+26·4	—23·4	+15·0	+11·4	151	119	156	135
Nander	+21·4	—17·6	+ 1·2	+ 1·3	186	153	186	183
Parbhani	+20·4	—19·6	+17·4	+13·6	152	126	157	134
Gulburga	+ 9·1	+11·9	+25·1	+53·0	171	157	140	112
Osmanabad	+19·8	—17·5	+19·4	+13·0	181	151	183	153
Raichur	+ 6·8	+ 3·9	+28·7	+43·0	147	137	132	108
Bidar	+18·9	—15·9	+14·3	+15·4	175	147	173	152

Note.—The figures of density for 1901 and previous censuses have been revised according to the latest figures for area.

II.—Variation in Natural Population.

District and Natural Division.	Population in 1911.				Population in 1901.				Variation per cent. 1901-1911 in natural population Increase + Decrease—
	Actual Population.	Immigrants.	Emigrants	Natural population.	Actual population.	Immigrants.	Emigrants.	Natural population.	
1	2	3	4	5	6	7	8	9	10
State	13,374,676	260,713	306,993	13,420,956	11,141,142	325,197	296,291	11,112,236	+ 20·7
Telingana ...	6,724,964	190,503	40,906	6,575,367	5,430,349	185,867	68,957	5,313,439	+ 23·7
Hyderabad City	500,623	113,172	27,576	415,027	462,821	118,412	52,634	396,543	+ 4·6
Atrafibalda ...	530,159	55,904	39,563	503,818	431,502	69,677	54,395	416,220	+ 21·0
Warangal ...	965,414	60,815	19,660	864,259	716,171	59,478	128,054	784,747	+ 10·1
Karimnagar ...	1,131,637	10,045	40,281	1,161,873	835,824	140,097	38,236	733,463	+ 58·4
Adilabad ...	620,426	65,282	4,493	559,637	434,281	29,923	2,195	456,553	+ 22·5
Medak	687,137	35,813	33,758	685,082	531,859	24,562	37,787	544,584	+ 25·8
Nizamabad ...	568,009	17,490	32,639	583,158	497,569	34,095	46,049	509,523	+ 14·4
Mahbubnagar ...	747,178	11,838	23,892	759,242	601,749	46,018	33,697	589,428	+ 28·8
Nalgonda ...	1,044,381	39,621	38,511	1,043,271	870,073	81,914	52,816	890,975	+ 17·0
Marathwara..	6,649,712	180,187	69,071	6,538,596	5,710,793	291,869	83,582	5,502,506	+ 18·8
Aurangabad ...	869,787	47,779	17,886	839,894	725,556	69,787	21,932	677,701	+ 23·9
Bhir	622,531	32,823	29,298	619,006	492,258	39,189	46,869	499,938	+ 23·8
Nander	704,549	42,207	38,149	700,491	580,345	43,709	37,785	574,321	+ 21·9
Parbhani ...	779,674	55,490	19,563	743,747	647,046	74,572	18,339	590,813	+ 25·8
Gulburga ...	1,150,983	37,181	18,285	1,132,087	1,054,145	64,215	41,145	1,011,089	+ 11·9
Osmanabad ...	635,977	40,450	13,785	609,312	530,577	50,508	17,900	497,969	+ 22·3
Raichur ...	996,684	14,219	7,726	990,191	938,015	81,931	32,396	888,468	+ 12·0
Bidar	889,527	22,933	37,274	903,868	747,951	28,070	50,787	770,668	+ 17·1

Note.—Figures for actual population of 1901 are adjusted figures (*see* Imperial Table II.)

III.—Comparison with Vital Statistics.

District and Natural Division.	In 1901-1910 total number of		Number per cent. of population of 1901 of		Excess + or deficiency — of births over deaths.	Increase + decrease — of population of 1911 compared with 1901.	
	Births.	Deaths.	Births.	Deaths.		Natural population.	Actual population.
1	2	3	4	5	6	7	8
State	823,984	928,040	7·3	8·3	—104,056	+ 2,303,720	+ 2,233,534
Telingana ...	415,067	428,716	7·6	7·8	— 13,649	+ 1,261,923	+ 1,294,615
Hyderabad City ...	77,035	83,371	16·6	18·0	— 6,336	— 18,484	+ 38,302
Atrafibalda... ...	20,470	24,270	4·7	5·6	— 3,800	+ 87,598	+ 88,657
Warangal	42,542	48,221	5·9	6·7	— 5,679	+ 79,512	+ 189,243
Karimanagar ...	81,771	69,627	9·6	8·3	+ 12,144	+ 428,410	+ 296,313
Adilabad	17,374	15,635	3·5	3·2	+ 1,739	+ 94,084	+ 136,145
Medak	44,310	44,701	8·3	8·4	— 491	+ 140,498	+ 155,778
Nizamabad... ...	40,450	40,728	8·1	8·1	— 278	+ 73,635	+ 70,440
Mahbubnagar .	26,969	27,511	4·4	4·5	— 542	+ 169,814	+ 145,429
Nalgonda	64,246	74,652	7·3	8·5	— 10,406	+ 152,296	+ 174,308
Marathwara ...	408,917	499,324	7·1	8·7	— 90,407	+ 1,036,090	+ 938,919
Aurangabad ...	66,603	93,609	9·1	12·9	— 27,006	+ 162,193	+ 144,231
Bhir	35,252	40,557	7·1	8·2	— 5,305	+ 119,068	+ 130,273
Nander	46,188	52,939	7·9	9·1	— 6,751	+ 126,170	+ 124,304
Parbhani	53,278	58,304	8·2	9·0	— 5,026	+ 152,934	+ 132,628
Gulburga	62,501	81,335	5·9	7·7	— 18,834	+ 121,020	+ 96,835
Osmanabad... ...	28,906	38,256	5·4	7·2	— 9,350	+ 111,448	+ 105,400
Raichur	78,749	85,085	8·4	9·1	— 6,336	+ 106,719	+ 63,669
Bidar	37,440	49,239	5·0	6·5	— 11,799	+ 133,200	+ 141,576

Note.—Returns for certain years not being available proportional figures have been used instead.

Chapter III.

MIGRATION.

48. Limitations of the subject as treated in this Chapter.

The main purpose of this Chapter is to find out what light the statistics of birth-place collected at the Census, throw on the subject of migration from and into the State. They tell us that a certain number of the population inhabiting these Dominions declared some locality outside these boundaries as their birth-place and that certain others who were enumerated outside this State, had given some town or village in it as their place of nativity. The number of such persons belonging to each sex is given, but no further particulars of them are available. Information regarding their age and civil condition would have been very helpful to our investigation. A person who was born in one place may go to another for widely different objects. He may be simply passing through the place where he is enumerated on the day of the Census; he may be visiting a friend for a few days; he may be a litigant having some temporary business in some Court in the locality; he might have gone there on a pilgrimage or to attend a wedding or a funeral. He will be an immigrant, for the purposes of this chapter, in the place where he was enumerated, equally with one who might have been brought into the State as an infant and has no recollection or knowledge of having been in any place outside the State. A young woman might have married outside her district. She would have figured as an emigrant at the first Census taken after she left her parents' house to join her husband. She goes back to her parental home for her first delivery, according to the general custom, and when she returns to her husband with her new-born baby, there will be two emigrants on one schedule, and two immigrants on the other. If particulars of age and civil condition were available, cases of this kind could be readily distinguished from those of what may be called economic migration. The only clue furnished by the available statistics to the nature of migration, is the proportion of sexes among the population enumerated in the State with birth-places outside it or enumerated outside but with birth-places in it. It may be mentioned here that the birth-place entered in the Schedule is sometimes not the right one, owing to the habit, prevalent among some classes, of regarding as their "native place" not the place where they were born but where their fathers or grand-fathers may live or might have lived.

49. Statistical Tables.

Imperial Table XI contains the statistics of birth-place. Five subsidiary tables are appended to this chapter, giving the actual figures of immigration and emigration by Natural Divisions and districts, the proportional migration between these areas, and the variations in the migration statistics relating to the movement of population between this State and other parts of the Indian continent.

50. Comparison with the previous Censuses.

An entirely misleading impression of the trend of migration in this State will be conveyed if, we do not carry our enquiry beyond the Census of 1901. There were some 65,000 more foreign-born persons enumerated in 1901 in the State than at the present Census and one is apt to infer that the excess was due to destitute people from other parts of India flocking to Hyderabad at a time of a dire famine. But a consideration of the figures for 1891 shows that this was not the case. The total numbers of immigrants and emigrants enumerated at the present and the two previous Censuses from and to countries and provinces outside the State, are compared in the marginal table. The number of immigrants in 1891 exceeded that at the 1901 Census by 60,076 and there were, in 1911, 64,484 fewer immigrants than in 1901. The foreign-born population amounted to 3·3 per cent. in 1891, 2·92 per cent. in 1901, and 1·9 per cent. in 1911, of the total population at the respective Censuses. Absolutely and proportionately, the foreign-born population in the State has been steadily diminishing during the last twenty years, at the rate of over 60,000 persons per decade. The number of emigrants from the State went down by about 90,000 between 1891-1901, and in 1911 it was about 10,000 more than in the latter year. If we regard the immigrant population as permanently settled in the State, we have to face the fact that in 20 years, it has decreased by 125,000, out of a total of 385,273 in 1891. We should regard the stream of immigration as having ceased, and expect the foreign-born population to dwindle into a few paltry hundreds in the next thirty or forty years. If, on the other hand, we regard it as consisting mostly of casual immigrants, there is still the equally significant fact that they do not find it worth while to come into the country in such large numbers as twenty years ago. The rapid economic and industrial developments which are changing the face of India, especially of Western and Central India, are absorbing the entire labour supply available in those parts of the country, so that little is left for immigration into other territories. Not only that, but they are exerting a powerful attraction on labour in these Dominions, as shown by the fact that, notwithstanding that our population is still less by about 2½ millions from what it should have normally been, the number of emigrants to Bombay Presidency continues to increase.

	Immigrants.	Emigrants.
1891	385,273	386,095
1901	325,197	296,291
1911	260,713	306,993

51. Migration between the State and Countries outside India.

It will be convenient to examine separately the migration statistics as they relate to countries outside India, to Provinces in India and to districts within the State. They are so classified in Subsidiary Tables I and II. The emigration to foreign lands is negligible, there being only 146 Hyderabadees enumerated in countries beyond India. But this figure is, of course, far from complete. Many pious Mussulmans from Hyderabad who undertake pilgrimages to the sacred shrines in Persia and to Mecca, not infrequently reside in those countries for some years and in some cases even settle there permanently, having severed all ties and interests with their native country. The table at the margin gives the totals and the number of immigrants from the most important centres, namely, Arabia and Afghanistan, in Asia, and the United Kingdom, in Europe. The total number of immigrants for 1901 was swollen by 601 persons from Turkestan and 1,195 from Persia. The number of Persians at the present Census was 90 and there was only one solitary native of Turkey in Asia. In 1901 the Afghan immigrants numbered 772 men and 114 women. The number of females has decreased only by 13 during the decade while the males have been reduced by 405. The Arabs in 1901 numbered 3,895 men and only 396 females, but in 1911 they are 2,394 men and 470 women. Apparently these persons have settled permanently in the State. Over 60 per cent. of the Arabs are found in Hyderabad City. More than 96 per cent. of the Europeans in the State are natives of the United Kingdom. They number 3,359 males and 431 females. A large proportion of them consists of British soldiers stationed in the State, and the rest are engaged in political, administrative and commercial capacities. The predominance of the Military element accounts for the proportionately small number of women.

Immigrants from outside India.

Total...	7,596
Arabia	2,864
Afghanistan	468
The United Kingdom	3,790

52. Migration to and from Provinces in India.

Subsidiary Table V analyses the statistics of migration between the Hyderabad State and other parts of India. The number of immigrants from Indian Provinces is 253,117, that of emigrants to them, 306,847. The corresponding figures at the two previous Censuses were, respectively, in 1891 : Immigrants 373,383, emigrants 386,095 ; 1901 : immigrants 312,314, emigrants 296,291.

53. Migration between the State and the Adjacent Provinces.

The Bombay and Madras Presidencies and the Central Provinces which adjoin the State, together account for 207,419 or over 81 per cent. of the total immigration from Indian Provinces. More than 56 per cent. of this number belongs to the Bombay Presidency, about 33 per cent. to Madras, and 11 per cent. to Central Provinces and Berar. The total number of emigrants to Indian provinces from the State is 306,847, of which 294,413 or 96 per cent. go to the three adjacent provinces. Bombay absorbs 48 per cent., Madras 21 per cent., and Berar 31 per cent. of the latter number. The State loses 94,123 persons in its migration transactions with Bombay and Berar, and gains 7,129 on the Madras side of the account. More than 15,000 immigrants from the Bombay Presidency were enumerated in each of the following districts which border on that Presidency :—Aurangabad, 25,491, Bhir, 15,441, Gulburga, 18,257, and Osmanabad, 24,792. Berarees are found in most numbers, in Adilabad, 8,085, Nander, 3,656, Hyderabad City, 3,112, and Aurangabad, 3,038. Madrassees are most numerous in Hyderabad City, 15,118, Warangal, 26,791, Nalgonda, 13,672 and Raichur, 5,572. Of emigrants from this State to the Bombay Presidency, over 9,000 were enumerated in Bombay City, and these were doubtless attracted thither by the several large works in progress. About 5,000 persons born in this State are reckoned among the inhabitants of the Poona district, and these, it is believed, are associated with military service. Otherwise, the largest number of Hyderabad-born in the Bombay Presidency are found in the contiguous districts of Ahmednagar (24,680), Khandesh East (12,631), Sholapur (34,516), Bijapur (23,368) and Dharwar (13,408). The emigrants to the Central Provinces and Berar, are found chiefly in the latter division where cotton-picking is the cause of a regular periodic emigration of labourers from this State, and many of the emigrants probably stay on for general labour and for the spring harvest. A considerable proportion of those who went to Berar ten years ago would seem to have permanently settled there. The following districts showed the largest number of Hyderabad-born :—Chanda, 11,616, Akola, 7,807, Buldana, 21,632, and Yeotmal, 31,651. In the Madras Presidency also Hyderabadees are mostly found in the districts adjoining the State : Krishna '23,601', Guntur '2,624', Kurnool '7,277', Bellary '12,894' and the Godavary Agency '6,322'. There are 2,318 of them in Madras City.

54. Migration between the State and Bombay.

Migration between the State and the Bombay Presidency.

Census.	Immigrants.	Emigrants.
1891	159,728	186,848
1901	164,185	129,278
1911	118,880	140,990

During the decade under review the number of Bombay-born in the State diminished by 45,355, while in the previous decade it increased by 4,457. The number of emigrants to the Presidency fell by 57,570 during 1891-1901 and increased by 11,712 during the last decade. The relatively small increase in immigrants and the considerable decrease in the number of emigrants during 1891-1901 is clearly connected with the great famine of 1899-1900. But while the number of immigrants shows a large decrease during the last 10 years, that of emigrants to Bombay shows no inconsiderable increase. In dealing with that part of our subject which relates to migration between contiguous districts, we shall have occasion to deal with some special features of the migration between this State and Bombay. Here, it need only be remarked h at the figures for the decade, of both immigration and emigration, confirm what has been said above, namely, that the industrial revolution in progress in the Bombay Presidency is absorbing all the labour available there, and besides is making large drafts on our population.

55. Migration between the State and the Central Provinces and Berar.

The statistics of migration between the Central Provinces and Berar and this State are compared in the table given at the margin. The figures for the Central Provinces and Berar are given separately in the Report of the Hyderabad Census of 1891, and have been put together for the marginal table. The immigration from the Central Provinces and Berar shows nearly the same features as that from Bombay, except that even in 1901, there was no increase of immigrants into the State. On the other hand, emigration to Berar is distinctly on the wane, as shown by the enormous disparity between the figures for 1891 and 1911.

Migration between Central Provinces and Berar, and the State.

CENSUS	Immigrants.	Emigrants.
1891	51,690	132,790
1901	39,871	94,978
1911	20,947	92,731

56. The statistics relating to migration between the State and the Madras Presidency present a different aspect. Immigrants from Madras decreased largely in 1901 and emigrants to the Presidency received a stimulus, both owing to the famine conditions which preceded the Census of that year. There was no famine in the Godavary and Krishna districts of the Presidency, which border on this State. With the return of normal conditions during the last 10 years, the figures show that the normal tendency at present is in favour of the State. The Madrasee population in Hyderabad City is largely a stationary one as is evident from the slight variation during the decade and by the proportion of its female population. The increase in Warangal by over 100 per cent. in 10 years suggests that the cause is connected with the principal industry of the district, coal mining. In the neighbouring district of Nalgonda, they have increased by over 11,000.

57. Migration between contiguous districts in other Provinces.

The adjoining table gives the totals of immigrants and emigrants from and to provinces outside the State in India, the three adjacent provinces of the Bombay Presidency, Central Provinces and Berar, and the Madras Presidency, and the districts of provinces contiguous to the State. These districts, of course, all belong to the three adjoining provinces, and the statistics relating to them are part of the statistics relating to these provinces. It will be noticed that, while allowance is made in the immigration figures for persons born in non-contiguous districts, the total number of emigrants to the adjacent provinces is assumed to have emigrated to contiguous districts. This is not, of course, literally correct, for as we have seen above, considerable numbers of Hyderabad-born persons were enumerated in Bombay, Poona and Madras Cities. The Census Reports of these Provinces give similar details of their immigrants as are furnished in this report for ours, and a reference to them shows that the actual number of Hyderabad emigrants to the contiguous districts in Bombay, Central Provinces and Berar, and Madras, is 255,739 (105,531 males and 150,208 females).

TERRITORIAL DIVISIONS.	Immigrants.	Emigrants
Total, India	253,117	306,817
Total, 3 adjacent provinces	207,419	294,413
Total, contiguous districts.	126,526	294,418

58. Preponderance of females in migration to contiguous districts in other provinces.

The most striking feature of the statistics of migration between the State and the contiguous districts of the three adjacent provinces is the preponderance of females both among immigrants and emigrants. The actual figures are given in the marginal table. Both as regards number and proportion, the predominance is far more pronounced among emigrants from this State than among immigrants into it. As the simultaneous migration to and from this State of several thousands of persons across the border, the majority of them, females, is not sufficiently explained by the ordinary causes connected with the demand and supply of labour, the statistics of this type of migration call for a somewhat detailed scrutiny.

Migration between the State and contiguous districts in adjacent provinces.

NATURE OF MIGRATION.	Males.	Females.
Immigrants	54,103	72,428
Emigrants	105,531	150,208

59. Bombay Presidency.

Let us first take the case of the Bombay Presidency. The number of immigrants from the Presidency to contiguous districts (Aurangabad, Bhir, Gulburga and Osmanabad) and that of emigrants from this State to such districts (Ahmednagar, Khandesh East, Nasik, Sholapur, Bijapur, Dharwar and Akalkot) are stated in the marginal table. It is surely improbable that on the 10th March 1911, over 83,000 persons had to be brought over to supply the needs of the labour market in the contiguous districts of this State, and that on the same day about 120,000 persons from these districts had to be taken over to the contiguous districts of the Presidency to meet the demand for labour. No doubt, there is an economic element in this migration as well as in others, but there is some other factor which may be said to be the dominant factor. The large number of females in these statistics points to the existence of a good deal of social solidarity, cemented by inter-marriages, between the populations on either side of the border. Administrative divisions do not cut across social life. There is no social convention, such as prevents intermarriage between members of one caste with those of another, which bars marriages between British subjects and subjects of his Highness the Nizam. The higher proportion of females among emigrants to the Presidency than among emigrants from it is noteworthy. In the United Provinces, Bihar and in parts of the Punjab, it was observed, in the last Census Report of India,* that the social status of a given caste decreased from west to east, and there was a sort of rule that a daughter must always be given in marriage to the west and a wife taken from the east. There does not seem to be any such express rule in the districts under reference, but, no doubt, marriages follow the same direction as economic interests. Wherever men go in search of work, there women will follow in search of husbands.

NATURE OF MIGRATION.	Males.	Females.	Females per 100 males
Immigrants ...	33,755	50,226	148·7
Emigrants	45,324	74,139	163·5

60. Central Provinces and Berar.

The number of immigrants from the Central Provinces and Berar is considerably smaller than that of emigrants to those provinces. The immigrants to the contiguous districts of Aurangabad, Parbhani, Nander and Adilabad, together number 16,819 (6,784 males and 10,035 females). The emigrants to the contiguous Berar districts and in Chanda number 35,617 males and 47,941 females. The number of female emigrants from the State is, proportionately to the male emigrants, smaller than the number of female immigrants to the number of male immigrants The position is thus somewhat different from that in

Migration between State and the Central Provinces and Berar.

NATURE OF MIGRATION.	Males.	Females.	Females per 100 males
Immigrants	6,784	10,035	147·9
Emigrants	35,617	47,941	134·6

* Census Report of India, 1901, para. 188, page 98.

regard to the Bombay districts. Women from Berar would seem to have a greater predilection for marrying in the Nizam's Dominions than the women of the latter to marrying in Berar. But the immense disparity between the number of immigrants and emigrants would show that the principal operative force in migration between these territories and the Central Provinces and Berar is at present economic.

61. Madras Presidency.

The number of male and female immigrants are about equal. The females outnumber the males by about 14 per cent. among emigrants to contiguous districts of the Madras Presidency. If the total number of immigrants from Madras, a large proportion of which is settled in Hyderabad City, is considered, the proportion of females falls below that of males.

Migration between the State and the Madras Presidency.

NATURE OF MIGRATION.	Males.	Females.	Females per 100 males.
Immigrants	23,102	23,830	103·1
Emigrants	24,590	28,128	114·3

62. Migration to and from non-contiguous Provinces.

Of the other provinces and States of India, the Rajputana Agency, the United Provinces of Agra and Oudh, Ajmer-Merwara, the Punjab and Mysore sent immigrants numbering over 1,000 each. There was a small increase in the number from the Rajputana Agency and a considerable increase in those from Ajmer-Merwara and the Punjab, but a decrease of nearly 15,000 in the number from the United Provinces, during the decade. The bulk of the United Provinces immigrants was enumerated in 1901 in three districts, namely, Hyderabad City, Warangal and Aurangabad, which shows that they were employed in some civic or industrial capacity. Their number in the City has undergone only a comparatively small diminution, but of 8,038 persons only 875 remain in Warangal, and of 2,795 only 698 in Aurangabad. The Madrassees in Warangal and Bombay men in Aurangabad have supplanted all others.*

63. Of the rest, Bengal which was represented by 1,602 persons in 1901 has only 734 at the present Census. The largest decrease is in the City where they have gone down to 388 from 936 ten years ago. The Central India Agency which has a meagre 565 persons at the present census had 4,347 in 1901. They, too, have been ousted from Warangal where they had nearly 1,000 persons at the previous Census.

64. Internal Migration.

We have now disposed of the several classes of external migration, and have now to deal with the more important subject of inter-State migration. As between the two Natural Divisions there is some but not much interchange of population. Subsidiary Table IV shows that 69,071 persons born in Marathwara have been enumerated in Telingana, and 40,906 born in Telingana, in Marathwara. In 1901, the corresponding figures were 83,582 and 68,957. The larger proportion of Marathwara persons in Telingana in both years is mainly due to the situation of Hyderabad City in that Division. The number of Marathwara-born enumerated in the City is 18,080, so that the normal immigration from this Division to Telingana is 50,991. Even this number is higher than that of the sons of Telingana found in Marathwara. Enough has been said in the two preceding chapters to show that the limits of expansion in Marathwara, both as regards population and cultivation, are within view, and that, in the absence of a striking industrial development, the population must seek other outlets through emigration. The surplus emigration from Marathwara to Telingana is only one phase of this movement. Outside the City, the largest numbers of Marathwara-born are found in Atraf-i-balda and in Adilabad. The

* The comparison instituted in this and the next paragraph between the district figures for 1911 and 1901, it is believed, is sufficiently accurate as a broad statement of fact. Owing to the general re-distribution of districts, however, it is made with reservation.

former district possesses some of the main attractions of the City which lies in its area, and is, besides, a well-watered district. The latter has large forest areas and its great need is more population. Telingana-born in Marathwara are found largely in Nander, Gulburga, Parbhani and Bidar. It is seen from Subsidiary Table I that, under all heads of immigration, with the significant exception of one, Telingana has larger figures than Marathwara. The exception is "Immigrants from contiguous parts of other Provinces." These immigrants, in Marathwara, are from the adjoining districts of the Bombay Presidency and the Central Provinces and Berar. Reference has been made in the previous paragraph to the character of the migration between these provinces and this State. Actual figures for emigration from Natural Divisions and Districts to outside districts and provinces are not available.

65. Proportion of Sexes in Migration between Natural Divisions.

From Subsidiary Table II, it is seen that the preponderance of women, which is such a feature of the migration between the State and the adjacent provinces, is entirely absent from the migration statistics between the Natural Divisions. It has been shown above that, in the immigrant population from the contiguous districts of the Madras Presidency, which is found almost entirely in Telingana, there are over 103 females to 100 males. When the contiguous Marathwara districts in the State are included, the proportion of immigrant females to Telingana sinks to 99 per 100 males. Similarly, as regards emigrants, while the proportion of females among emigrants from Telingana to contiguous districts outside the State, is 114·3 for 100 males, when Divisional emigration is taken into account it falls to 102. This feature of inter-Divisional migration is duly reflected in the statistics of Marathwara. Immigrants from the contiguous districts of Bombay and Berar have about 148 females per 100 males; when contiguous districts of Telingana are included, the proportion is reduced to 125. Emigrants to the former districts have 163 females in Bombay and 184 per 100 males in Berar districts: with the inter-State figures, the proportion is only 95. It is obvious that there is much less social intercourse as between the Natural Divisions than as between the populations of the State and of the adjoining political divisions.

66. Migration by districts.

Of the total population of the State, 981 in every 1,000 have their birthplaces within its borders. Of these 948 were born in the districts where they were enumerated, and with these stay-at-homes we have nothing to do in this chapter. 25 persons out of 1,000 inhabitants of the State, had the necessity or enterprise or energy or curiosity to travel so far as the districts contiguous to those in which they were born. Many of the 25 were doubtless born in villages and talukas bordering on the district where they were enumerated, but of movements between villages and talukas we have no data. 8 persons in 1,000 were enumerated in districts not contiguous to their own. This is less than the proportion enumerated outside the State. There is less reason for a man to go from, say, Osmanabad to Karimnagar—there were two such persons enumerated—than from Raichur to Bombay City. The native of Hyderabad fully shares the sentiment of his countrymen in other parts of India that it is wisest and best to stick to one's native village if one can help it.

67. Internal Migration.

The City of Hyderabad has the largest proportion of immigrants (226 per 1,000) in the State. Only 33 of this number are from contiguous districts. Amongst the remaining 193, immigrants from foreign countries outside India are about 12. Immigrants from non-contiguous parts of the State and from other provinces of India are represented in almost equal proportions, amongst the remaining portion of the non-Hyderabad-born. Next to the City, the largest proportions of immigrants are in Atrafibalda (107), Adilabad (105), Parbhani (71) and Warangal (67). These figures are inclusive of immigrants born in non-contiguous districts and outside the State. The border districts show, as might be expected, the largest proportion of foreign immigrants, the City always excepted. We have dealt with this aspect of the subject in the preceding paragraphs. The high proportion of immigrants in Hyderabad City are due to obvious reasons. Atraf-i-balda has the largest percentage of irrigated land in the State and the high proportion of immigrants enumerated therein, is partly due to the usual movement of agriculturists in Telingana, when the water-supply in their own places is exhausted after the Abi crops, of proceeding to places where large sources of irrigation exist for Tabi cultivation. The high proportion of immigrants in Adilabad is similarly to be partly accounted for by the seasonal movements of pastoral communities to forest areas where they find plenty of fodder and water for their cattle. Both these movements were in progress about the time of the Census and they have no doubt had some influence on the proportion of immigrants enumerated in these districts and in others offering like facilities. Atraf-i-balda is unique in that it has the highest proportion not only of immigrants, but also of emigrants, in the State, the former excluding, and the latter including, the capital city. The immigrants are mostly natives of Hyderabad City and the contiguous districts of the Medak Division, Bidar, and Gulbarga, and the proportion of females among them, from 102 to 144 per 100 males, would show that many of them are more or less permanent settlers. Adilabad has the lowest density of population in the State, and it is not surprising that, while it has one of the largest proportions of immigrants, it has the smallest proportion of emigrants in the State. The bulk of immigrants to this district are from Aurangabad and from Bombay and Berar. A special circumstance which caused the influx of 5,663 labourers in the Parbhani district, was the construction of the railway extension line known as the Purna-Hingoli Branch. Even otherwise, the district is one of the low density districts in the State and is dependent to a large extent on the influx of labour from neighbouring districts to carry on its agricultural operations. Bhir and Nander are its principal sources of supply within the State and outside the State, the Bombay Presidency. The Jatra of Korvi in the Warangal district, which occurred at about the time of the Census, attracted a large concourse of Hindus from the neighbouring districts of the State and of the Madras Presidency. Warangal, next to Adilabad, has the fewest persons to the square mile, and with its coal-mining industry, is always thirsting for more population. It has also a low proportion of emigrants, 22 per 1,000. The Urus at Khuldabad, in the Aurangabad district, also held at about the time of the Census, is estimated to have been attended by over 4,000 pilgrims, mostly Musalmans, from different parts of the State and from the Bombay Presidency. Aurangabad also draws a considerable supply of labour from Bhir, but it is dependent to a much larger extent for its supply on the Bombay Presidency. Bhir and Nander are the largest exporters of labour in Marathwara, the largest importers being Parbhani, Osmanabad and Nander. In Telingana, Nizamabad and the City show the highest proportion of emigrants, next to Atraf-i-balda. The City-born are represented in all the districts. They serve, it may be supposed, to impart some of the refinement of the capital to the rustics of Marathwara and Telingana. The causes of the larger or smaller proportion of migration, in the absence of special circumstances, are closely associated with those adduced in dealing with the densities of population and its movements in the two previous chapters.

68. Proportion of females in internal migration.

The proportion of women among immigrants in Bhir is 222 per 100 males and in Osmanabad 205. These are the two highest percentages in the State and they occur only in the immigrant population from contiguous districts, whether within or without the State. As Osmanabad also sends out a high proportion of women among its emigrants, 210 per 1,000 males, it may be concluded that this exchange of females has reference to some aspects of its social life. The explanation with regard to Bhir would seem to be that its position as a Labour Exchange in Marathwara has attracted a number of immigrant settlers, and that at the time of the Census, the male settlers had gone in search of work to the neighbouring districts, leaving their women behind.

SUBSIDIARY TABLE I.—Immigration (Actual Figures).

District and Natural division where enumerated.	Born in																	
	District.			Contiguous district in State.			Other parts of State.			Contiguous parts of other Provinces.			Non-contiguous parts of other Provinces.			Outside India.		
	Total.	Males.	Females.	Total.	Males.	Females.	Total.	Males.	Females.	Total.	Males.	Females.	Total.	Males.	Females.	Total.	Males.	Females.
1	2	3	4	5	6	7	8	9	10	11	12	13	14	15	16	17	18	19
State	13,113,963	6,665,244	6,448,719	..	.. .	....	....	....	....	126.526	54,103	72.423	126.591	71,334	55.257	7.596	6.437	1,159
Telingana ..	6,534,461	3,336,868	3.197,593	52.169	26,364	25.805	16,902	9,230	7,672	71,474	35,661	35,813	43,316	26,791	16.525	6,642	5,707	935
Hyderabad City..	387,451	190,292	197,159	16,563	8,632	7,931	45,609	27,093	18,516	....	....	....	45,165	27,858	17,307	5,835	5,079	756
Atraf-i-balda ..	464,255	237,581	226,674	43,704	21,614	22,090	9,645	4,196	5.449	....	....	....	2,399	1,683	716	156	110	46
Warangal ..	844,599	435,472	409,127	26,327	13,938	12,389	5,576	3,541	2,085	19,209	8,167	11,042	9,574	6,195	3,379	129	100	29
Karimnagar ..	1,121,592	581,169	540,423	7,787	3,668	4,119	1,469	879	590	55	17	38	703	504	199	31	23	8
Adilabad	555,144	279,514	275,630	30,677	18,177	12,500	15,480	8,110	7,370	3,965	1,469	2,496	15,046	7,063	7,983	114	95	19
Medak	651,324	332,604	318,720	31,628	13,436	18,192	1,932	1,031	901	....	....	....	2,101	1,222	879	152	117	35
Nizamabad ..	550,519	276,413	274,106	13,858	5,035	8,823	2,562	1,453	1,129	....	....	....	955	639	316	95	81	14
Mahbubnagar ..	735,350	374,226	361,124	9,490	4,148	5,342	765	395	370	160	131	29	1,347	762	585	66	50	16
Nalgonda ..	1,004,760	517,345	487,415	24,843	12,124	12,719	603	376	227	6,598	3,383	3,215	7,513	3,859	3,654	64	52	12
Marathwara .	6,469,525	3,271,376	3,198,149	38,527	19,743	18,784	2,379	1,663	716	120,829	51.086	69,743	17.498	11,899	5.599	954	730	224
Aurangabad ..	822,008	414,236	407,772	8,133	3,791	4,342	4,059	1,942	2,117	17,695	6,929	10,766	17,646	10,418	7,233	246	184	62
Bhir	589,706	303,596	286,112	14,401	4,651	9,750	1,156	638	518	12,391	4,544	7,847	4,784	1,243	3,541	91	66	25
Nander	662,342	331,632	330,710	27,184	12,387	14,797	6,112	3,496	2,616	3,230	1,585	1,645	5,554	3,429	2,125	127	109	18
Parbhani ..	724,184	362,282	361,902	29,271	14,385	14,886	7,837	4,909	2,928	366	30	336	17,849	9,488	8,361	167	137	30
Gulbarga	1,113,802	562,924	550,878	15,766	8,582	7,184	1,313	873	440	14,744	7,151	7,593	5,247	2,832	2,415	111	85	26
Osmanabad ..	595,527	310,963	284,564	12,993	4,153	8,840	1,402	761	641	22,792	8,247	14,545	3,183	791	2,392	80	54	26
Raichur	982,465	496,391	486,074	2,474	1,154	1,320	1,242	739	508	7,787	3,780	4,007	2,627	1,412	1,215	89	65	24
Bidar	866,594	438,275	428,319	19,726	9,775	9,951	732	247	485	634	280	354	1,798	831	967	43	30	13

SUBSIDIARY TABLE II.—Emigration (Actual Figures.)

District and Natural division of birth.	Enumerated in																	
	District.			Contiguous districts in State.			Other parts of State.			Contiguous parts of other Provinces.			Non-contiguous parts of other Provinces.			Outside India.		
	Total.	Males.	Females.	Total.	Males.	Females.	Total.	Males.	Females.	Total.	Males.	Females.	Total.	Males.	Females.	Total.	Males.	Females.
1	2	3	4	5	6	7	8	9	10	11	12	13	14	15	16	17	18	19
State	13.113.963	6.665.244	6448.719	....	....	....	....	....	....	294.413	127.391	167.022	12.434	7.782	4.652	146	134	12
Telingana ..	6.534.461	3.336.868	3.197.593	30.710	15.237	15.473	10.196	6.169	4.027	Figures for districts not available.	Figures for districts not available.	Figures for districts not available.	Figures for districts not available.	Figures for districts not available.	Figures for districts not available.	Figures for districts not available.	Figures for districts not available.	Figures for districts not available.
Hyderabad City..	387,451	190,292	197,159	5,257	2,938	2,319	22,319	13,205	9,114									
Atraf-i-balda ..	464,255	237,581	226,674	37,699	18,344	19,355	1,864	868	1,056									
Warangal ..	844,590	435,472	409,127	13,904	6,861	7,043	5,756	2,927	2,829									
Karimnagar ..	1,121,592	581,169	540,423	34,969	18,505	16,464	6,312	3,266	2,046									
Adilabad	555,144	279,514	275,630	2,791	1,376	1,415	1,702	910	792									
Medak	651,324	332,604	318,720	30,996	15,592	15,404	3,212	1,733	1,479									
Nizamabad ..	550,519	276,413	274,106	23,271	10,953	12,318	9,368	6,023	3,345									
Mahbubnagar ..	735,350	374,226	361,124	20,554	9,939	10,615	3,338	1,597	1,741									
Nalgonda ..	1,004,760	517,315	487,415	38,114	18,656	19,458	397	243	154									
Marathwara .	6.469.525	3.271.376	3.198.149	67.183	34.392	32.791	1.888	1.202	686									
Aurangabad ..	822,008	414,236	407,772	9,894	4,293	5,601	7,992	4,784	3,208									
Bhir	589,708	303,596	286,112	24,822	9,961	14,861	4,476	2,032	2,444									
Nander	662,342	331,632	330,710	31,922	18,016	13,906	6,227	3,041	3,186									
Parbhani ..	724,184	362,282	361,902	13,975	5,574	8,401	5,588	3,459	2,129									
Gulbarga.. ..	1,113,802	562,924	550,878	14,421	7,034	7,387	3,864	1,887	1,977									
Osmanabad ..	595,527	310,963	284,564	10,754	3,468	7,286	3,031	1,201	1,830									
Raichur	982,465	496,391	486,074	4,125	2,026	2,099	3,601	2,161	1,440									
Bidar	866,594	438,275	428,319	33,859	15,872	17,487	3,915	1,862	2,053									

SUBSIDIARY III—PROPORTIONAL MIGRATION TO AND FROM EACH DISTRICT.

District and Natural division.	Number per mille of actual population of						Number of females to 100 males amongst			
	Immigrants.			Emigrants.			Immigrants.		Emigrants.	
	Total.	From contiguous districts.	From other places.	Total.	To contiguous districts.	To other places.	From contiguous districts.	From other places.	To contiguous districts.	To other places.
1	2	3	4	5	6	7	8	9	10	11
State	19	9	10	23	22	1	120	42	131	59
Telingana ...	28	18	10	6	5	1	99	60	102	65
Hyderabad City	226	33	193	55	10	45	92	62	79	69
Atraf-i-balda ...	107	84	23	76	72	4	102	104	106	131
Warangal ...	67	50	17	22	15	7	94	50	103	97
Karimnagar ...	9	7	2	36	31	5	113	55	89	63
Adilabad ...	105	56	49	7	4	3	81	96	103	87
Medak	52	46	6	50	45	5	136	91	99	85
Nizamabad ...	31	24	7	57	41	16	175	67	112	56
Mahbubnagar ...	16	13	3	32	28	4	121	85	107	109
Nalgonda ...	38	30	8	37	37	...	102	55	104	63
Marathwara...	27	24	3	10	10	...	125	46	95	57
Aurangabad ...	55	30	25	21	12	9	119	70	130	67
Bhir	53	43	10	47	40	7	222	60	149	120
Nander	60	43	17	54	45	9	116	69	77	105
Parbhani ...	71	38	33	25	18	7	107	75	151	62
Gulbarga ...	32	27	5	16	12	8	95	53	105	105
Osmanabad ...	63	56	7	22	17	5	205	66	210	152
Raichur	14	11	3	8	4	4	109	56	104	67
Bidar	26	23	3	42	38	4	102	13	110	110

IV—MIGRATION BETWEEN NATURAL DIVISIONS (ACTUAL FIGURES) COMPARED WITH 1901.

Natural Division in which born.		Number enumerated in Natural Division.	
		Telingana.	Marathwara.
1		2	3
Telingana ...	1911...	6,655,893	40,906
	1901...	5,346,767	68,957
Marathwara ...	1911...	69,071	6,608,806
	1901...	83,582	5,641,836

V.—Migration between the Hyderabad State and other parts of India.

Province or State.	Immigrants to the Hyderabad State.			Emigrants from the Hyderabad State.			Excess (+) or deficiency (—) of immigration over emigration.	
	1911.	1901.	Variation.	1911.	1901.	Variation.	1911.	1901.
1	2	3	4	5	6	7	8	9
Total ...	**253,117**	**312,314**	**— 59,197**	**306,934**	**296,291**	**+ 10,643**	**— 53,817**	**+ 16,023**
Provinces	**229,385**	**291,490**	**— 26,105**	**299,605**	**291,416**	**+ 8,189**	**— 70,220**	**+ 74**
Ajmer-Merwara	6,698	3,517	+ 3,181	...	110	— 110	+ 6,698	+ 3,407
Andamans and Nicobars ...	...	...	......	87	...	+ 87	— 87	...
Assam	5	...	+ 5	119	150	— 31	— 114	— 150
Baluchistan	115	18	+ 97	76	49	+ 27	+ 34	— 86
Behar and Orissa	17	1,602	— 868	204	662	— 214	— 187	+ 940
Bengal	717			244			+ 473	
Bombay...	118,653	164,185	— 45,532	140,990	129,278	+ 11,712	— 22,337	+ 34,907
Burma	185	114	+ 71	1,575	600	+ 975	— 1,390	— 486
Central Provinces and Berar...	20,945	39,871	— 18,926	92,731	94,978	— 2,247	— 71,786	— 55,107
Coorg	1	...	+ 1	66	...	+ 66	— 65	...
Madras	67,821	55,369	+ 12,452	60,692	62,507	— 1,815	+ 7,129	— 7,138
North-West Frontier Provinces	364	2,429	+ 2,405	94	849	+ 625	+ 3,362	+ 1,580
Punjab	4,470			1,878				
United Provinces of Agra and Oudh	9,399	24,390	— 14,991	1,349	2,233	— 884	+ 8,050	+ 22,157
States and Agencies ...	**19,729**	**19,722**	**+ 47**	**7,329**	**4,875**	**+ 2,454**	**+ 12,440**	**+ 14,847**
Baluchistan (Agency-tracts)...	71	...	+ 71	...	...	...	+ 71	...
Baroda	204	156	+ 48	164	223	— 59	+ 40	— 67
Bombay States...	177	...	+ 177	...	...	...	+ 177	...
Central India Agency ...	565	4,347	— 3,782	2,177	2,627	— 450	— 1,612	+ 1,720
Central Provinces States ...	2	...	+ 2	...	...	...	+ 2	...
Cochin	10	...	+ 10	...	...	...	+ 10	...
Kashmir	83	1	+ 82	11	18	— 7	+ 72	— 17
Mysore	3,880	1,360	+ 2,520	4,342	1,876	+ 2,466	— 462	— 516
Punjab States	399	...	+ 399	...	...	...	+ 399	...
Rajputana Agency	14,271	13,858	+ 413	568	131	+ 437	+ 13,703	+ 13,727
Travancore	6	...	+ 6	67	...	+ 67	— 61	...
United Provinces State ...	101	...	+ 101	...	...	...	+ 101	...
French and Portuguese Settlements	**288**	**18**	**+ 270**	**...**	**...**	**...**	**+ 288**	**+ 18**
India Unspecified... ...	**3,675**	**1,084**	**+ 2,591**	**...**	**...**	**...**	**+ 3,675**	**+ 1,084**

Chapter IV.

RELIGION.

PART I.

69. Scope of the Chapter.

The first two chapters dealt with the distribution of the population, and their variations in number, according to the areas occupied by them. Its distribution according to religions—the several kinds of faith in God and a future life, and the conduct and worship appropriate thereto—forms the subject-matter of this chapter. It is worthy of note that the entire population is accounted for under the several religions, so that there is no standing room left for the Atheist or the Agnostic. Every religion, ancient, medieval and modern, is represented in the State. The Hindu, the Buddhist and the Jain, the Jew, the Christian (Syrian, Roman Catholic and Protestant) and the Musulman, the Parsi, the Sikh, the Arya Samajist and the Brahmo Samajist, as well as the Animist, enjoy equal toleration and protection under the Government of His Highness the Nizam.

70. Statistical Tables.

The statistical materials for this chapter are contained in Imperial Tables V and VI. The first table gives the distribution of persons professing each religion in urban and rural areas ; the second, shows their actual numbers in the State and in the districts. Imperial Table XVII contains particulars as to sect and race of the Christian population. Of the six subsidiary tables appended to this chapter, the first two indicate the general distribution of the population by religion in the State and in the districts at the present and previous Censuses. Subsidiary Tables III, IV, and V are specially devoted to the variations in number and distribution by sects and races of persons professing the Christian faith. The sixth and the last subsidiary table is intended to show the proportions in which the several religions are represented in the urban and rural population.

71. Distribution of the population by religion.

The marginal table gives the actual number of persons following each of the six religions which have a following of more than 20,000 in the State. Of the others, the Sikhs number 4,726, the Parsis, 1,529, the Arya Samajists are represented by 173 and the Brahmo Samajists by 36 individuals, while 20 Buddhists and 12 Jews uphold the name of these ancient religions in His Highness's territories.

Religion.	Population.
Hindu	11,626,146
Musalman	1,380,990
Animist	285,722
Christian	54,296
Jain	21,026

72. Variation in the number and proportion of Hindus.

The Hindu population shows an increase of 17·7 per cent. since the last Census. Since 1881, it has increased by 30·7 per cent. As the total population has grown by 20 per cent. during the last 10 years and by 35·8 per cent. since 1881, the Hindu rate of increase has not kept pace with that of the population as a whole. Owing to this disparity between the rates of increase of the population as a whole, and of the Hindus, the latter who, in 1881, showed a proportion of 9,033, have since then steadily declined to 8,693, in 10,000 persons, which is their proportion at the present Census. This set-back, 340 in 10,000 persons, is accounted for as follows:—Musulmans + 92, Animists + 214, Christians + 26, Jains + 7, and others + 1. The separate enumeration of Animists since 1891, and conversions chiefly to Christianity are responsible for the bulk of the decline in the Hindu proportion. If we take the Hindus and Animists together, as was done in 1881, we find that their combined population at the present Census, represents an increase of 33·9 per cent. in 30 years. But this is not all. Since 1891, the first year when Animists were accorded a distinctive position on the Census Schedule, the line between Hinduism and Animism has been sought to be drawn with increasing precision at each Census, with the result that the increases noted against the Animists have been quite phenomenal; and, of course, the effect on the strength of the Hindu population, as shown in the Census, has been the reverse, though, owing to the vast numbers of the latter, the decrease shows only as a small percentage. At the present Census, the enumerators were instructed not to enumerate as "Hindu" persons who could not state what their religion was, and simply returned some tribal name, but to write down the name of their tribe, in the column for religion in addition to writing it down in the column for caste and race. The result has been to swell the number of Animists by 337·4 per cent. on the total recorded at the Census of 1901. If we take the Animists as in 1901, and after allowing them a 20 per cent. increase—the rate of the general population during the decade—add the rest to the Hindu population, the increase of the latter during the decade would be 19·9 per cent. Thus, it is seen that the classification of Animism as a distinct religion, has had the effect of showing the increase of the Hindu population since 1881 to be 3·2 per cent. less than what it would have been if the plan of 1881 had been throughout followed; and that the rule introduced at the present Census of classifying as Animists all who could not state what their religion was, has affected the Hindu increase during the last decade to the extent of 2·2 per cent. But for this innovation, the Hindu rate of increase during the decade would be slightly higher than that of the Musulman.

73. Loss by Conversions from Hinduism.

The other source of leakage from the Hindu population, arises from conversions to other religions. The number of persons enumerated as Aryas and Brahmos is too insignificant to affect the statistics. There is no considerable or systematic proselytising on the part of Mahomedanism in these Dominions. The only religion which is actually engaged in making converts is Christianity.

74. Re-admission of Converts.

It is well-known that, while Hinduism is a non-proselytising religion, converts to Christianity are mostly drawn from Hindus especially of the lower castes. The only attempts which Hindus have made to stem the tide of proselytism, have so far taken the shape of a movement for relaxing the rules against the re-admission of repentant converts.

75. Probable number of Converts to Christianity.

Allowing 20 per cent. for the natural increase of the Christian population, there is a balance of 26,700 for converts from other religions. If, as is probable, the whole or the larger proportion of this number were converts from Hinduism, it would mean a loss of 0·27 per cent. calculated on the Hindu population in 1901.

76. The effect of migration.

Migration, too, is likely to have detrimentally affected the rate at which the Hindu population has increased. It was shown in the previous chapter that there was an excess of emigrants over immigrants during the decade. What proportion of these were Hindus, there is no means of knowing, as there is no entry as regards religion in the table relating to birth-place. But it is reasonable to assume that the Hindus were represented amongst them in as large a proportion as in the total population of the State, and the bulk of the loss must necessarily fall to them.

77. The influence of social customs and religious ideals.

The causes set forth in the preceding paragraphs, especially the first two, have operated with varying force during the last thirty years but never more strongly than during the last ten, to bring about a disparity between the rate at which the total population has been increasing and that at which the Hindu population has been increasing. There are other causes, depending on social customs and religious ideals, which tend to exert a retarding influence on the rate of growth of population among Hindus. These causes work in a steady and uniform manner as they are independent of instructions to enumerators and of the conditions, material and moral, which control the operations of missionary propaganda. Their effect is seen in the slower rate of growth over long periods of the Hindus as compared with communities like the Musulman, for instance, which are not affected, at any rate, to the same extent, by similar customs and ideals. These are social customs such as infant and too early marriages and enforced widowhood, and, generally, the predominance of ascetic ideals in the social and religious outlook of the Hindus as a community. Early marriages, though they lead to a large number of births, also lead to a large number of deaths among infants and children, so that, in the net result, such marriages are less calculated to help the growth of population than marriages between persons of mature ages. The large number of deaths among child-mothers, which is also a consequence of too early marriages, also unfavourably affects the numerical strength of the Hindu population, actually and potentially. Enforced widowhood, by arbitrarily withdrawing a considerable proportion of women in the child-bearing ages from fulfilling the function of motherhood, greatly handicaps the race in its growth. Ascetic ideals of life leading to inattention to health and comfort, conduces to lowered vitality and increased mortality. In the face of these discouraging circumstances, the wonder is not that the Hindu population grows at a somewhat less rapid rate than the population of other creeds, but that it has managed in spite of them all, to grow as much as it has grown during the last decade. It is a noteworthy fact that, as shown in the margin, the rate of increase of the Hindu population in the Nizam's Dominions exceeds that in the Madras and Bombay Presidencies, and in the Central Provinces and Berar, both during the decade and since 1881.

Percentage of increase of Hindu population.

Province.	1901-1911.	1881-1911.
Madras	8·1	24·3
Bombay	5	18
Central Provinces & Berar	16	16
Hyderabad...	17·7	30·7

78. Hindus in Natural Divisions.

The distribution and movement of the Hindu population in the Natural Divisions and Districts, only serve to confirm the foregoing observations. The number of Hindus in Telingana and in Marathwara is about equal but, while the Hindus in Telingana have increased by 42·6 per cent. since 1881 as against only 20·6 per cent. in Marathwara, their proportion in the former Division at the present Census is lower than in Marathwara. In all the three previous Censuses it was higher in Telingana than in the other Division. This seemingly paradoxical result is due almost entirely to the separate enumeration of the Animists, about 90 per cent. of whom are inhabitants of Telingana. In 1881 when the term 'Hindu' included the Animist, there were 9,053 Hindus in every 10,000 persons in Telingana. Since 1891 the Hindu proportion has gradually waned while that of the Animists has waxed. In Marathwara, too, the Hindus have lost ground but less than in Telingana. There has been no landslide such as has taken place in Telingana during the last ten years. There are 300 Hindus less than in 1901 for every

Natural Division.	Hindus.	Proportion per 10,000.	Increase per cent. in 1901-11.
Telingana... ...	5,793,527	8,615	+17·2
Marathwara ...	5,832,619	8,771	+18·3

10,000 persons in Telingana, whereas the Marathwara Hindus have lost only 15. The marginal table shows that Animism and Christianity together have gained more than Hinduism has lost in each of the Divisions. The bulk of the converts in Marathwara would seem to have come from among Animists, while in Telingana the converts would seem to have come in about equal proportions from among Hindus and Animists.

Variation in 10,000 persons since 1901.

Religion.	Telingana.	Marathwara.
Hindu	—300	—15
Animist	+281	+24
Christian	+34	+8

79. Distribution of Hindus by Districts.

In seven districts out of the sixteen there are more than 9,000 Hindus to every 10,000 persons. Four of them are in Telingana and three in Marathwara. Karimnagar has had the largest proportion of Hindus in its population at every Census since 1881. Even there, however, their proportion is lower now than it was in previous years. Their proportion at this Census is 92 per 10,000 less than in 1901. Animists appear in the district figures for the first time at this Census, the proportion being 85 per 10,000 of the population. The Christian element also rose from 2 per 10,000 to 5. In Nizamabad the Hindu proportion increased from 9,152 at the previous Census to 9,211. This is mainly due to a rather sharp decline in the Musulman proportion as also in that of Animists. The latter who rose from 8 per 10,000 of the population in 1891, to 57 in 1901, declined to 32 at the present Census. In Bhir also, the proportion of Hindus showed a notable increase during the decade. The proportion of Animists also increased but there was a reduction in the Musulman element, and the Christian population, which was always insignificant, 2 per 10,000, disappeared altogether. Raichur, also, showed an increased proportion of Hindus during the decade, in spite of a considerable increase in the proportion of Christians, and the appearance for the first time of an Animist element in the Census population. In Nalgonda, the Hindu decline is very heavy. There are 494 less Hindus in 10,000 of the population than in 1901. The Animist and Christian columns contain the explanation. There were no Animists in the district at previous Censuses, but at this, 365 out of every 10,000 of its population were of this community. The Christian religion also increased its followers from 17 in 1901 to 101 in 10,000 persons. In Mahbubnagar also, Animists were enumerated for the first time at the present Census, with a detrimental effect on the Hindu proportion. In Osmanabad the increased proportion of Hindus is simply the reverse aspect of a corresponding decline among Musulmans and Jains.

Hindus per 10,000 persons

District.	Population.
Karimnagar	9,496
Nizamabad	9,211
Bhir	9,093
Raichur	9,084
Nalgonda	9,017
Mahbubnagar	9,004
Osmanabad	9,000

80. In the other nine districts, the Hindu proportion in the population was as stated in the margin. In Warangal it fell from 9,472 at the last Census to 7,995, while that of the Animists increased from 14 to 1,315, and that of the Christians from 16 to 132. The cases of Gulbarga and Aurangabad are very similar to that of Warangal. In Adilabad, on the other hand, occurred a remarkable increase of the Hindu proportion accompanied by as noteworthy a decrease of the Animists. The latter declined from 1,860 to 1,063 per 10,000 of the population during the decade, while the Hindus rose from 7,608 to 8,454.

Hindus in 10,000 of the Population.

District.	Population.
Warangal	7,995
Gulburga	8,481
Aurangabad	8,442
Adilabad	8,454
Bidar	8,564
Atrafibalda	8,751
Nander	8,909
Medak	8,958
Parbhani	8,974

There was an increase in the Hindu proportion in Atrafibalda, due to a reduction in that of the Musulmans. The decrease of the Hindu proportion in other districts is explained by the same reasons as those given in the case of Warangal.

81. Musalmans.

Next to the Hindus, the Musalmans constitute the largest section of the population. Numerically, they increased by 19·4 per cent. during the decade and by 49·1 per cent. since 1881. Proportionately, however, they have not kept up the progress made up to 1901. In the ten-year period under review, the proportion of Musalmans in the population declined from 1,037 to 1,032 for every 10,000 persons. The Musalman rate of increase is only very little less than that of the whole population. It is unlikely that any Musalman was enumerated as an Animist. Conversions to Christianity from followers of Islam are not common. The loss is too small to be of any significance except as an indication that the tide of increase which has been flowing since 1881 has reached, for the time being, its high-water mark. Incidentally, it also shows that conversions to Mahomedanism are as rare in these Dominions as conversions from it.

82. Musalmans in Telingana.

Variation in the number and proportion of the Musalman population in the natural Divisions.

Natural Division.	Increase per cent. in 1901-11.	Variations in 10,000 persons.
Telingana	19·1	—15
Marathwara	19·7	—8

Musalmans per 10,000 of population.

	1901.	1911.
Atrafibalda	1,244	1,141
Medak	1,005	947
Mahbubnagar	831	796
Nizamabad	785	737
Adilabad	524	478

The rate of increase of the Musalman population is slightly smaller and the decline in its proportion considerably larger in Telingana than in Marathwara, as is seen from the marginal table. Except in Hyderabad City, in Warangal, in Nalgonda and, to a small extent, in Karimnagar, the Musalman proportion has receded in all the districts of Telingana, nowhere so much as in the prosperous agricultural districts of Atrafibalda and Medak. The Musalman proportion per 10,000 of the population at this and the previous Census are given in the margin. It is remarkable that the Musalman factor in the population should exhibit a tendency to decline most where irrigation and agriculture are yielding the richest results. The proportion of Musalmans in Hyderabad City has for the first time for the last 20 years exceeded that of 1881. There are exactly 100 Musalmans more in every 10,000 of the population of the City than there were 30 years ago. In Warangal and Nalgonda they have improved their proportion by 59 and 44 respectively, while in Karimnagar the increase is but 2 per 10,000 of the population.

83. Musalmans in Marathwara.

Musalmans per 10,000 of the population.

	1901.	1911.
Bhir...	882	834
Gulbarga	1,508	1,471
Osmanabad	953	935
Raichur	1,014	988

The Musalman population of Marathwara has, as noted above, declined by 8 in every 10,000 of the population since 1901. The decline is confined to four districts, Bhir, Gulburga, Osmanabad and Raichur. The proportional figures are given in the marginal table. Elsewhere the Musalman proportion has increased : in Aurangabad from 1,267 to 1,282, in Nander from 980 to 1,025, in Parbhani from 904 to 930 and in Bidar from 1,374 to 1,403. Marathwara contains many historical centres of the Musalman population as shown by the fact that there is a far larger proportion of it classed as rural than in Telingana.

84. Animists.

In discussing the variations in the number and proportion of Hindus, it was necessary to deal largely with the position of the Animists as disclosed by the statistics. Animists as such were not separately enumerated at the first census of the State taken in 1881. The variation in their numbers and proportion to the total population since 1891 is shown in the marginal table. The increase amounts to 337·4 per cent. in the last ten, and to 880·8 in the last twenty, years. Compared with the variations in the neighbouring provinces, these percentages are very high, which shows that a considerable proportion of the Animists was enumerated for the first time at the present Census in this State. This conclusion is borne out by the fact, which appears from Subsidiary Table II, that in 9 districts of the 16, the Animist column is a blank at all previous Censuses. It is interesting to note, on the other hand, that, in the district of Adilabad, which had the largest Animist population in the State in 1901, their proportion per 10,000 of the total population at the present census is 797 less than in 1901 and 170 less than in 1891. Nizamabad is another district where the proportion of Animists has declined since 1901. The largest proportional increase of this group is in Warangal, which now supersedes Adilabad as the district with the largest number and proportion of Animists in the population. In Nalgonda 365 persons in every 10,000 of the population are shown as Animists. There were none at the previous Census. All the above are Telingana districts. The proportion of Animists in the urban population of the State, as a whole, is 8 per 10,000 of the population. In Telingana it is only 3, while in Marathwara it is 15.

Animists.

Census.	Number.	Proportion per 10,000 persons.
1891...	29,130	25
1901...	65,315	59
1911...	285,722	214

Percentage of variations.

Province.	Since 1901.	Since 1881.
Madras	— 0·5	+35·0
Bombay	+238	—66
Central Provinces and Berar	+ 30	+46

85. Animists in Marathwara.

Compared with Telingana, Marathwara has a much smaller Animists population. In the former division, 382 in 10,000 of the population are Animists against 43 in Marathwara. No Animists were enumerated in Marathwara in the 1891 census. In 1901 there were only 4 districts which had an Animist element in the population, whereas at the present Census it is found in every district. Aurangabad has the largest Animist population in Marathwara, with Gulbarga for a distant second.

86. Christians.

The Christian population of the State numbers 54,296 at the present Census. Subsidiary table III gives the actual numbers of Christians and the variations per cent. in them at each Census. The Christian population, is classified according to race into European, Anglo-Indian and Indian. The number of European Christians at this Census was 5,384, of Anglo-Indians, 3,004, and of Indian Christians, 45,908. The Christian population as a whole, increased by 136·1 per cent. during the last 10 years and by 298·8 per cent. since 1881. But this large increase is confined to Indian Christians, as conversions do not play any part in the increase of the other communities. The marginal table shows the numbers and variations therein of the three groups of Christians at this and the previous Censuses. The increase in the European Christian population calls

Variation in Christians by race.

—	1901.	1911.	Per cent.
European	4,347	5,384	23·8
Anglo-Indian ...	3,292	3,004	—8·7
Indian	15,357	45,908	198·9
Total ...	22,996	54,296	136·1

for no remark. It is composed of officials, merchants and missionaries, and its movements depend on the exigencies of administration, trade and proselytism. The Anglo-Indian Community has declined in numbers, and this is, perhaps, partly referable to the tendency among some members of it to return themselves as Europeans. The large majority of European Christians belong to the Church of England which also claims about one-third of the Anglo-Indian. The larger half of the latter community, however, owe allegiance to the Roman Catholic Church. Of the other sects, the Methodist has the largest following among these two communities.

87. Indian Christians.

Indian Christians of the Roman Catholic Church are more numerous than those of any Protestant Sect. They number 16,322 as against 9,037 at the previous Census, an increase of 80·6 per cent. Next to Hyderabad City, where there are 7,308 Indian Catholics, their chief centres are the Nalgonda and Aurangabad districts. Of the Protestant Sects, the Baptist, the Anglican and the Methodist have the largest number of Indian followers, and have increased most during the decade. 992 out of 1,000 Baptists are Indians. Their principal centres in this State are the Warangal and Nalgonda districts. The Warangal district has the largest number of Indian Christians of the Anglican Communion, and Medak, that of the Methodist Sect. Out of 1,000 Indian Christians, 356 are Roman Catholics, 208 are Baptists, 193 are Anglicans and 177 Methodists. It may be a mere coincidence, but it is worthy of note that the additions to these four sects of Indian Christians seem to be in an inverse ratio to the number of them that were already in it. The Presbyterian is the only other Christian Mission which has a following of about 1,000 Indians, but it does not seem to have been especially active during the decade. The Presbyterians are almost entirely confined to the Aurangabad district. Taking all sects together, Indian Christians are found in the largest numbers in the districts of Warangal, Nalgonda and Aurangabad. The bulk of the Christians are town-dwellers, there being only 28 Christians in 10,000 of the rural population, as against 161 in the same number of the urban.

Variation in Christian by Sect.

Sect.	1901.	1911.	Increase per cent.
Baptists	844	9,557	+1,032·3
Anglican Community ...	2,412	8,857	+ 267·2
Methodists	1,037	8,121	+ 683·1

88. Jains.

The Jains in the State number 21,026. They increased by 3·3 per cent. during the decade, but as they had decreased by 26·9 during the previous decade, their proportional place in the population has continued to decline. In 1891, the Jain proportion was 24 in 10,000 of the population, in 1901, it was 18, and in 1911 it is 16. All but 857 of the Jains are inhabitants of Marathwara. The districts where they are most numerous are Aurangabad, Parbhani, Osmanabad and Bhir. Over 40 per cent. of the Jains in Telingana are found in Hyderabad City. Adilabad and Medak have 127 and 120 persons respectively of this creed. There are twice as many Jains living in towns as there are in villages.

89. Sikhs.

The Sikh population of the State has remained remarkably steady as regards its proportion to the total population since 1881. At all the four censuses, this has been about 4 to every 10,000 of the population. Their number is 4,726, which is 9 per cent. more than that at the previous census. Since 1881 the Sikh population has increased by 28 per cent. As their increase from 1881 to 1891 was 26·5 per cent, their growth in the last 20 years is only 1·5 per cent. They are about equally distributed between Telingana and Marathwara, the actual number in the two divisions being 2,270 and 2,456 respectively. This is due to an increase of 45·5 per cent. in the former and a decrease of 11·5 in the latter division. About 28 per cent. of the Sikhs are found in the Nander district. The next largest number is centred in Hyderabad City. Bhir, Parbhani, Warangal, Nizamabad and Karimnagar are other districts where there are more than 200 members of this faith.

90. Parsis.

The number of Parsis in the State is 1,529, of which 808 were enumerated in Hyderabad City and 85 in Atrafibalda. Of the rest 225 are in the Aurangabad, and 101 in the Warangal district.

91. Other Sects.

The numbers of adherents which the Arya Samaj, the Brahmo Samaj, Buddhism and Judaism possess are too few to merit comment. Of these the first had 173 (90 in Hyderabad City and 61 in Nizamabad), the second 36 (35 in Hyderabad City), the third 20 (13 in Hyderabad City) the fourth 12, all in Hyderabad City.

PART II.

92. Caste and Sect.

In the first part of this Chapter, the statistics of the several religions professed in this State, have been reviewed. Only in the case of Christianity has there been a separate enumeration of sects. The Hindus, Musulmans, Jains and Sikhs have sects of their own, though they are shown all together for census purposes. The Hindus are divided into numerous castes and several sects, and it is not always easy to say whether a certain group, the Lingayats for instance, should be regarded as a caste or a sect. The Lingayats have been treated as a caste for census purposes. But there can be no doubt that they also form a distinct sect, and some of them would, perhaps, claim that their religion is as much entitled to be regarded as a separate religion as Jainism or Sikhism. However that may be, the broad principle of distinction between a caste and a sect is that, while the latter originated with some difference of religious doctrine, the former is generally associated with some original, or acquired, differences of occupation or function in the Hindu social system. As a rule, the principal Hindu sects concern themselves with only the higher castes. The occupational groups called castes belong to the lower strata of Hindu society. A special chapter of this report is devoted to Castes.

93. Brahmanical Sects.

There were probably several sects of *pre*-Buddhistic Hinduism, but under the name of Vedic Hinduism, they are generally treated as one. All the Hindu sects, recognised at present, belong to the *post*-Buddhistic period, that is to say, they are less than a thousand years' old. It may be added that all these sects are founded not on the *pre*-Buddhist Brahmanism, of which animal sacrifices were a prominent feature, but on the philosophical part of the Vedas, known as the Upanishads. The crusade against animal sacrifices started by Buddha had done its work. *Post* Buddhistic Brahmanism set its face as rigorously against animal sacrifice as did Buddhism. Indeed, the revived Brahmanism was so largely permeated, both in its philosophical and practical aspects, by Buddhist influences, that Sankaracharya the great protagonist of the revival, was taunted by his opponents of the older school, with being a Buddhist in the guise of a Brahman *revivalist.* Sankaracharya was a native of Malabar in Southern India. He travelled all over the country preaching his gospel that the individual soul and the Universal Soul were one and identical, and that the goal of the former was absorption in the latter. This is known as ***Advaitism,*** and it is the largest and best known Brahmanical sect even at the present day. A later reformer, Ramanuja, also from the South country, qualified to some extent the doctrine taught by Sankaracharya, and the sect which he founded is known as the ***Visishtadwaita.*** Ramananda, Kabir and Chaitanya carried and developed Ramanuja's philosophy in Northern India and in Bengal. Both these main sects are largely represented in the Hindu population of this State. The third-important sect of Brahmanism, pure Dwaitism or dualism, was founded by Madhavacharya, and this has many followers in the Karnatak districts. Of these three main sects, only the second made a direct effort to include non-Brahmins in its ministrations. These sects, originally based on philosophical and metaphysical differences, are in practice associated with the worship of one of the two gods of the Hindu Trinity, Siva and Vishnu, the third, Brahma, for some reason or other, having long ceased to figure as an object of popular worship. Brahma is the creator, while Vishnu and Siva are the Protector and Destroyer, respectively, and it might be that the pessimistic frame of mind of the Indian suggested to him that while Brahma deserved no thanks for creating, it would be expedient to propitiate Vishnu and Siva who had the power to protect and to destroy. The sectarians of Sankaracharya's school worship Siva and Vishnu, with a preference for the former; while the followers of Ramanuja and Madhava are worshippers of Vishnu only. While, owing to the study of the Vedas being forbidden to Sudras, philosophical interpretations and the disputes arising therefrom concern only the Brahmins, the worship of Siva or Vishnu is common ground for all Hindus.

94. The Lingayats.

The Lingayats, to whom reference has already been made, are worshippers of Siva and regard the worship of Vishnu and other deities as heretical. The origin of this sect has a special interest for us, as its early history as well as that of its founder Basava is associated with Kalyan, which was the capital of the Western Chalukyas in the latter half of the twelfth century, and which is now included in the district of Bidar in these Dominions. Basava's teachings were a combination of pure Theism and liberal principles of social reform. He taught that all men were holy if they led a pure life ; that there was no inequality due to birth ; that women had the same rights and responsibilities as men; that infant and child marriages were sinful and that the re-marriage of widows was permissible. The Lingayats are one of the largest Hindu sects in the State, numbering over three-quarters of a million souls. Notwithstanding the doctrine of equality of all men preached by the founder of the sect, several Lingayat castes were enumerated at the 1901 Census such as Lingayat Gowlis, Lingayat Vakkaligaru, Lingayat Koli, Lingayat Seelawant, Malli Lingayat, Lingayat Sonar, Lohar Sutar, Teli, Kumbhar and so on. The Lingayats hold the Vedas in reverence but they reject the commentaries and glosses of later writers. They are strict vegetarians and teetotallers. They are a steady, law-abiding race, exceedingly conservative in their habits and ideas.

95. The Manbhav Sect.

Another Hindu sect, also said to have had its origin in the Bidar district of His Highness the Nizam's territories, is one founded by a Sanyasi, named Bhikshumuni, in the last century. The founder of this sect was a native of the village of Nyalkal. This is said to be a sub-sect of the Manbhav sect which was founded by Shri Chakradhar, a Karhada Brahmin, who flourished about the beginning of the thirteenth Century at Paithan in the Aurangabad district. This sect has a *Math* at Kabul. Its present headquarters are in Ritpur in Berar. The chief temple of the Manbhavs is that of Panchaleshvar in these Dominions, which every newly installed Mahant or spiritual head of the sect, has to visit before assuming his powers, and after worshipping the god there, to give a feast to the members of the sect. The principal tenets of the sects are said to be celibacy, maintenance by begging alms, abstaining from taking life, abstinence from flesh and liquor ; devotion to God ; and constant movement from place to place. These apply only to the Sanyasis of the sect who are drawn from both sexes. The Manbhavs admit converts from all castes except the very lowest. These particulars are taken from Monograph, No. 131, in the Ethnological Survey of Bombay Series. Recently the Manbhavs were annoyed by statements questioning their claim to belong to the recognised Hindu sects, and the Mahant Shree Dutt-Laksharaj Kavistwar Mahanubhav of Sansthan Matapur, district Adilabad, in the Nizam's Dominions, submitted an application to the Sankaracharya of Karawir, requesting the latter to declare that the sect was constituted in accordance with the principles laid down in the Hindu scriptures. The Sankaracharya of Karawir, accordingly, issued an order stating that, having carefully gone through the religious books of the sect, he was satisfied that the Manbhavs were followers of the Vedic religion. The history of this sect is of special interest as showing, firstly, that new sects are constantly being formed, and secondly, that they are anxious, however much they may deviate from the customs of Hindu orthodoxy, to be recognised as true limbs of the ancient religion of the Hindus. There is another important fact which emerges from the history, so similar in essential respects, of both the Lingayats and Manbhavs. Both sects in the beginning professed to be against distinctions of caste. But both have gradually come to adopt such distinctions among themselves.

96. The Arya Samaj and the Brahmo Samaj.

Persons professing these faiths were enumerated for the first time in this State at the present Census. The Arya Samaj, with its belief in the infallibility of the Vedas, is without doubt a Hindu sect, though it accepts converts from all races and creeds. The point of difference between the Arya Samaj and orthodox Hinduism, is that the former rejects all the Puranas and later sacred literature of the latter, and is opposed to idol worship. It is rather doubtful how far the Brahmo Samaj can be called a Hindu sect. There are, no doubt, sections of the Brahmo Samaj which claim that it is the purest form of Hinduism, but it rejects all authority except that of the individual conscience in matters of religion. It does not accept the Vedas as a divine revelation, and it is opposed to caste and the worship of idols.

97. Jainism.

Jainism, like Buddhism, is an ancient off-shoot of Hinduism. It has however, unlike Buddhism, managed to survive in the land of its birth, owing partly to the more accommodating and less aggressive character of its followers. There are three sects of Jainism—the Digambaras, the Svetambaras and the Dhondiyas. The most distinctive feature of Jainism is its great regard for the sanctity of life. The Jains are chiefly engaged in commerce as that is the one occupation which involves no injury to even the minutest animals. Their charity is proverbial. Their numbers have shown a tendency to decline throughout India, as in this State, which is probably due to some extent to a disposition among them to return themselves as Hindus.

98. Sikhism.

The Sikhs, too, have two sects, one the older and original sect of Sikhs who are little distinguishable from the Hindus, and the Singhs, or those who have received the baptism instituted by Guru Govind, the tenth and the last Guru. The Singhs are required to abstain from smoking, to wear turbans and the following five Kakars or things whose names begin with K ; *Kesh* or long, hair and beard, Kangha, comb, Kripan, a sword or knife, Kara, a steel bracelet and Kachh, a kind of short drawers. When Guru Govind Singh was defeated and pursued by the Moghals, he fled to the Deccan where he founded a monastery at Nander in these Dominions. He died there in 1708 A. D. It was at Nander that he met Banda whom, on his death-bed, he appointed as the secular leader of the Sikhs. He had previously ordained that all Sikhs should regard the Granth as their Guru, and look upon it as the person of the living Guru. At the time when Guru Govind Singh met him, Banda, a native of Poonch, was living as a *bairagi* at Nander, in expiation of the sin, it is said, of having killed a doe. Nander is still a holy place of the Sikhs.

99. Characteristics of Hinduism.

The sects of Hinduism which are either numerically important in or have historical associations with these Dominions, have been briefly described above. Most, if not all, of them aim, or aimed originally, at overthrowing idol-worship and caste. The only sect which achieved any considerable success in these directions is Sikhism, and its success was due to the measures deliberately adopted by the Gurus, especially by the last and, in some respects, greatest of them, to keep their followers apart from the mass of Hindus. It may be also due partly to the political position attained by the Sikbs as a distinct community. In the altered conditions of these times, when peace and security of life and property reign from end to end of the land, the vast mass of Hinduism is able to exert steadily its enormous power of gravitation on the smaller communities which sprang from its loins. The Jains, the Lingayats, and even the Sikhs, are feeling the effect of this force. On the other hand, movements are at work within Hinduism itself to infuse into it the spirit of modernism by means of social reforms and the simplification of religious ceremonies. This movement is not as yet much felt in these Dominions, but there can be no doubt that it will be so in course of time. Whatever Hinduism is or is not, its spirit of adaptibility is very great. This is the secret of its vitality. While it resists as far as possible innovations and puts innovators out of its pale, it is always ready to accept and adapt itself to accomplished facts. All that it asks is that the new order of things should establish itself on a footing of some sort of historical continuity with the past. It was just because Buddhism failed or neglected to observe this principle, that it was not accepted as a Hindu sect, while Jainism which, in all essential respects, bears a close resemblance to Buddhism, has managed to live on terms of peace with the parent creed, owing to its greater spirit of accommodation. Hinduism, as has been observed so frequently, does not consist in any particular dogma or convention. It embraces all beliefs from the most ethereal to the coarsest. It tolerates and even sanctifies practices which stand at opposite poles of the moral compass. But one thing it always insists on: it always stands for one principle and that is the principle of historic continuity. It does not oppose changes : no religion has changed more than it has done in the past. But it abhors all violent changes and sets its face sternly against revolution in any shape or form. If this is realized, there will be less surprise and disappointment at the apparent contradictions of the beliefs and practices to be found within the comprehensive precincts of Hinduism.

100. Animism.

In some respects, the most important religion of the present Census of this State, is Animism. It shows the largest proportional increase, as compared with other religions. No one, of course, returned himself as an Animist, but all those who did not say that they professed any of the other religions, if they belonged to certain castes, have been classed as Animists. The chief castes of Animists are given in Imperial Table XIII. They are Andh, Bhil, Erkula, Gond and Lambada. The two last are by far the most numerous sections of Animists, each numbering over 120,000 persons. The numbers of persons belonging to the above castes who returned themselves as Hindus and as Animists, are compared in the marginal table. Animism, broadly speaking, consists in the worship of inanimate objects. But the inanimate objects should be worshipped as such and not as representing a higher power. The former is Animism and the latter, the first step towards anthropomorphism. This is the view taken by Westermarck* and as he expressly refers to the anthropomorphism of the Vedas and of Hinduism generally as being distinct from Animism, his opinion has an important bearing on the Indian aspect of the problem. If the mere worship of an inanimate object is Animism, the bulk of the population of India should be returned as Animists. It follows, therefore, that what distinguishes the Indian Animist from the mass of his fellows, is not the object of his worship but his mental conception of it. Now, it is easy to see how it is that Animism gradually becomes absorbed in the surrounding mass of Hinduism. The Animist continues to worship his rock or tree, only instead of regarding it as a god in itself, he learns to regard it as the vehicle, body or symbol of a higher power.

Caste.	Hindu.	Animists.
Andh	3,276	2,625
Bhil...	...	9,921
Erkula	40,467	2,018
Gond	24,090	124,341
Lambada	1,19,259	142,044

* Westermarck : "The origin and development of Moral Ideas," Vol. II, pages 595—598.

The change involves no outward breach with his past form of worship. It is noteworthy in this context that, both in this State and in other Provinces, the Animistic population, when once it has been completely enumerated, tends thereafter to decline, showing that Animism is essentially a transitional creed in our days. The Erkula and Lambada, it is evident, have come largely under the influence of Hinduism and it has been noted that an increasing proportion of the Savara caste in Madras, of the Bhils in Bombay and more than one caste in the Central Provinces and Berar, had been returning themselves as Hindus, at successive Censuses.

101. Islam (Mohamedanism.)

In direct contrast to Hinduism is the monotheistic creed of Islam which for eight centuries has been more or less in contact with Hinduism. It encourages a firm faith in and resignation to one Controlling Power and absolute submission to the Heavenly Master. Its dogma "There is no God but God and Muhammad is His apostle" is so simple and comprehensive that the followers of the Prophet are easily distinguished, be they pure-blooded Musalmans or local converts. A very full account of the sects of Islam was given in the Census Report for 1891, and there is no need to add anything to it here.

SUBSIDIARY TABLE I.—General Distribution of the Population by Religion.

Religion and Locality.	Actual Number in 1911.	Proportion per 10,000 of Population in				Variation per cent. Increase + Decrease —			Net Variation.
		1911.	1901.	1891.	1881.	1901-1911.	1891-1901.	1881-1891.	1881-1911.
1	2	3	4	5	6	7	8	9	10
1. Hindu.									
State	11,626,146	8,693	8,860	8,941	9,033	+ 17·7	— 4·3	+ 15·9	+ 30·7
Telingana	5,793,527	8,615	8,915	8,985	9,058	+ 17·2	+ 3·9	+ 17·0	+ 42·6
Marathwara	5,832,619	8,771	8,786	8,897	9,012	+ 18·3	— 11·3	+ 15·0	+ 20·6
2. Musalman.									
State	1,380,990	1,032	1,037	987	940	+ 19·4	+ 1·5	+ 22·0	+ 49·1
Telingana	625,936	931	946	921	915	+ 19·1	+ 7·6	+ 18·9	+ 52·5
Marathwara	755,054	1,136	1,144	1,047	984	+ 19·7	— 3·1	+ 26·1	+ 46·4
3. Animist.									1891-1911.
State	285,722	214	59	25	...	+ 337·4	+ 124·2	...	+ 880·8
Telingana	257,056	382	101	55	...	+ 361·2	+ 91·3	...	+ 782·6
Marathwara	28,666	48	19	...	...	+ 198·9	+159,733·3	...	+477,666·4
4. Christian.									
State	54,296	40	21	18	14	+136·1	+ 12·5	+ 50·0	+ 298·8
Telingana	44,064	66	32	31	27	+ 135·2	+ 11·4	+ 46·8	+ 269·3
Marathwara	10,232	15	7	6	3	+ 139·6	+ 17·7	+ 115·3	+ 507·9
5. Jain.									
State	21,026	16	18	24	9	+ 3·3	— 26·9	+ 226·7	+ 146·7
Telingana	857	1	1	2	...	+ 18·0	— 0·8	+2,644·8	+ 255·1
Marathwara	20,169	30	38	46	17	+ 2·0	— 27·4	+ 306·7	+ 137·5
6. Sikh.									
State	4,726	4	4	4	4	+ 9·0	— 6·5	+ 26·5	+ 28·0
Telingana	2,270	3	3	5	4	+ 45·5	— 38·9	+ 42·2	+ 27·1
Marathwara	2,456	4	5	3	4	— 11·5	+ 32·3	+ 11·5	+ 30·7
7. Parsi.									
State	1,529	1	1	1	...	+ 4·5	+ 38·2	+ 65·8	+ 139·6
Telingana	1,033	2	2	1	1	+ 0·7	+ 40·8	+ 80·1	+ 155·6
Marathwara	496	1	1	1	...	+ 13·2	+ 82·7	— 31·5	+ 14·2
8. Arya.									
State	173	...	...	...	...	...	...	...	...
Telingana	160	...	...	...	...	...	...	...	...
Marathwara	13	...	...	...	...	...	...	...	...
9. Brahmo.									
State	36	...	...	...	...	...	...	...	...
Telingana	36	...	...	...	...	...	...	...	...
Marathwara	...	...	...	...	...	...	...	...	...
10. Buddhist.									
State	20	...	...	...	...	+ 566·6	...	...	...
Telingana	13	...	...	...	...	+ 166·6	...	...	...
Marathwara	7	...	...	...	...	...	...	...	...
11. Jew.									
State	12	...	...	...	...	— 7·6	— 50·0	— 44·6	— 74·4
Telingana	12	...	...	...	...	— 7·6	— 50·0	— 44·6	— 74·4
Marathwara	...	...	...	...	...	...	...	...	...

SUBSIDIARY TABLE II.—Distribution by Districts of the main religions.

District and Natural Division.	Number per 10,000 of the population who are											
	Hindu.				Musalman.				Animist.			
	1911.	1901.	1891.	1881.	1911.	1901.	1891.	1881.	1911.	1901.	1891.	1881.
1	2	3	4	5	6	7	8	9	10	11	12	13
State	8,693	8,860	8,941	9,033	1,032	1,037	987	940	214	59	25	...
Telingana	8,615	8,915	8,985	9,053	931	946	921	915	382	101	55	...
Hyderabad City	5,236	5,424	5,466	5,867	4,892	4,218	4,165	4,292	1	1	...	...
Atrafibalda	8,751	8,746	8,386	8,840	1,141	1,344	1,094	1,181	78	...	...	...
Warangal	7,995	9,472	9,476	9,539	553	494	503	459	1,815	14	...	...
Karimnagar...	9,496	9,588	9,593	9,609	411	409	402	389	85	...	...	...
Adilabad	8,454	7,608	8,322	9,605	478	524	432	394	1,063	1,860	1,233	...
Medak	8,9 8	8,984	8,945	8,993	947	1,005	1,043	1,004	59	...	...	...
Nizamabad	9,211	9,152	9,195	9,298	737	785	785	696	32	57	8	...
Mahbubnagar	9,004	9,164	9,173	9,166	796	831	824	831	193	...	...	...
Nalgonda	9,017	9,511	9,501	9,517	316	472	495	483	365	...	...	...
Marathwara	8,771	8,786	8,897	9,012	1,136	1,144	1,047	964	43	19	...	...
Aurangabad...	8,442	8,489	8,744	8,879	1,382	1,267	1,137	1,078	136	124	...	...
Bhir	9,093	9,039	9,123	9,223	834	892	806	758	13	8	...	...
Nander	8,909	8,981	9,080	9,140	1,025	980	886	831	33	...	...	...
Parbhani	8,974	9,034	9,098	9,187	930	904	828	788	40	1	...	...
Gulbarga	8,431	8,465	8,504	8,649	1,471	1,508	1,466	1,341	74	1	...	...
Osmanabad	9,000	8,980	9,034	9,105	935	953	894	858	5	...	...	...
Raichur	9,034	8,977	8,977	9,130	938	1,014	1,012	860	3	...	...	...
Bidar	8,564	8,610	8,709	8,885	1,403	1,374	1,272	1,151	17	...	...	...

District and Natural Division.	Number per 10,000 of the population who are											
	Christian.				Jain.				Others.			
	1911.	1901.	1891.	1881.	1911.	1901.	1891.	1881.	1911.	1901.	1891.	1881.
	14	15	16	17	18	19	20	21	22	23	24	25
State	40	21	18	14	16	18	24	9	5	5	5	4
Telingana	66	32	31	27	1	1	2	...	5	5	6	5
Hyderabad City	224	310	332	318	8	7	5	...	39	40	32	22
Atrafibalda	25	9	12	15	2	1	3	...	3	...	6	14
Warangal	132	16	17	...	...	...	...	...	5	4	4	2
Karimnagar...	5	2	1	...	1	...	1	...	2	1	3	2
Adilabad	1	...	...	...	2	6	11	...	2	2	3	1
Medak	32	10	3	...	2	1	3	...	2	...	6	3
Nizamabad	13	1	1	...	1	1	2	...	6	4	9	6
Mahbubnagar	6	5	2	...	...	...	...	...	1	...	1	3
Nalgonda	101	17	2	...	...	...	...	...	1	...	2	...
Marathwara	15	7	6	3	30	38	46	17	5	6	4	4
Aurangabad...	73	37	28	9	63	71	91	27	4	12	5	7
Bhir	...	2	2	1	54	60	65	15	6	9	4	3
Nander	1	...	...	...	18	19	16	14	19	20	18	15
Parbhani	5	1	1	8	47	53	68	21	4	7	5	1
Gulbarga	9	3	5	6	14	21	23	8	1	2	2	1
Osmanabad	4	1	3	1	54	66	69	36	2	...	...	...
Raichur	17	5	6	6	7	3	4	2	1	1	1	2
Bidar...	4	2	...	...	10	12	18	12	2	2	1	2

SUBSIDIARY TABLE III.—Christians—Number and Variations.

District and Natural Divisions.	Actual number of Christians in				Variation per cent.			
	1911.	1901.	1891.	1881.	1901-1911.	1891-1901.	1881-1891.	1881-1911.
1	2	3	4	5	6	7	8	9
State	**54,296**	**22,996**	**20,429**	**13,614**	**+ 136·1**	**+ 12·5**	**+ 50·0**	**+ 298·8**
Telingana... ...	**44,064**	**18,727**	**16,982**	**11,931**	**+ 135·2**	**+ 10·2**	**+ 42·3**	**+ 269·3**
Hyderabad City ...	16,240	14,201	14,375	11,270	+ 14·3	— 1·2	+ 27·5	+ 44·0
Atrafibalda	1,291	513	468	584	+ 151·6	+ 9·6	— 19·8	+ 121·0
Warangal	11,979	1,649	1,544	18	+ 626·4	+ 6·8	+ 8,477·7	+ 66,450·0
Karimnagar... ..	586	214	193	2	+ 173·8	+ 10·8	+ 9,550·0	+ 29,200·0
Adilabad	28	10	...	7	+ 180·0	......	......	+ 300·0
Medak	2,203	441	106	8	+ 399·5	+ 316·0	+ 1,225·0	+27,437·5
Nizamabad	720	127	40	1	+ 466·8	+ 217·5	+ 3,900·0	+71,900·0
Mahbubnagar ...	451	359	121	13	+ 25·6	+ 196·6	+ 830·7	+ 3,369·2
Nalgonda	10,566	1,213	135	28	+ 771·0	+ 798·5	+ 382·1	+37,635·7
Marathwara ...	**10,232**	**4,269**	**3,447**	**1,683**	**+ 139·6**	**+ 23·8**	**+ 104·8**	**+ 507·9**
Aurangabad... ...	6,869	2,873	1,929	669	+ 121·6	+ 48·4	+ 188·3	+ 852·0
Bhir	2	92	148	57	— 97·8	— 37·8	+ 159·6	— 96·4
Nander	69	9	2	...	+ 666·6	+ 350·0	......	......
Parbhani	409	72	67	159	+ 468·0	+ 7·4	— 57·8	+ 157·2
Gulbarga	1,044	419	426	507	+ 149·1	— 1·6	— 15·9	+ 105·9
Osmanabad	252	50	214	49	+ 400·0	— 76·6	+ 336·7	+ 414·2
Raichur	1,711	739	640	242	+ 131·5	+ 15·4	+ 164·4	+ 607·0
Bidar	376	15	21	...	+ 2,406·6	— 28·5	......	... ..

SUBSIDIARY TABLE IV.—Races and Sects of Christians (Actual Numbers).

Sect.	European and allied races.		Anglo-Indian.		Indian.		Total.		Variation Increase + or Decrease —
	Male.	Female.	Male.	Female.	Male.	Female.	1911.	1901.	
1	2	3	4	5	6	7	8	9	10
All denominations ...	**4,311**	**1,072**	**1,548**	**1,456**	**23,636**	**22,273**	**54,296**	**22,996**	**+31,300**
Anglican Communion ...	3,586	718	550	550	4,545	4,312	14,261	6,813	+ 7,448
Armenian	......	......	......	......	......	......	......	14	— 14
Baptist	23	16	14	20	5,038	4,519	9,630	885	+ 8,745
Congregationalist... ...	3	2	2	......	181	167	355	315	+ 40
Greek	1	......	1	......	......	......	2	3	— 1
Lutheran	......	......	1	......	14	9	24	5	+ 19
Methodist	234	77	78	104	4,172	3,949	8,614	1,468	+ 7,146
Minor Protestant denominations	3	5	......	3	236	190	427	953	— 526
Presbyterian	89	43	9	8	475	524	1,148	610	+ 538
Protestant (unsectarian or sect not specified) ..	9	9	42	25	637	624	1,346	275	+ 1,071
Roman Catholic	358	201	848	744	8,347	7,975	18,473	11,649	+ 6,824
Syrian (Romo)	......	......	2	2	......	1	5	......	+ 5
Indefinite Belief	5	1	1	......	1	3	11	6	+ 5

SUBSIDIARY TABLE V.—Distribution of Christians per mile (a) races by sect and (b) sects by race.

Sect.	Races distributed by sect.				Sects distributed by race.			
	European and allied races.	Anglo-Indian.	Indian.	Total.	European and allied races.	Anglo-Indian.	Indian.	Total.
1	2	3	4	5	6	7	8	9
All denominations	1,000	1,000	1,000	1,000	99	55	846	1,000
Anglican Communion ...	830	866	198	263	302	77	621	1,000
Baptist...	7	11	208	177	4	4	992	1,000
Congregationalist	1	1	8	7	14	6	980	1,000
Greek	...	...	...	...	500	500	...	1,000
Lutheran	...	...	1	...	...	42	958	1,000
Methodist	58	61	177	159	36	21	943	1,000
Minor Protestant Denominations	1	1	9	8	19	7	974	1,000
Presbyterian	25	6	22	21	115	15	870	1,000
Protestant (Unsectarian or sect not specified)	8	28	26	25	13	50	937	1,000
Roman Catholic	104	530	356	340	30	86	884	1,000
Syrian (Romo)	...	1	...	...	...	800	200	1,000
Indefinite Belief	1	...	...	...	545	91	364	1,000

SUBSIDIARY TABLE VI.—Religion of urban and rural population.

Natural Division.	Number per 10,000 of urban population who are.						Number per 10,000 of rural population who are.					
	Hindu.	Musalman.	Animist.	Christian.	Jain.	Others.	Hindu.	Musalman.	Animist.	Christian.	Jain.	Others.
1	2	3	4	5	6	7	8	9	10	11	12	13
State	6,381	3,390	8	161	29	31	8,940	780	236	28	14	2
Telingana	6,160	3,559	3	238	7	33	8,938	590	431	48	1	2
Marathwara	6,708	3,140	15	47	63	27	8,947	964	45	13	28	3

Chapter V.

AGE.

102. Statistics.

Imperial Table VII, giving particulars of the distribution of the population by age, sex and civil conditions, is the principal table for this and the two subsequent chapters. Imperial Table XIV contains the same kind of information for selected castes, and Imperial Table XVIII furnishes particulars of the age distribution of Europeans, Armenians and Anglo-Indians. Eight Subsidiary Tables are appended to this Chapter. They are intended to illustrate (1) the age distribution of 100,000 of each sex by annual periods, (2) the age distribution of 10,000 of each sex in the State and in each Natural Division, (3) the age distribution of 10,000 of each sex in each main religion, (4) the age distribution of 1,000 of each sex in certain castes, (5) proportion of children under 10 and of persons over 60 to those aged 15-40, and also of married females aged 15 to 40 per 100 females, (6) variations in population at certain age periods, (7) reported birth-rate by sex and (8) reported death-rate by sex.

103. Anomalies of the Age Statistics.

In normal conditions, a population would show the largest number of individuals at the earliest age periods. The number would decline progressively at each successive period, dwindling down as we approach extreme old age. But this is far from being the case with age statistics, even in countries far more advanced than India. Even in England it has been noticed that many adults are ignorant of their exact age. "There is a great tendency," observes a well-known writer, "to return ages at some exact multiple of 10, when really a year or two one side or the other of the precise figure (30, 40, 50, etc). For this reason decennial age-periods are preferable in calculating death-rates, and 25-35, 35-45, etc., should be chosen in preference to 30-40, 40-50, etc. This tendency does not appear until adult life, and quinquennial periods can therefore be safely used up to the age of 25 years. Among children under 5 years of age, the vagueness with which parents use the terms "one year old," "two years old," etc., when the children are only in their first or second year, respectively, is a cause of considerable error. Wilful misstatement of age occurs more especially among women : thus at every Census the young women of 20 to 25 years of age have invariably been more numerous than were the girls aged 10 to 15 at the immediately preceding Census. The tendency of old persons to overstate their ages throws some doubt on the figures for ages over 85, and it is preferable to make a single group for all ages over 85*." It is remarkable how exactly these tendencies to erroneous statement of age, noticed in the English Census returns, are reproduced in this country. Subsidiary Table I shows that there is the same tendency here to return ages as some exact multiple of 10, the same vagueness in the ages assigned by parents to children under 5, the same wilful misstatement of age by persons at certain periods of life, the same tendency among old persons to overstate their ages. The accompanying charts illustrate in a graphic form the erratic manner in which the figures for both sexes rise and fall at the several age-periods. Taken by quinquennial periods, the figures fall, though unevenly, from 0-5 to 15-20. From 20-25 there is a rise, which increases at the next age-period. Then for two periods the numbers fall, to rise again at 40-45. Thenceforward, they fall and rise in every alternate period. There are three times more persons living at age 70 and over than at 65-70. The number of children living at each year in the first quinquennial period is separately shown in the tables, and there, again, we encounter the same arbitrary variations.

* *Vital Statistics.*—A Newsholme, 3rd Edition, pp. 2, 4.

104. Some special features of the Hyderabad Returns.

In addition to the anomalies noted above, there are some special ones characteristic of Hyderabad, and generally of Indian age-statistics. The first of these is the tendency, as illustrated in Subsidiary Table I, for the number of children at one year of age to be smaller than that at age 2. This is partly due to the fact that the vernacular equivalents of the term "infant" being generally understood to mean children who derive their nourishment from their mothers, a number of unweaned children at age one are often wrongly returned as infants. One gratifying feature of Indian life, more especially in the villages, is that the practice of rearing infants on artificial food is altogether unknown. On the contrary, the tendency is for the weaning to be postponed to as late a date as possible, perhaps, in the belief, noticed in some parts of the country, that suckling infants have in some way the effect of preventing conception. Even with this addition, the number of infants returned at the Census, there is some reason to believe, is less than the actual number in the population. It is believed that the proportion of persons who escaped enumeration is exceedingly small, but it is most likely that children of tender age formed a majority of such persons. The preliminary Census Record was prepared some five or six weeks before the final Census. It is probable that some of the births which occurred in the interval escaped the notice of the enumerators at the final count. The small number of children at the age of one, as compared with that of infants and children at the age of two, suggests that there is also a tendency to return as being two years of age, children who are, perhaps, eighteen or twenty months old. When a woman bears children in quick succession she tries to avert the "evil eye" or the jealousy of less prolific wives in her neighbourhood by exaggerating the difference in the ages of her little ones. It is, moreover, not uncommon to state the current and not the completed year as the age of a child. The third year of age is a favourite, it may be owing to some sort of sentiment that a child which has attained the third year has acquired comparative immunity from some of the risks which beset the lives of infants and children just past infancy. The number of children living at the 3rd, 4th and 5th years of life is larger than that living at the first two years. As soon as a female child approaches her 5th year, the necessity of finding a suitable bridegroom within the customary caste-group begins to loom on the horizon of the parents. To understate her age gives them more time to look about them for a proper youth to whom she may be dedicated betimes. Except as a preliminary to marriage, the Indian woman is absolutely careless about her age. When once she has secured a husband, or lost him, she rather likes to make herself out to be older than she really is, because in India age still carries with it some title to respect. "Even a Sudra should be reverenced if he is eighty years old," a great Hindu Lawgiver has declared. The tendency for old people to exaggerate their age, noticed in other countries, gains additional strength from the veneration felt for old persons as such both among Hindus and Mussulmans. The old people are, in fact, the universal referees in respect of social customs and of family usage. Generally speaking, there is more likelihood of the ages of males being more accurately returned than those of females. There are many more occasions in the life of a man than of a woman when he may be asked about his age. If he went to school as a boy, there would be a record of his age on the school register to warn him against any subsequent erroneous statement of it. If he appeared as a party or a witness before a Civil or Criminal Court, if he had to register a document or to apply for the reduction of his assessment on his land, he will have to give his age and to stick to it in all his future transactions. The ages of persons, especially of children, belonging to castes which have horoscopes cast at each birth in the family, are likely to be more accurate than those of persons belonging to castes which have no such custom. The preference shown for certain ages is to be accounted for by the fact that certain ceremonies or sacraments have been traditionally prescribed for performance at these ages; for example, 7 in the case of Brahman boys for the investiture of the sacred thread, and 8 in the case of Brahmin girls as the age when she becomes *Kanya*, *i.e.*, begins to be a marrigeable maiden.

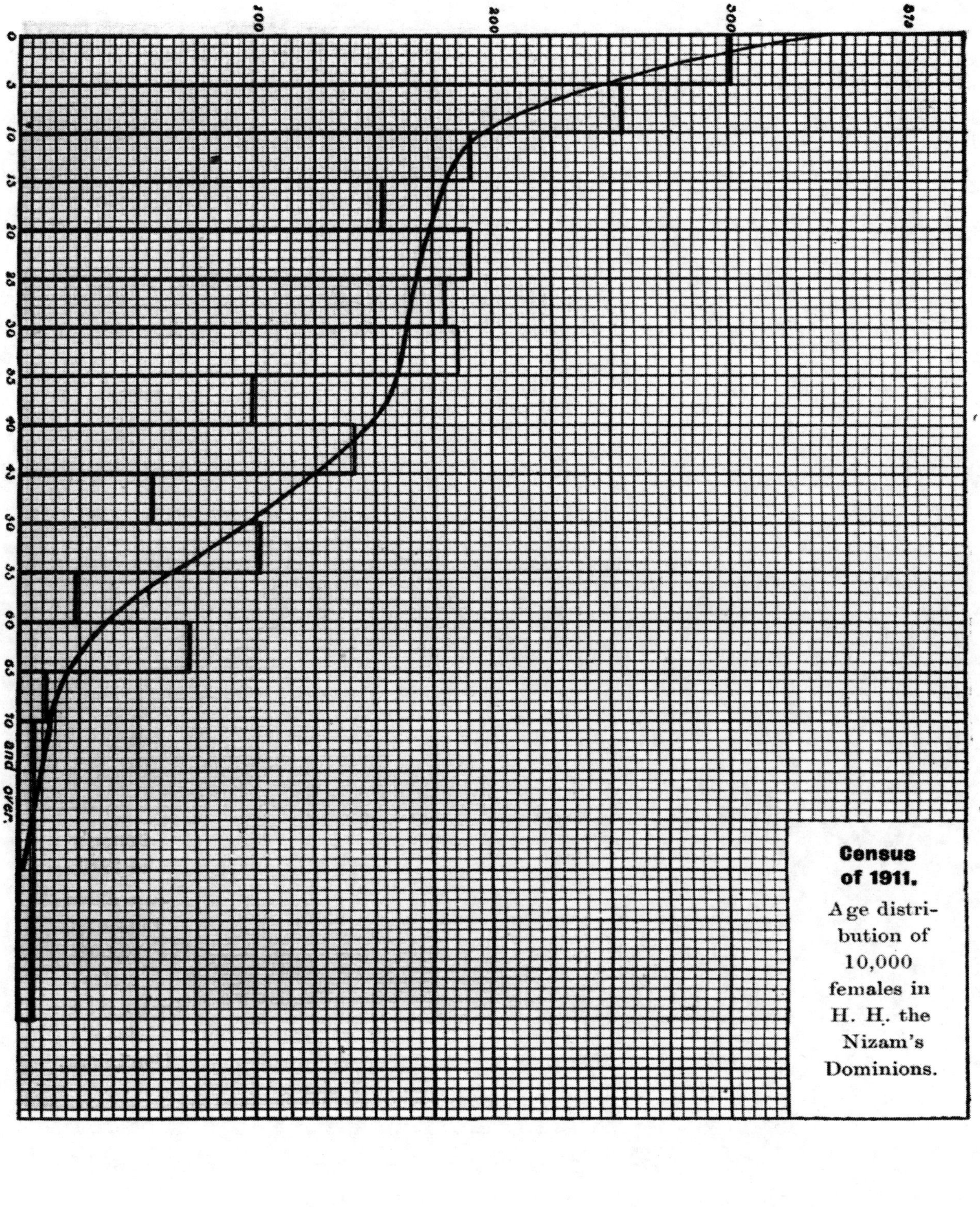

Census of 1911.

Age distribution of 10,000 females in H. H. the Nizam's Dominions.

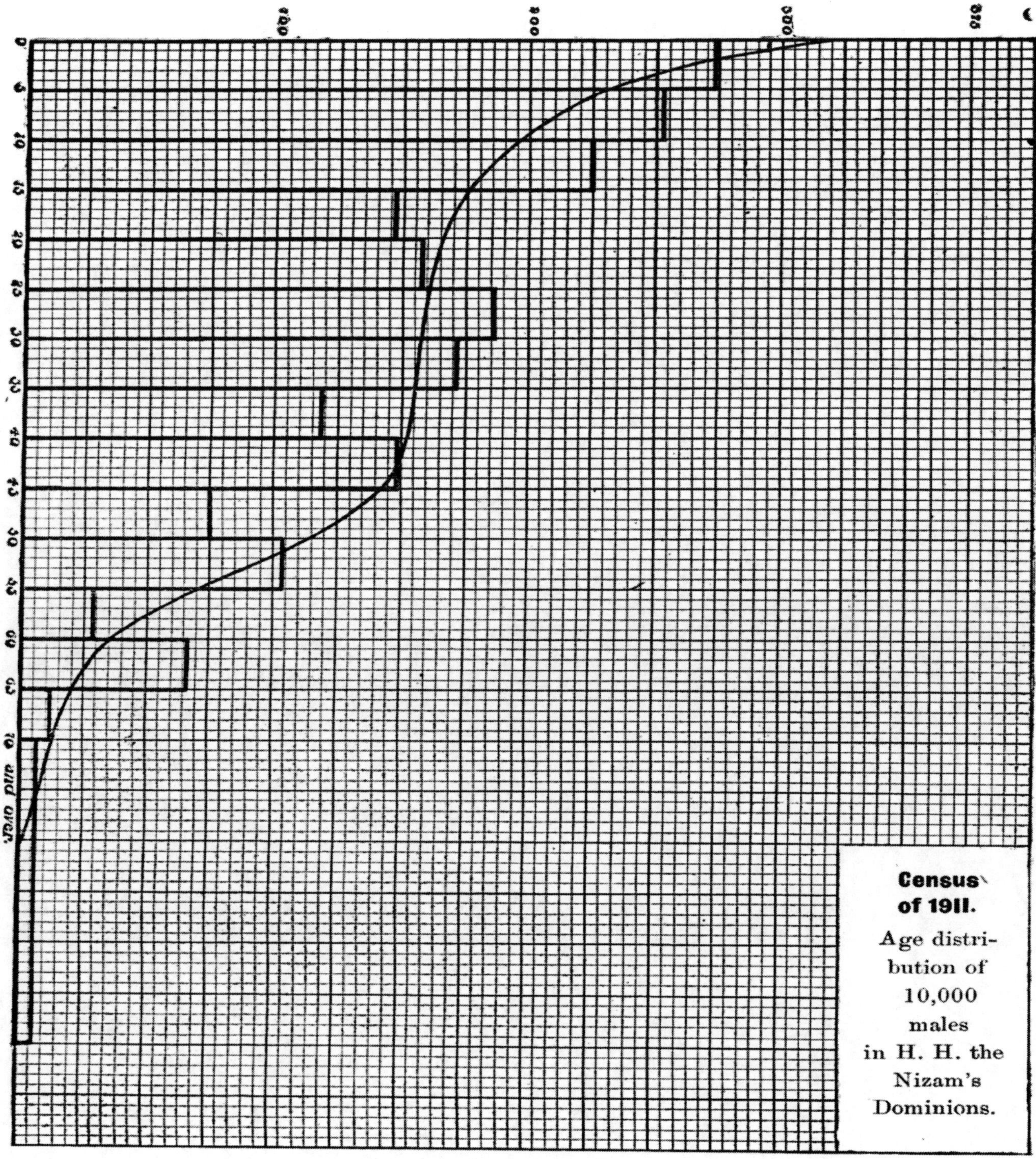

Census of 1911.

Age distribution of 10,000 males in H. H. the Nizam's Dominions.

105. Adjusted Ages.

There are several "smoothing processes" usually employed for the purpose of adjusting the population at the different ages. A rough idea of what the adjusted population at the several ages will be is given by the curved lines in the accompanying two diagrams.* The actual and adjusted figures are compared in the following statement. All adjustments with the help of "smoothing processes" are merely approximations to the actual age distribution of the population, and ours has no pretence to be the most approximate of them. Much of this chapter will consist of deductions from a comparison of the unadjusted figures at the several Censuses. As the errors are likely to be constant, these conclusions are likely to represent in large part the actual changes and tendencies in each decade.

Age-period.	Number per 10,000 males.		Number per 10,000 females.	
	Actual.	Adjusted.	Actual.	Adjusted.
0—1	264	319	291	340
1—2	178	299	203	315
2—3	333	276	370	294
3—4	291	256	328	275
4—5	303	247	316	260
0—5	1,369	1,397	1,508	1,484
5—10	1,262	1,080	1,273	1,124
10—15	1,125	939	955	946
15—20	785	861	767	891
20—25	790	824	954	859
25—30	929	801	901	831
30—35	860	785	922	811
35—40	593	772	493	783
40—45	741	752	712	694
45—50	874	667	281	567
50—55	521	494	506	422
55—60	146	284	115	264
60—65	328	151	364	148
65—70	62	89	58	85
70—over	165	104	191	91

106. Mean age of the Male Population.

Subsidiary Table II gives the age distribution of 10,000 of the population by sexes at the four Censuses since 1881. The mean age is given in bold type at the bottom of each column. The mean age is the average of the ages of the persons living at a given time. A higher mean age means that more persons were living at the later than at the earlier ages. The steady increase of the mean age of males from 24·5 in 1881 to 25·5 in 1911 calls for comment. The marginal table compares the figures for males in three age-groups for each year, 10 to 15, 15 to 45, and 45 and upwards. It is somewhat startling to find that there are fewer persons at the first two age-groups and more persons in the third period at the present Census than in any of the three previous Censuses. Moreover, the numbers at the first two age-periods have been steadily going down since 1891, that at the second age-period since 1881, and that in the last period as steadily increasing. Let us compare the figures in a different manner, taking the age-groups, 0-10, 10-20 and

Age distribution of 10,000 males.

Census.	0-15	15-45	45 & over.
1881...	3,820	4,808	1,373
1891...	3,838	4,710	1,452
1901...	3,796	4,698	1,506
1911...	3,756	4,648	1,596

* The principle followed in the diagrams is an adaptation of the one explained in Newsholme's *Vital Statistics*, 3rd Edition, page 265. The rectangles contained by the dark lines denote the population as enumerated in each age group, while the curved lines indicate the adjusted population. The latter are so drawn as to include the same amount of total space as the rectangles, while co[illegible]forming to such marked tendencies as the higher rates of mortality among children and old persons. The curves, [illegible]ourse, steadily decline from infancy to old age.

20-40 and 40-60 and 60 and over. The first group will represent the children born during the decade, the second the youths who have survived from among the children enumerated at the Census of 1901, the third, the persons in the prime of their reproductive powers, and the fourth those past middle age, and the last, old persons. The conclusions which are indicated by this table are what might have been expected. The Censuses of 1881 and 1901 were both preceded by severe famines. The largest mortality in a famine occurs among the aged and the very young. The number of young children is further reduced by the falling off in the birth-rate at such a time. The falling off in the numbers enumerated between 0-10 and at 60 and over in 1881 and 1901, thus accords with expectation. The smallness of the numbers in the next age-period, 10-20, in 1891 and 1911 is a necessary corollary of the small number of children under 10 in 1881 and 1901. The fourth column in the table gives the number of persons between the ages of 20-40, the best part of the 'useful' period of life. This group has steadily decreased during the last 30 years. The next age-period (40-60) shows a steady increase during the same period. If we take the period, 15-40, which is regarded as the 'useful' period of life in India, we find again the same steady decline during the last 30 years. Look at it how we will, there is no escaping the fact that the proportion of males at the "useful" ages in the population has gone on decreasing during the last thirty years.

Age distribution of 10,000 males.

Census	0-10	10-20	20-40	40-60	60 & over
1881... ...	2,583	2,025	3,302	1,624	466
1891... ...	2,760	1,801	3,249	1,677	513
1901... ...	2,498	2,058	3,192	1,779	478
1911... ...	2,631	1,860	3,172	1,782	555

107. Mean age of Females.

While the mean age of males has steadily increased since the Census of 1881, the mean age of females has very slightly fallen since 1901. Both for males and females, the mean ages in 1901 and 1911 are higher than those in 1881 and 1891. The famine of 1899-1900 changed the age-constitution of the population and by cutting off a large proportion of children, raised the mean age of the population from 24·6 to 25·2 in the case of males and from 24·3 to 25·1 in the case of females. The marginal table shows that the mean age of females has remained less than that of males at all the four Censuses; that in the famine Censuses of 1881 and 1901 the difference between the two was the least, only ·1; and that, in itself, the mean age of females tends to increase in famine times and to fall in prosperous years, the inferior and superior limits being ·1 and ·5 respectively, unlike the male mean age which has risen in good years and in bad since 1881. In other words, in normal years there are proportionately more females living at the earlier than in the later age-periods. It may be that in famine years comparatively fewer female children are born or more female children die than in ordinary years, and probably also the mortality among male adults is greater than that among females. These probabilities will be in accord with the observed tendencies in India and elsewhere. The number of females at certain age-periods for every 10,000 of the sex at the four Censuses of the State is given in the marginal table. The proportion of females between the ages of 20-40 has remained remarkably constant since 1881, except for a sudden rise in 1901, when at all ages except 0-10, and 60 and over,

Mean age of population.

Census.	Males.	Females.
1881	24·5	24·4
1891	24·6	24·3
1901	25·2	25·1
1911	25·5	25·0

Per 10,000 females.

Census.	0-10.	10 20.	20-40.	40-60.	60 over.
1881	2,749	1,849	3,272	1,561	569
1891	2,917	1,670	3,271	1,525	617
1901	2,549	1,892	3,357	1,653	549
1911	2,781	1,722	3,270	1,614	618

the proportion of females was the highest of any Census. This would seem to offer a striking confirmation of the belief that the vitality of the female population is greater than that of the male in times of famine. The numbers of males and of females living at the reproductive or "useful" period 15-40, are compared in the marginal table. Except in 1881, the proportion of women at this age-period is higher than that of men, though by itself it has been declining. The exceptionally high proportion of women at the productive ages in 1901 is the direct cause of the large increase in the number of children under 10 years of age during the last decade, which is a record one for this State. Subsidiary Table VI furnishes information regarding variations in population at the several age-periods. The increase in the number of children during the decade previous to the present Census is 28·8 per cent. as against 26·9 between 1881 and 1891.

Per 10,000 persons at 15-40.

	Males.	Females.
1881	4,090	4,077
1891	3,972	4,051
1901	3,947	4,132
1911	3,907	4,037

108. Proportion of Children in the Population.

Subsidiary Table V gives interesting particulars regarding the proportion of children under 10 to married females aged 15-40 and also of married females aged 15-40 per 100 females of all ages. The proportion of children under 10 to 100 married females at this age-period is 157. The number of married women between 15-40 was 35 per cent.of the females of all ages in 1891 and 1911 and 33 per cent.in 1901. These percentages of married women at this age-period seem too low at first sight for an Indian State where marriage is universal and obligatory,especially for women, but it must be remembered that the widowed are separately enumerated, and that they form a considerable proportion of the female population. The exclusion of widowed women of between 15-40 in calculating the proportion of children, exaggerates the productive capacity of married women. Many of the widows are no doubt mothers. Then, again, eminent writers on Vital Statistics have held that the correct manner of showing the birth-rate is to distinguish between the births in marriage and out of it. It may be doubted, whether, in the absence of statistics of illegitimate births, the more satisfactory way is not to give the proportion for the whole female population at the productive ages, especially in a country like India where a small proportion—3·6 per cent.—of women of these ages remain unmarried. There are as we have seen 4,037 females at between 15-40 in every 10,000 of that sex, and the number of unmarried women among them would be 146.

109. Proportion of old persons in the Population.

The same Subsidiary Table has a column giving the proportion of persons of 60 and over per 100 persons in the age-period 15-40. At the present as well as at the two previous Censuses the proportion of old women has been in excess of that of old men. In 1891 the males at 60 years and over were 13 per cent. of those at 15-40; in 1901, the proportion was 12, and at this, it is 14. Never before during the last 30 years have there been so many old men in the State as at the present Census. The percentage of women at 60 and over in 1891 and 1911 is the same, namely, 15; in 1901, it had fallen to 13 per 100 persons at 15-40. Subsidiary Table VI which contains particulars of the variations in population at the several age-periods shows that the largest proportionate increase—36·6 per cent.—during the decade preceding the present Census, was among persons at 60 years and over. Between 1891 and 1901, their numbers had gone down by 12·2 per cent.,—the largest proportionate decrease in the population, omitting children under 10 years of age.

110. Variations in the population under 10 years.

The greatest proportionate increase in the number of children under 10 years in the last 30 years, occurred during 1901-1911. In 1881-1891, when also the State was recovering from the effects of a great famine, the number of children increased by 26·9 per cent. In the last decade, the increase was 28·6 per cent. In 1891 to 1901 the child population had decreased by 14·2 per cent. In the age-period 0-5, the increase at the present Census is very striking. The famine which reduced the population of 1901 occurred at the end of the decade, and proved most disastrous to tender children. The difference in the numbers at the first five years of life, whether taken singly or together, is remarkable. These are compared in the marginal table. Assuming that errors of statement in regard to the age of children are constant, the combined effect of a lowered birth-rate and enhanced death-rate is evident in the extremely meagre figure of the population at 0-1 in 1901. The figures for the second year of life, so entirely at variance with those of the other years, are puzzling. It is evident that a considerable proportion of children under 1 year was returned as belonging to the next year of age, for some reason or other, in 1901. However that may be, the table shows that the increase per cent. in the population at the ages 0-5 was larger even than that of old persons at 60 and over, during the decade previous to the present Census. Another noteworthy feature of the statistics of children, at the present and previous Censuses, is that the number of females shows a proportionately larger increase than that of males.

Age.	Census of		Variation per cent.
	1901.	1911.	
0—1	175,786	371,040	+ 111·0
1—2	236,893	254,336	+ 7·3
2—3	323,459	470,646	+ 45·5
3—4	286,702	413,504	+ 44·2
4—5	332,827	414,183	+ 24·4
Total ...	1,355,667	1,923,659	+ 41·0

111. Variations at other age-periods.

The population at the age-period 10-15 increased during the decade by only 3·1 per cent. This, as has been explained above, is because this section of the population consists of survivors from those born in the latter half of the decade preceding the Census of 1901, a period when both the birth-rate and death-rate were affected by two famines. The population at the age-periods 15-40 and 40-60 showed increases of 18 and 18·9 per cent. respectively. This, as well as the increase in the number of old men over 60, is due to the low death-rate during the decade preceding the present Census, as compared with that of the decade prior to the Census of 1901.

112. Vital Statistics.

Subsidiary Tables VII and VIII contain particulars of the reported birth and death-rates during the decade. Though they are obviously unreliable as an accurate record of the actual number of births and deaths, they have some value as indicating the variations in the vital conditions of the State from year to year. The accompanying diagrams present in a graphic form the reported birth and death-rates in the State and the City of Hyderabad. The lowest death-rate in the State was recorded in 1902. In 1901 it was 1·1, in 1902 it was 6·9 per mille. In 1903 there was a sharp rise to 8·3, and in 1904 it was 8·9. The plague, it may be recalled, was at its worst in these years. In 1905, there was a fall, but it rose again next year to the same rate as in 1904. In 1907 the registered death-rate was 8·7. In 1908 and 1909, there was a further decline in the death-rate. In 1910 it reached the highest point registered in the decade, 9·4 per mille of the Census population of 1901. It is worthy of note that after 1905, the death-rate never fell below 8 per mille and only once rose above 9. The death-rate of Hyderabad City was throughout higher than that of the State. The sharp rise in the death-rate in 1908 and the equally steep fall in the birth-rate in the following year shown in the diagram are the results of the disastrous floods in the Musi river in the latter year. The higher death-rate of the female than of the male population of Hyderabad City in almost all the years of the decade, preceding the present Census, is what should be expected from the fact that the City populations consists of a proportionately larger number of adults than the

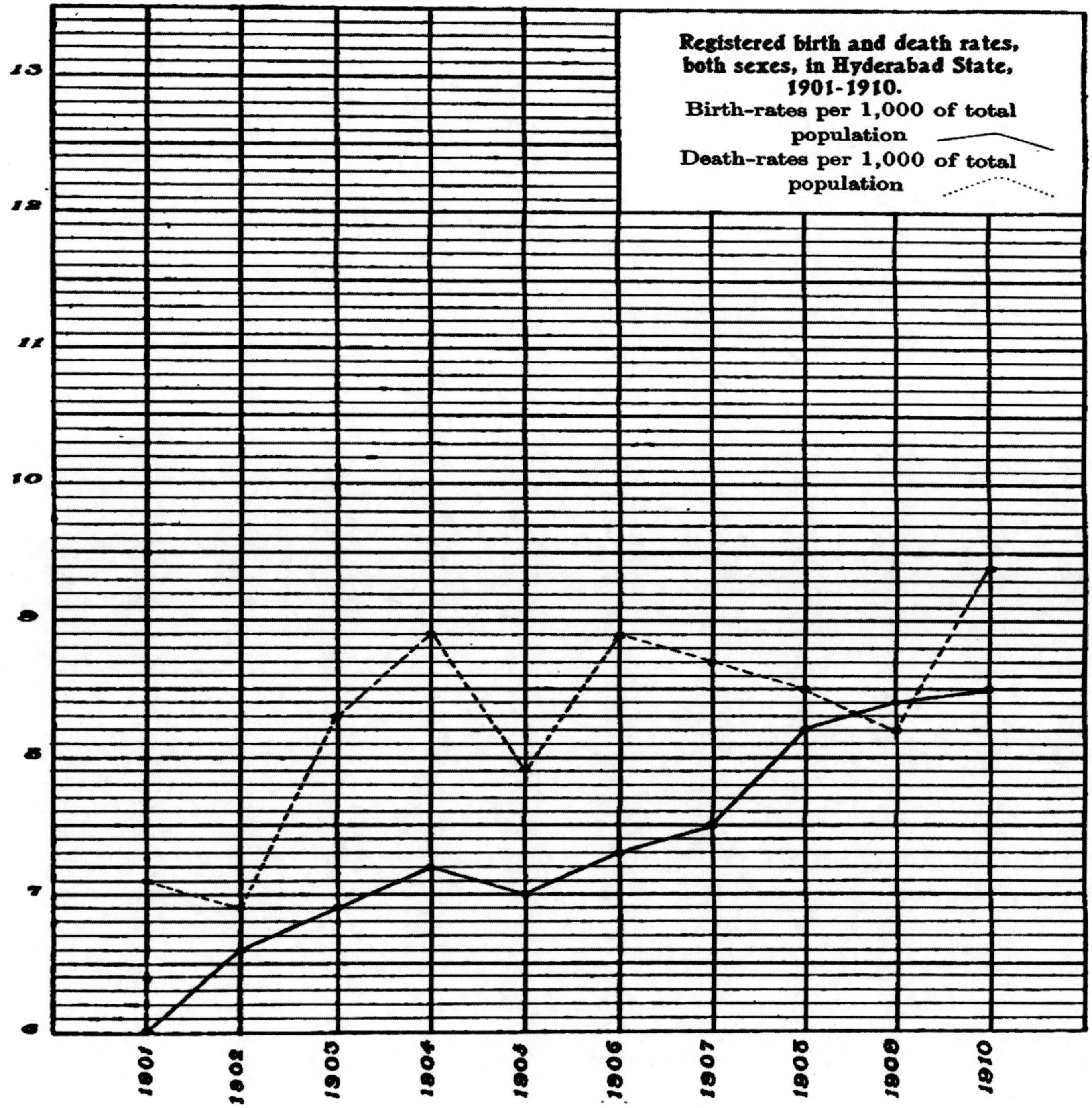
Registered birth and death rates, both sexes, in Hyderabad State, 1901-1910.
Birth-rates per 1,000 of total population
Death-rates per 1,000 of total population
13
12
11
10
9
8
7
6
1901
1902
1903
1904
1905
1906
1907
1908
1909
1910

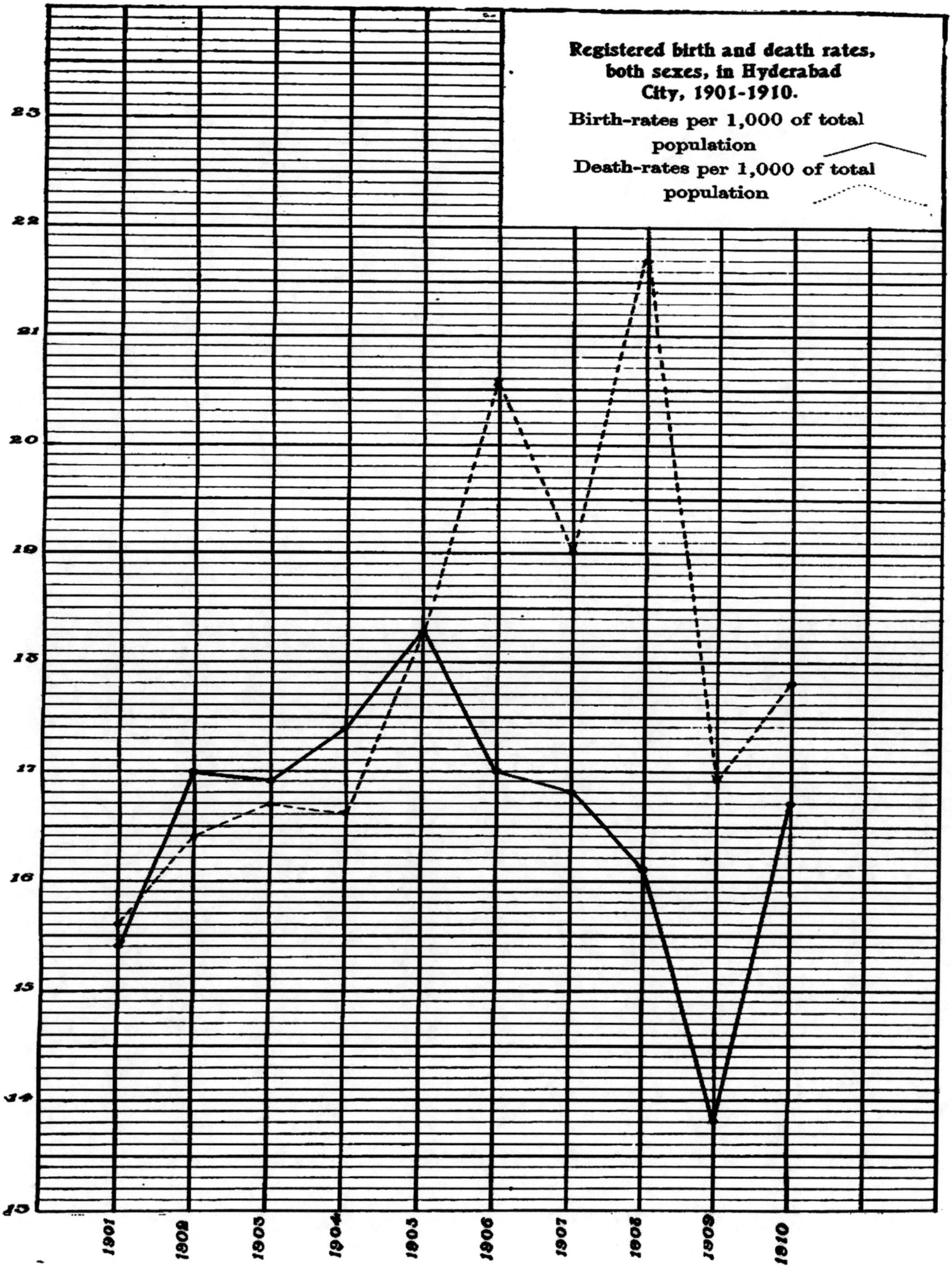

Registered birth and death rates, both sexes, in Hyderabad City, 1901-1910.
Birth-rates per 1,000 of total population
Death-rates per 1,000 of total population
23
22
21
20
19
18
17
16
15
14
13
1901
1902
1903
1904
1905
1906
1907
1908
1909
1910

State. Though the death-rate among males and females is lowest at the 'useful' period of life, the female death-rate at this period tends to be higher than the male, owing to the dangers attendant on child-bearing. Hence there is need for caution in accepting the death-rate of the City of Hyderabad as an index to the different rates of male and female mortality in the State. As regards the reported birth-rates, it is evident that they are much less reliable than the death-rates. If we assume that the reported death-rate is approximately near the actual, the birth-rate must have exceeded it by, on an average, 2 per cent. per annum, in order that the population might increase, as it has done by 20 per cent. in the decade. The reported birth-rate, in the State is, on the other hand, uniformly lower than the death-rate, except in one year when it was slightly higher. It is also impossible, in view of the excess of the female population, at infancy and early childhood throughout the State, to accept the City figures which show a uniformly higher male birth-rate, as correct. It is probable that female births are more often not reported than male births. The birth of a male-child is always a matter of pride and rejoicing, while that of a female-child is often a cause of regret and perplexity. The reported birth-rates in the last six years of the decade are higher in Marathwara than in Telingana.

113. A rough estimate of the actual birth and death-rate.

In the foregoing paragraph, some general tendencies to which the reported death and birth-rates point have been indicated. It is easy to see that the reported births and deaths are only a small proportion of the actual number of these occurrences. The population at the Census of 1911 is the population at the Census of 1901 *minus* the number of deaths *plus* the number of births during the decade, leaving out of consideration emigrants and immigrants who form an inconsiderable fraction of the population. The problem may be stated thus :—

$$X = Y \text{—the deaths} + \text{the births during the decade.}$$

X standing for the population of 1911 and Y for that of 1901. The number of reported deaths is 928,040 and that of births 823,984. The population at the Census of 1901 was 11,141,142. If we substitute these figures on the right-hand side of the equation, we get :

$$X = 11,141,142 - 928,040 + 823,984 \text{ or } 11,037,086,$$

whereas X, according to the enumeration at the present Census, is 13,374,676. We must, therefore, have recourse to indirect means of arriving at an approximate estimate of the death and birth-rates which prevailed during the decade. One such means is as follows : The equation stated above may be stated in another way. The population of 1911 is made up of the survivors from the population of 1901 and survivors from amongst the births during the decade. The survivors from the population of 1901 are the persons living in 1911 at 10 years of age and over. The survivors from among the births in the death are the persons living in 1911 under 10 years. If the number of persons living at 10 years and over in 1911 be deducted from the total number of persons living in 1901, we arrive at the number of deaths from amongst the latter in the decade. The former number is 9,755,996 : the Census population in 1901 was 11,141,142. The difference, 1,385,146, represents the number of persons who were living in 1901 and who died during the decade. But this number does not include all the deaths which occurred in the decade, and the death-rate must be deduced from the aggregate of deaths in the decade. The deaths among the children under 10 years of age, born during the decade, must be added to the number of deaths amongst the population of 1901 to get this total. The number of children under 10 at the present Census is 3,618,680. The problem is, how many children should have been born in the decade for this number to survive at the end of it? The population most nearly analogous to this child population in respect of age-distribution and therefore, of rate of mortality, is the population under 10 at the 1901 Census. The youngest infant at that Census might have been one day or even one hour old, when the population was enumerated : the oldest child, just 10 years old or a day or two less. But there is one essential difference between the life-history of the population under 10 in 1901 and the corresponding population in 1911 during the intervening decade. The first year of life is notorious for its high mortality. The bulk of the child population of 1901 had passed this ordeal, while every year's crop of children during the decade had to pass through it. The number of deaths during the decade amongst the child population of 1901 would, therefore, only give us a standard for estimating that among the children born during the decade. The difference between the number of persons living in 1911 between 10 and 20 years of age, and the number in 1901, 10 years old and under, represents the number of deaths during the decade in the latter population. The latter number was 2,808,521, the former is, 2,396,924 : the difference, 411,597. The proportionate number for the child population of 1911 is 621,396. This may be taken to be the number of deaths among all children born during the decade, with the exception of deaths in infancy, that is, in the first year of life. Adding this number to the difference between the population of 1901 and the number of living in 1911 at ages 10 and over, we get 2,006,542 as the total of deaths during the decade, excepting deaths in infancy. This, on the Census population of 1901, gives a death-rate of 180·1 per mille in 10 years. If we allow 200 per mille for deaths in infancy—a modest allowance—the total death-rate will be 380 per 1,000 persons or 38 per mille per annum. The birth-rate is arrived at by adding the estimated number of deaths among children (including infants) during the decade to the number living under 10 years of age in 1911, and working out its proportion to the Census population of 1901. This gives 580·4 per mille for 10 years or 58 per mille per annum. The difference between the estimated death and birth-rates is, it will be noted, about 20 per cent., the rate at which the population has increased during the decade. Mr. Ackland's estimates, deduced by actuarial methods from more precise data than is available here, for the adjoining provinces of Madras and Bombay are birth-rate, 41 and 41·9, and death-rate, 35·8 and 33·4 respectively. The birth-rate in this State is certainly much higher, considering that the increase of population during the decade was 20 per cent. here, while in Madras and Bombay it was only 6 and 8·3 per cent. respectively. A higher birth-rate necessarily means a somewhat higher death-rate also.

114. Age-distribution of the Population in the Natural Divisions.

The mean age of both the male and female population is distinctly higher in Marathwara than in Telingana. The deficiency in the proportion of persons at between 10 and 20 years of age in Marathwara as compared with Telingana, is explained by the deficiency in the number of children at the Census of 1901. But it might have been expected that, as the part of the Dominions which bore the brunt of the famines which preceded that Census, Marathwara would show a larger proportion of children under 10 years at the present Census than Telingana. As has been said above, the effect of a famine is, by destroying the very young and the very old, to leave a population with a large proportion of persons in the adult ages, and thus to bring about a high birth-rate. The proportion of persons at ages ranging from 20 to 40 is higher in Marathwara than in Telingana, and this is the more remarkable in that, at the 1901 Census, the proportion of persons over 20 in Marathwara was lower than in Telingana. That notwithstanding the larger proportion of persons at the productive ages in Marathwara, there is a smaller proportion of children under 10 years of age in that Natural Division than in Telingana, would seem to require explanation. The plague has been off and on causing havoc in the Marathwara districts, and the plague, unlike famine, is most dangerous to adult life. But it is not known that it has the effect of impairing the reproductive powers of the adults whom it spares. In the face of the larger proportion of persons living at the productive ages in Marathwara than in Telingana, it seems farfetched, therefore, to bring in plague a cause of the lower proportion of children in the former Division. The proportion of married women in the productive ages in Marathwara is higher than in Telingana, there being 36 married women in the former as against 34 in the latter for 100 females of all ages. The proportion of children per 100 married females at between 15 and 40 years of age, however, is only 150 in Marathwara, while in Telingana it is 165. In 1891 it was 159 and 173 respectively in the two divisions. It may be that the large Animist element in the population of Telingana gives it a higher birth-rate. And it may be also that there were among the married females enumerated in Marathwara many young women who, having married outside the State, had come home on a visit to their parents, leaving behind their children with their husbands' parents and relatives. We have seen in the last Chapter that there is a great deal of social intercourse between the population of Marathwara and the contiguous British Districts.

115. Age distribution by Religion.

The Jains have the highest mean age of the religious communities of the State, as shown in the marginal table, and the Animists, the least. As pointed out in the foregoing paragraphs, this means that the Jains, and next to them, the Mussulmans, have a proportionately larger number of persons living at the later than at the earlier age-periods. The Jains have the largest proportion of persons at from 40 to 60, and they would have the largest proportion also between 15 and 40 years of age but for the Christian males who number 3,900 in 10,000 persons as against 3,356 of the Jains. The marginal table exhibits the age-constitution of the male population of the principal religions in the State in four age-groups. The Animists have the largest proportion of children, and would have the smallest proportion of old men and men past middle age, but for the Christians. The low proportion both of persons under 15 and of persons over 40, and the very high proportion of persons at the ages 15-40, amongst Christians, is due to the fact that the community contains a large proportion of converts who are generally of the 'useful' ages. Old people do not generally change their habits of thought or life. As compared with the Christian male population at between 15-40, the female population is small, which shows fewer women are converted from other religions than men. This accounts for the small proportion of children among Christians. The converts are either single men or if they are married and have children, the children usually remain in the old faith with their mothers. In view of the fact that the Musulmans have the largest proportion of men living at the age of 60 and over, they would seem to enjoy the highest degree of longevity of the religious communities of the State. Among Hindus and Musulmans, the proportion of old females has remained higher than that of old males at all the Censuses. In the marginal table are given proportionate figures, for each religious community, of females between 15 and 40 years of age and of children (males) under 10 per 10,000 of the population. The Animist women, it is evident, are the most prolific in the State. Next to them come the Hindus. The Jains have the lowest proportion of children, though they have the highest proportion of women in the productive age-period. The Jains marry early but it is evident that early maternity is not common among them.

Religions.	Males.	Females.
Jains	27·2	25·6
Musalman	26·1	25·3
Hindu	25·2	24·8
Christian	24·8	23·3
Animist	23·3	22·0

Per 10,000 males.

Religions.	0-15.	15-40.	40-60	60 and over.
Hindus	3,765	3,905	1,784	546
Musulmans	3,574	3,952	1,826	648
Christians	3,500	4,628	1,441	431
Jains	3,274	4,128	1,970	628
Animists	4,364	3,583	1,551	502

Per 10,000 persons.

Religions.	Females, 15-40.	Male children under 10 per 10,000 of population.
Hindus	4,040	2,642
Musulmans	4,047	2,437
Christians	4,198	2,438
Jains	4,200	2,151
Animists	3,752	3,181

116. Age-distribution of certain castes.

The particulars given in Subsidiary Table IV of the age-distribution of 1,000 of each sex in certain castes are of special interest in connection with the subject-matter of the next chapter. Here it is only relevant as indicating the relative age compositions of the castes mentioned therein. The Gonds are by far the most prolific caste in the State and next to them are the Lambadas who are also Animists. They breed fast but die soon as shown by the fact that they have both very low proportions of persons living at the age of 40 and over. The Sayyed among Mussulmans and the Lingayat among Hindus have the highest proportions of males past middle age in the State. The two castes have only one thing in common, namely, certain definite, though widely different, religious beliefs and their faith in them amounts to fatalism. This, no doubt, saves them from much of the worry to which people with a less absolute acquiescence in things as they are, are exposed. The Brahmins have the largest proportion of females at 40 and over of any caste. The Lingayats come second in the list. Both these castes have a large proportion of widows at these ages, and widowhood seems to have the effect of prolonging female life. The Pathans and Shaikhs among Mussulmans and the Kolis among Hindus have over 400 females at between 15-40 years in every 1,000 of the sex. Theirs are the largest proportions in the State. The two Musulman castes, however, have relatively a small proportion of children under 10. It is obvious that the birth-rate in these castes is low as compared with most others in the State.

SUBSIDIARY TABLE I.—Age Distribution of 100,000 of each Sex by Annual Periods (all religions).

Age.	Persons.	Males.	Females.	Age.	Persons.	Males.	Females.
Total ...	200,000	100,000	100,000				
0	5,392	2,591	2,801	50	9,497	4,770	4,727
1	3,680	1,617	2,063	51	406	239	167
2	6,403	2,743	3,660	52	324	185	139
3	5,616	2,658	2,958	53	214	120	94
4	5,460	2,724	2,736	54	231	124	107
5	6,372	3,016	3,356	55	1,918	1,097	821
6	5,232	2,587	2,645	56	130	62	68
7	4,087	1,943	2,144	57	95	26	69
8	5,613	2,768	2,845	58	207	83	124
9	3,319	1,540	1,779	59	51	26	25
10	6,908	3,604	3,304	60	6,613	3,153	3,460
11	2,483	1,130	1,353	61	64	30	34
12	6,850	4,067	2,783	62	247	134	113
13	1,832	860	972	63	75	39	36
14	3,142	1,592	1,550	64	83	44	39
15	4,657	2,325	2 332	65	928	498	430
16	4,308	2,025	2,283	66	45	21	24
17	1,519	668	851	67	78	13	65
18	5,066	2,446	2,620	68	54	16	38
19	1,354	794	560	69	31	13	18
20	11,413	5,045	6,368	70	2,094	1,011	1,083
21	1,069	728	341	71	15	6	9
22	3,147	1,653	1,494	72	44	15	29
23	923	472	451	73	14	9	5
24	1,206	607	599	74	15	10	5
25	13,312	6,629	6,683	75	432	196	236
26	1,481	851	630	76	76	68	8
27	832	468	364	77	7	1	6
28	2,006	1,096	910	78	24	12	12
29	500	238	262	79	24	11	13
30	14,861	7,143	7,718	80	1,016	440	576
31	1,256	657	599	81	13	8	5
32	1,852	1,070	782	82	30	15	15
33	510	309	201	83	17	9	8
34	527	314	213	84	17	8	9
35	8,058	4,543	3,515	85	99	43	56
36	734	402	332	86	14	3	11
37	267	97	170	87	1	......	1
38	792	454	338	88	1	1	......
39	219	97	122	89	3	2	1
40	12,742	6,541	6,201	90	189	73	116
41	375	218	157	91	3	......	3
42	653	394	259	92	......	......	......
43	236	127	109	93	......	......	......
44	335	190	145	94	2	2	......
45	4,899	2,793	2,106	95	22	8	14
46	322	152	170	96	1	1	......
47	192	53	139	97	1	1	......
48	382	217	165	98	4	......	4
49	116	76	40	99	1	......	1
				100	20	12	8

Note.—This return was prepared from a few units taken at random in different parts of the State. It is merely designed to illustrate the tendency of the people to pitch on certain numbers and not to how the general age distribution of the population

SUBSIDIARY TABLE II—Age Distribution of 10,000 of each Sex in the State and each Natural Division.

Age.	1911.		1901.		1891.		1881.	
	Males.	Females.	Males.	Females.	Males.	Females.	Males.	Females.
1	2	3	4	5	6	7	8	9
State.								
0—1 ...	264	291	151	165	268	297	204	226
1—2 ...	178	208	204	222	219	251	207	228
2—3 ...	338	370	274	306	333	374	257	291
3—4 ...	291	328	241	274	298	342	290	325
4—5 ...	303	316	291	307	311	328	348	382
Total 0—5 ...	1,369	1,508	1,161	1,274	1,429	1,592	1,306	1,452
5—10 ...	1,262	1,278	1,332	1,275	1,331	1,325	1,277	1,297
10—15 ...	1,125	955	1,303	1,117	1,078	890	1,237	1,044
15—20 ...	735	767	755	775	723	780	788	805
20—25 ...	790	951	715	893	806	983	817	986
25—30 ...	939	901	923	965	971	915	958	918
30—35 ...	860	922	950	976	914	932	958	910
35—40 ...	593	493	604	528	558	441	569	463
40—45 ...	741	712	751	719	738	702	718	679
45—50 ...	374	281	354	286	323	286	312	269
50—55 ...	521	506	5:0	511	497	495	461	479
55—60 ...	146	115	164	137	119	92	138	134
60—65 ...	328	364						
65—70 ...	62	58	478	549	513	617	466	569
70 and over ...	163	191						
Mean Age ...	25·5	25·0	25·2	25·1	24·6	24·3	24·5	24·4
Telingana.								
0—5 ...	1,374	1,532	2,504	2,765	1,386	1,550	1,389	1,570
5—10 ...	1,309	1,380			1,367	1,361	1,302	1,305
10—15 ...	1,172	981	1,291	1,084	1,174	975	1,224	1,041
15—20 ...	761	795	807	840	788	845	810	886
20—40 ...	3,091	3,181			3,135	3,135	3,152	3,094
40—60 ...	1,713	1,557	5,598	5,311	1,604	1,482	1,599	1,508
60 and over ...	580	624			546	652	524	646
Mean Age ...	24·9	24·4	...	...	24·4	24·0	24·3	24·2
Marathwara.								
0—5 ...	1,364	1,488	2,675	2,341	1,465	1,627	1,288	1,357
5—10 ...	1,218	1,216			1,300	1,292	1,257	1,291
10—15 ...	1,077	929	1,315	1,149	995	818	1,247	1,044
15—20 ...	708	738	705	718	669	725	771	782
20—40 ...	3,254	3,357			3,347	3,389	3,424	3,419
40—60 ...	1,854	1,671	5,305	5,797	1,739	1,562	1,644	1,600
60 and over ...	580	601			485	587	419	507
Mean Age ...	25·6	25·2	...	...	24·6	24·9	24·7	24·6

SUBSIDIARY TABLE III—Age Distribution of 10,000 of each sex in each main religion.

Age.	1911. Males.	1911. Females.	1901. Males.	1901. Females.	1891. Males.	1891. Females.	1881. Males.	1881. Females.
1	2	3	4	5	6	7	8	9
Hindu	10,000	10,000	10,000	10,000	10,000	10,000	10,000	10,000
0—5 ...	1,381	1,518	1,173	1,285	1,445	1,609	1,322	1,447
5—10 ...	1,261	1,267	1,341	1,261	1,339	1,328	1,282	1,284
10—15 ...	1,123	946	1,310	1,117	1,085	895	1,237	1,035
15—20 ...	734	766	753	778	721	777	785	801
20—40 ...	3,171	3,274	3,177	3,359	3,286	3,262	3,271	3,235
40—60 ...	1,784	1,621	1,778	1,659	1,668	1,518	1,608	1,534
60 and over ...	546	608	468	541	506	611	500	664
Mean Age ...	25·2	24·8	25·1	25·1	24·3	24·2	24·4	24·4
Mussalman ...	10,000	10,000	10,000	10,000	10,000	10,000	10,000	10,000
0—5 ...	1,226	1,359	1,061	1,164	1,293	1,442	1,105	1,060
5—10 ...	1,211	1,259	1,264	1,386	1,262	1,280	1,180	1,023
10—15 ...	1,187	1,015	1,260	1,117	1,011	836	1,179	799
15—20 ...	761	790	768	743	747	804	781	604
20—40 ...	3,191	3,257	3,282	3,341	3,338	3,367	3,334	2,641
40—60 ...	1,826	1,643	1,809	1,619	1,767	1,595	1,748	1,321
60 and over ...	648	677	565	630	582	676	628	2,552
Mean Age ...	26·1	25·3	26·0	25·3	25·6	25·1	25·8	25·2
Christian ...	10,000	10,000	10,000	10,000	10,000	10,000	10,000	10,000
0—5 ...	1,286	1,588	1,031	1,341	1,085	1,486	941	1,460
5—10 ...	1,202	1,413	1,142	1,496	1,107	1,415	938	1,453
10—15 ...	1,062	1,135	1,071	1,234	801	1,133	871	1,181
15—20 ...	728	931	719	1,014	689	1,087	660	1,047
20—40 ...	3,900	3,267	4,302	3,275	4,835	3,276	5,009	3,173
40—60 ...	1,441	1,254	1,361	1,317	1,154	1,204	1,280	1,266
60 and over ...	431	412	384	323	329	399	301	420
Mean Age ...	24·3	22·3	24·6	22·4	24·0	22·2	25·3	22·4
Jain	10,000	10,000	10,000	10,000	10,000	10,000	10,000	10,000
0—5 ...	1,066	1,359	984	1,190	1,072	1,304	1,073	1,142
5—10 ...	1,085	1,201	1,015	1,158	1,022	1,137	988	1,030
10—15 ...	1,123	962	1,248	1,125	1,059	915	940	875
15—20 ...	772	805	848	801	769	818	790	806
20—40 ...	3,356	3,395	3,413	3,457	3,562	3,447	3,682	3,505
40—60 ...	1,970	1,664	1,989	1,750	1,961	1,629	1,915	1,796
60 and over ...	628	614	503	519	555	660	612	846
Mean Age ...	27·2	25·6	26·8	25·7	27·1	25·6	27·2	27·6
Animistic ...	10,000	10,000	10,000	10,000	10,000	10,000	...	...
0—5 ...	1,621	1,907	1,377	1,586	1,501	1,793	...	...
5—10 ...	1,560	1,582	1,533	1,480	1,540	1,456	...	...
10—15 ...	1,183	998	1,288	1,147	1,190	1,032	...	...
15—20 ...	668	650	705	831	581	672	...	...
20—40 ...	2,915	3,102	3,112	3,215	2,959	3,123	...	...
40—60 ...	1,551	1,253	1,651	1,389	1,706	1,432	...	...
60 and over ...	502	508	484	452	523	502	...	...
Mean Age ...	23·3	22·0	23·5	22·8	24·1	22·8	...	...

SUBSIDIARY TABLE IV.—Age Distribution of 1,000 of each Sex in certain Castes.

Caste.	Males—Number per mille aged.					Females—Number per mille aged.				
	0—5	5—12	12—15	15—40	40 and over.	0—5	5—12	12—15	15—40	40 and over.
1	2	3	4	5	6	7	8	9	10	11
Hindu.										
1 Brahman	155	128	84	401	232	156	133	82	359	270
2 Dhangar	157	141	106	360	236	201	131	101	382	185
3 Golla	147	165	108	366	214	178	138	103	370	211
4 Goundla	144	178	99	354	225	171	123	111	383	212
5 Kapu	166	134	112	387	201	141	166	93	362	238
6 Koli	162	144	115	370	209	173	125	100	401	201
7 Komati	161	129	106	367	237	141	154	98	360	247
8 Lingayet	170	134	113	326	252	171	125	88	353	263
9 Madiga or Mang	190	144	81	366	219	200	154	74	333	239
10 Mahar or Mala	174	143	99	362	226	174	148	86	389	203
11 Mahratta	148	137	93	391	231	146	148	96	367	243
12 Munuer	177	136	80	399	208	170	130	110	371	219
13 Mutrasi	168	142	76	370	244	182	122	97	384	215
14 Sale	189	158	86	346	226	178	171	67	357	227
15 Telaga	164	151	82	371	232	171	151	79	362	237
Musalman.										
16 Pathan	132	142	73	416	237	149	142	77	409	223
17 Sayyed	129	142	75	393	261	134	149	87	391	239
18 Shaikh	146	126	98	389	241	144	130	79	406	241
Christian.										
19 Indian Christian	158	167	73	388	214	177	149	76	395	203
Animist.										
20 Gond	301	186	63	279	171	245	147	71	371	166
21 Lambada	245	168	73	311	203	244	188	53	339	181

SUBSIDIARY TABLE V.—Proportion of Children under 10 and of Persons 60 and over to those aged 15—40, also of Married Females aged 15—40 per 100 Females.

District and Natural Division.	Proportion of children (both sexes) per 100.						Proportion of persons at 60 and over per 100 aged 15—40.						Number of married Females aged 15—40 per 100 females of all ages.		
	Persons aged 15—40.			Married females aged 15—40.			1911.		1901.		1891.				
	1911.	1901	1891.	1911.	1901.	1891.	Males	Females.	Males.	Females.	Males.	Females.	1911.	1901.	1891.
1	2	3	4	5	6	7	8	9	10	11	12	13	14	15	16
State	68	62	71	157	157	165	14	15	12	13	13	15	35	33	35
Telingana	71	...	72	165	...	173	15	16	...	...	14	16	34	...	33
Hyderabad City ...	47	...	41	122	...	113	15	16	...	...	13	16	35	...	36
Atrafibalda	66	...	66	153	...	187	18	18	...	...	16	19	34	...	29
Warangal	75	...	78	177	...	187	15	15	...	...	14	16	34	...	33
Karimnagar	76	...	80	177	...	186	14	14	...	...	13	14	35	...	34
Adilabad	82	...	83	187	...	190	11	14	...	...	12	15	34	...	33
Medak...	67	...	64	152	...	150	19	18	...	...	18	19	35	...	34
Nizamabad	65	...	66	150	...	158	14	17	...	...	13	17	35	...	35
Mahbubnagar ...	69	...	72	159	...	171	16	16	...	...	12	16	34	...	34
Nalgonda	77	...	83	178	...	196	15	15	...	...	15	17	34	...	33
Marathwara ...	66	...	70	150	...	159	13	15	...	...	12	14	36	...	36
Aurangabad	68	...	69	153	...	153	12	13	...	...	14	15	36	...	37
Bhir	67	...	68	149	...	151	12	13	...	...	13	14	37	...	38
Nander	65	...	71	146	...	159	12	16	...	...	12	15	36	...	36
Parbhani	66	...	71	147	...	158	12	14	...	...	12	14	37	...	37
Gulbarga	65	...	67	150	...	156	16	16	...	...	11	16	35	...	36
Osmanabad	65	...	70	147	...	154	13	13	...	...	12	13	37	...	38
Raichur	65	...	76	161	...	183	13	14	...	...	9	13	32	...	35
Bidar	65	...	68	146	...	153	15	17	...	...	14	17	36	...	36
(Lingsugar)	...	...	72	...	...	175	...	...	...	...	9	12	...	...	35
(Railways)	...	...	38	...	...	128	...	...	...	...	4	7	...	...	45

SUBSIDIARY TABLE VI—Variation in population at certain age periods.

District and Natural Division.	Period.	Variation per cent. in population (Increase + decrease—). All Ages.	0—10.	10—15.	15—40.	40—60.	60 and over.
1	2	3	4	5	6	7	8
State...	1881-1891	+ 19·2	+ 26·9	+ 2·7	+ 17·0	+ 19·9	+ 30·1
	1891-1901	— 3·4	— 14·2	+ 18·7	— 2·8	+ 3·4	— 12·2
	1901-1911	+ 20·0	+ 28·8	+ 3·1	+ 18·0	+ 18·9	+ 36 6
Telingana ...	1881-1891	+ 17·5	+ 25·5	+ 15·2	+ 21·6	+ 20·5	+ 24·4
	1891-1901	+ 4·7	— 2·4	+ 13·8	...	...	...
	1901-1911	+ 21·3	+ 26·8	+ 11·9	...	...	...
Hyderabad City	1881-1891	+ 12·9	+ 63·2	+ 32·2	+ 48·8	+ 37·2	+ 40·5
	1891-1901	+ 8·0	+ 16·1	+ 24·3	...	...	...
	1901-1911	+ 11·6	+ 12·1	+ 12·1	...	...	...
Atrafibalda	1881-1891	+ 9 5	+ 14 6	— 6·7	+ 2·1	+ 0·8	+ 10·3
	1891 1901	+ 7·9	+ 6·4	+ 31·4	...	...	...
	1901-1911	+ 23·6	+ 37·2	+ 8·8	...	...	...
Warangal	1881-1891	+ 26·2	+ 34·1	+ 22·5	+ 27·0	+ 30·0	+ 23·6
	1891-1901	+ 11·6	+ 2·8	+ 18·3	...	...	...
	1901-1911	— 4·9	— 1·2	— 9·8	...	...	...
Karimnagar	1881-1891	+ 16·5	+ 15·2	+ 18·9	+ 15·8	+ 19·9	+ 14 4
	1891 1901	— 5·3	— 12·8	— 0 7	...	...	...
	1901-1911	+ 9·2	+ 11 5	— 4·7	...	...	...
Adilabad	1881-1891	+ 7·9	+ 2·2	+ 18·3	+ 8·5	+ 14·7	+ 7·4
	1891-1901	+ 17·7	+ 9·6	+ 15·1	...	...	...
	1901-1911	+ 127·0	+ 146·9	+ 95 5	...	...	...
Medak...	1881-1891	+ 11·6	+ 37·5	+ 20·4	+ 27·6	+ 16·2	+ 30·6
	1891-1901	+ 0·5	— 2·9	+ 17 3	...	...	...
	1901-1911	+ 87·3	+ 101·9	+ 66·6	...	...	...
Nizamabed	1881-1891	+ 10·7	+ 11·0	+ 17·1	+ 16	+ 11·6	+ 19·9
	1891-1901	— 0·7	— 11·1	+ 4·4	...	...	...
	1901-1911	— 10 4	— 0·7	— 21·8	...	...	...
Mahbubnagar	1881-1891	+ 23·1	+ 45·3	+ 9·0	+ 23·7	+ 22·3	+ 58·7
	1891-1901	+ 4·6	— 5·3	+ 31·0	...	...	...
	1901-1911	+ 5·8	+ 9·0	— 3·6	...	...	...
Nalgonda	1881-1891	+ 26·3	+ 32·0	+ 13·2	+ 37·9	+ 29 9	+ 21·6
	1891-1901	+ 12·0	+ 5·9	+ 12·5	...	...	...
	1901-1911	+ 49·2	+ 47·2	+ 58·2	...	...	...
Marathwara	1881-1891	+ 16·7	+ 29·2	— 8·1	+ 13·1	+ 12·5	+ 33·4
	1891-1901	— 10·4	— 24·5	+ 23·8	...	...	...
	1901-1911	+ 18·6	+ 31·2	— 4·8	...	...	...
Aurangabad	1881-1891	+ 13·4	+ 14·7	+ 7·5	+ 11 8	+ 12·7	+ 41·2
	1891-1901	— 12·9	— 22·6	+ 6·7	...	...	...
	1901-1911	+ 20 5	+ 34·8	— 1·6	...	...	...
Bhir	1881-1891	+ 15·0	+ 19·9	— 7·3	+ 12·6	+ 21·3	+ 38·3
	1891-1901	— 23 4	- 33·[illegible]	+ 4·9	...	...	...
	1901-1911	+ 26·4	+ 43·8	— 8·3	...	...	...
Nander	1881 1891	— 0·5	— 13·7	— 17·8	— 18·3	— 11·9	— 6·2
	1891-1901	— 20·3	— 34·6	— 1·6	...	...	...
	1901-1911	+ 39 8	+ 61·7	— 2·0	...	...	...
Parbhani	1881-1891	+ 17·5	+ 41·6	+ 31·0	+ 36·2	+ 39·5	+ 66·4
	1891-1901	— 19·8	- 32·7	+ 5 9	...	...	...
	1901-1911	+ 20·7	+ 37·9	— 15·4	...	...	...
Gulbarga	1881-1891	+ 23·9	+ 5·5	— 40·6	— 17·5	— 14·1	— 2·0
	1891-1901	+ 14·3	— 26 6	+ 78·0	...	...	...
	1901-1911	+ 54·9	+ 121·9	+ 86·5	...	...	...
Osmanabad	1881-1891	+ 19·4	+ 39·7	— 11·7	+ 14·7	+ 27·1	+ 35·9
	1891-1901	— 17 5	— 27·5	+ 20·7	..	...	...
	1901-1911	+ 18·8	+ 25.0	— 8 9	...	...	...
Raichur	1881-1891	+ 28·5	+ 119·9	— 13·2	+ 49·5	+ 67·7	+ 108·8
	1891-1901	— 0·6	— 17·4	+ 63·6	...	...	...
	1901-1911	+ 95·7	+ 91·8	+ 90·2	...	...	...
Bidar...	1881 1891	+ 14·3	+ 20·8	+ 2·8	+ 11·7	+ 17·2	+ 34 8
	1891-1901	— 15·0	— 23·8	+ 5·5	...	...	...
	1901-1911	+ 16·1	+ 24·0	— 5·1	...	...	...
(Lingsugar)	1881-1891	+ 28·9	+ 145·5	+ 4·4	+ 79·9	+ 88·3	+ 85·8
	1891-1901	+ 8·2	— 0·01	+ 93·6	...	...	...
	1901-1911	...	...	...	...	...	...
(Railways)	1881-1891	+ 776·3	...	...	...	...	...
	1891-1901	+ 81·9	+ 75·9	+ 214·5	...	...	...
	1901-1911	...	...	...	...	...	...

SUBSIDIARY TABLE VII.

Reported Birth rate by sex and natural division.

Year.	Number of births per 1,000 of total population (Census of 1901).				
	State.	Hyderabad City.		Telingana (districts).	Marathwara.
	Both sexes.	Male.	Female.	Both sexes.	Both sexes.
1	2	3	4	5	6
1901	6·0	8·3	7·1	5·9	5·3
1902	6·6	9·1	7·9	6·6	5·8
1903	6·9	9·2	7·7	6·5	6·4
1904	7·2	9·3	8·1	6·5	7·0
1905	7·0	9·8	8·5	6·5	6·6
1906	7·3	9·1	7·9	7·3	6·6
1907	7·5	8·8	8·0	6·7	7·5
19:8	8·2	8·6	7·5	7·0	8·1
1909	8·4	7·4	6·4	7·3	8·8
1910	8·5	8·8	7·9	7·2	8·9

NOTE.—Figures for districts by sex are not available.

SUBSIDIARY TABLE VIII.

Reported death-rate by sex and natural division.

Year.	Number of deaths per 1,000 of total population (Census of 1901).				
	State.	Hyderabad City.		Telingana (districts).	Marathwara.
	Both sexes.	Male.	Female.	Both sexes.	Both sexes.
1	2	3	4	5	6
1901	7·1	7·6	8·0	6·1	7·2
1902	6·9	8·0	8·3	6·5	6·5
1903	8·3	8·3	8·4	6·4	9·2
1904	8·9	8·3	8·3	6·3	10·6
1905	7·9	9·2	9·3	5·5	9·1
1906	8·9	10·1	10·5	8·5	8·3
1907	8·7	9·2	9·8	7·4	9·0
1908	8·5	10·7	10·9	7·6	8·1
1909	8·2	8·4	8·4	6·9	8·6
1910	9·4	8·6	9·1	7·7	10·2

NOTE.—Figures for districts by sex are not available. Figures for the City a·e worked out from proportionate figures.

Chapter VI.

THE PROPORTION OF THE SEXES.

117. There is no special Imperial table compiled for this Chapter but the Tables VII, XIV and also XI are the principal ones dealt with. Five sub-tables have been prepared to illustrate the main features of the relevant statistics. Sub-table VI could not be prepared as the returns of deaths contain no record of age. The subject-matter of this chapter is one of considerable interest, and has been discussed with much display of learning and ingenuity, if without much practical result, in Census Reports for the last thirty years. The female population in most European countries is more or less in excess of the male population. In India, on the contrary, it is less. Why should this be so? The answer to the question which most readily suggested itself, was that the female population was not accurately enumerated owing to the disposition of the people to conceal their womankind. This explanation by itself has been found inadequate. There are three other sources which either singly or together may contribute to the elucidation of this sex-constitution of our population. These are a large immigrant population, consisting mainly of males or a considerable emigration of females; a larger number of male than of female births; a higher mortality rate for women than men.

118. Concealment as a cause of the deficiency of the female population.

One of the reasons given in the last Census Report of India against attaching too great importance to the theory of concealment, was that, if there was any concealment, it was more likely to occur amongst Mussulmans than amongst Hindus, but that in most provinces the former had a larger proportion of women than their Hindu neighbours. So far as these Dominions are concerned, the proportion of females amongst Mussulmans is less than that amongst Hindus, whether we take the figures for the whole State or for each of the two Natural Divisions. For the whole State, the Mussulman proportion of females was less than that of the Hindu in 1891 and in 1901 also. If these facts seem to militate against one of the principal arguments brought forward against the theory of concealment, it has to be pointed out, on the other hand, that by far the most numerous Mussulman caste in the Nizam's Dominions, the Shaikh has a higher proportion of females than 9 out of 15 selected Hindu castes, few of which would be expected to cherish a disposition to conceal their women. Among these 9 castes, are the Brahmans and the Komati with 961 and 957 females respectively per 1,000 males as against the Shaikh's 972. Notwithstanding this fact, it seems probable that concealment does play an appreciable part in reducing the number of the female population enumerated at the Census of this State. In the next chapter on Civil Condition, reasons are given which suggest the possibility of some omission of supernumerary wives in polygamous marriages. It is sufficient to state here that, whatever might be the case elsewhere, it is impossible to discard altogether the theory of concealment in considering the question of the proportion of the sexes in these territories.

119. Migration.

The outstanding feature of the Statistics of migration as they affect the subject-matter of this chapter, is that the number of the male immigrants in the State exceeded that of females by 3,035, and that, of emigrants from the State, there were 36,379 more women than men. In Subsidiary Table I, will be found the proportion of females in the natural population—that is, persons born within the State wherever they may happen to have been enumerated—at the present and the two preceding Censuses. These proportions are higher than those of the actual population at this and the previous Census but not than that of 1891. It is on the face of it extraordinary that a State which suffers from a chronic scarcity of women, should export about 40,000 of them in excess of the male emigrants. It is impossible to imagine any compelling cause for this drain on the womanhood of these territories. The fact, however, is unquestionable, and it induces the doubt if, after all, Hyderabad is really so deficient in women as the statistics make out. This, again, goes to show that the theory of omission should not be lightly set aside in dealing with the proportion of the sexes in His Highness the Nizam's Dominions.

120. Vital Statistics in relation to the Sexes.

We have now to consider the two most important factors of births and deaths as affecting the proportionate distribution of the sexes. First, as to births, it will be seen from Sub-table II that the male population under one year of age, both of Hindus and Mahomedans, has been uniformly lower than the female, at every Census of this State. Not only that, but it continues to be so up to the fifth year of life. We have, therefore, to give up without further consideration the theory of a larger proportion of male births as an explanation of the deficiency of women. Vital Statistics, so far as any are collected in the State, are on the face of them unreliable, more especially in the case of births. But even if, as shown in Subsidiary Table V for the City of Hyderabad, there were actually more male births than female births, the greater mortality among male infants inclines the balance in favour of the female within the first year.

121. The Female Death-rate.

The admitted prevalence of polygamy ; the emigration of a considerable number of females in excess of males ; a population of female infants and children from 0-5 years far more numerous than that of males of the same age—these are circumstances which tend to throw doubt on the very existence of any deficiency in the female population in this State. Is there any other circumstance calculated to neutralise their significance ? If there is, it must be sought only in a greater mortality of women. In the absence of reliable statistics of mortality, the only evidence of the existence of such a factor is that furnished by the numbers enumerated at the several age-periods. We have seen above that the female population up to five years of age continues in excess of the male. Between 5 and 10, however, the position is reversed and the male population gains a decided advantage over the female. This preponderance is accentuated at the next five-year period. So far the statistics of 1901 and 1911 move hand in hand. Between 15 and 20, the female again leads in 1911, while in 1901, the male continued to maintain his advantage. Between 20 and 25, the number of females exceed that of males at both Censuses. The 1901 figures continue this predominance at the next five year period. But beyond that, till the sixtieth year is reached, women remain in a position of numerical inferiority. These movements are shown by means of proportional figures in Subsidiary Table II. It would be against all experience to attach excessive importance to the precise age-periods, especially in the case of females, but the broad fact stands out, namely, that the male population above the age of 5 is in as marked excess of the female population of that age as it is in defect below that limit. It is evident that some influence comes into play at some point after the fifth year is passed, rendering the conditions of life less favourable to women than to men. Subsidiary Table II shows the number of females per 1,000 males at different age-periods at the present and two previous Censuses. The fact that the number of females of the ages 0-30 at all the Censuses is smaller than that of men, while up to 5 years it is higher, shows that the apparent preponderance at the age-period 20-25, and less consistently at the immediately previous and subsequent five year periods, is due to aberrations in the age-record. Every woman in this State, who can possibly do so, would seem to have a fancy for returning herself as between 20 and 25 years of age. These variations in the Hyderabad statistics confirm the conclusion of the eminent Actuary, Mr. T. G. Ackland, formed on a study of the statistics of British India at the current census that "the general trend, as indicating a superior mortality for female, as compared with male, lives in the early years, and after middle life, with an inferior mortality in the intermediate years, appears to be well marked and unmistakable."

122. The discussion so far has brought us to this point: There is a possibility of omission, especially of supernumerary wives of polygamous marriages; there is no ground for thinking that such deficiency of females as there is, is due to an excess of male births; that even, if there were such an excess, its effect is more than neutralised by the higher mortality of male infants in the first year; that the large female emigration from the State is incompatible with the existence of a considerable deficiency of women; and that the female rate of mortality is lower than male mortality except in the intermediate years of life between infancy and old age. It is evident that the rate at which women die during this interval should be so high as to counteract the effects of their superiority at the earlier and the later age-periods. This intermediate period is the period when women bear children, when the strain and stress of maternity, aggravated by drudgery at the home and, for a large proportion of women, in the field, and by the almost total absence of skilled assistance at the most crucial period in a women's life, tells heavily upon them.

123. Conditions unfavourable to female life.

Owing to the erratic character of the recorded ages, it is futile to attempt to take the question further on the basis of the age statistics. For the rest it only remains to add that most of the conditions, tending to produce a relatively high mortality amongst females, found to prevail in other parts of India, exist and have full scope in the Nizam's Dominions. The exceptions are female infanticide and neglect of female infant life. With a higher proportion of females than males at every age under 5, these two causes of a deficiency of females are not to be thought of. The other conditions which cannot be less common in this State than elsewhere are (1) infant marriage and premature sexual intercourse and child-bearing; (2) a very high birth-rate; (3) unskilful midwifery; (4) abortions in the case of pregnant widows; (5) confinement and bad feeding of women at puberty, during their menstrual period and after child-birth; (6) the hard life of widows, and (7) the hard labour which women of the lower classes have to perform. The prevalence of infant and too early marriages is attested by the fact that there are 211,006 married females and 6,792 widows under 10 years of age: 27,913 married and 1,258 widows are returned as being under 5 years of age. The number of married females under 15 years of age is 623,339, and that of widows 17,979. It is necessary here to add a word of warning. Attention was called in the last Census Report of India to the necessity of discriminating between the physiologically unobjectionable form of early marriages prevalent among the Jats of the Punjab and the Rajputs, and the form of early marriage which was said to be the established usage in Bengal. In the former kind of marriage, the marriage is merely a betrothal and the husband and wife do not begin to live together until after several years. In the latter marriage, there is no such interval and maternity is forced on girls not physically fitted to undergo the ordeal. There is reason to believe that both kinds of early marriage are prevalent in the State. Except where counteracted by an active, outdoor life, the tendency is for the less objectionable form to degenerate into the more objectionable one. Unskilful midwifery is an outstanding feature of the conditions of female life here as elsewhere in India. With a large number of young widows, compelled by custom to lead a celibate life, abortions and suicides are to be expected. The other causes do not call for comment.

124. Progressive increase in the proportion of females.

The proportion of the female to the male population has increased during the last decade. In 1891 and 1901, there were the same number, namely, 964 females, to 1,000 males, but at the present Census it has risen to 968. For the natural population it stands even higher. There are 974 females to every 1,000 males born in the State, including those who were enumerated outside the State. No definite reason can be assigned for the increase, part of which is probably due to a decreasing tendency to conceal women from the Census schedules. The decade was on the whole a prosperous one from the point of view of the agricultural industry which supports the bulk of the population. The increase in the population under 10 years shows that the birth-rate was higher and the increase at all ages shows that the death-rate was lower than at the preceding decade. An increased proportion of male births has been observed to happen in times of scarcity in some countries, the classic illustration being the siege of Paris, when the shortage of food caused the direst distress, and when many more boys than girls were born ; and perhaps the prosperous seasons of the last decade led to the converse result of an increase in the number of female births. The statistics of the male and female population under 10 years of age in the 1901 and the 1911 Censuses, lends countenance to this proposition. In 1901, the male and female populations under this age, numbered 1,414,820 and 1,393,701 : that is, there were 21,119 less female children than male. In 1911, the figures were 1,788,219 and 1,830,461 respectively : that is, there were 42,242 more female children than male.

125. Comparison with other Provinces.

The number of females for every 1,000 males in the neighbouring British provinces is given in the marginal table.

Province.	Number of females per 1000 males.
Bombay	920
Central Provinces	1,008
Madras	1,032
Hyderabad	968

It may be pointed out that though the proportions for Madras, Bombay and the Central Provinces and Berar, vary considerably from that of Hyderabad, the ratios for the Natural Divisions of these provinces which lie contiguous to this State, bear a more or less close resemblance to it. The proportion for Marathwara is 981 per 1,000 males. The nearness to it of the proportion for the Bombay Deccan districts, is unmistakable. Aurangabad, Parbhani and Nander which are contiguous to the Maratha Plain Division of the Central Provinces have the highest proportion of females in the State. These facts show that sex proportions tend to be uniform in blocks of areas possessing the climatic and other peculiarities which constitute them into a Natural Division. The subjoined map shows the number of females to 1,000 males in each of the districts.

MAP OF HYDERABAD.

Showing proportion of females to 1,000 males in each district.

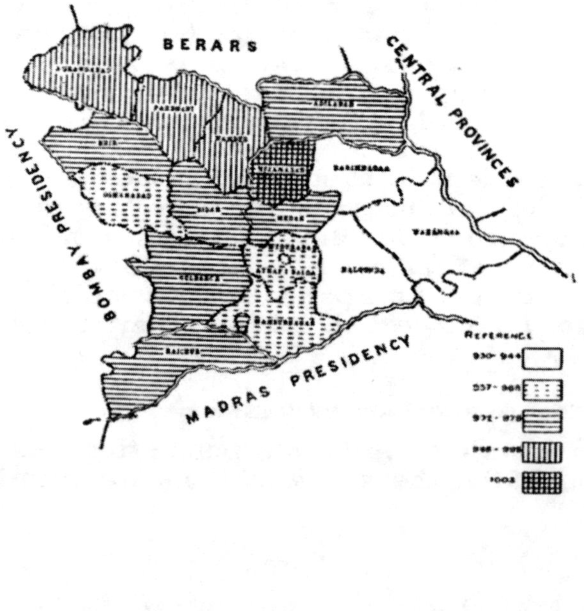

126. Low Proportion of Females in Telingana.

Telingana has only 955 females per 1,000 males, while Marathwara has 981. The three lowest proportions in the State occur in Telingana. They are Nalgonda 944, Hyderabad City 937, Warangal 937 and Karimnagar 930. The City-born population of Hyderabad has 1,036 females for every 1,000 males. The deficiency of females in the total population of the City, is plainly due to the large immigrant population which has only 660 females per 1,000 males. As the Capital of the State, Hyderabad City is the temporary home of thousands of persons from the districts and from outside the Dominions, who do not bring their women with them. A deficiency of females is characteristic of most city populations and Hyderabad is no exception. But the case of the districts is different. Of the three districts which have the lowest proportion of females in Telingana and, indeed, in the whole State, Warangal is the only one where the natural, that is, the district-born population shows a slightly higher proportion than the actual population. In Nalgonda and Karimnagar, where there is very little immigration, we have populations which have a large natural deficiency of women. Karimnagar, indeed, offers exceptional opportunities to the study of the phenomenon we are discussing. It has the lowest proportion of females in the State, it has few immigrants. There is considerable emigration to neighbouring districts but in about equal proportions of men and women. Its population consists almost wholly of Hindus, speaking Telugu. Unlike Warangal and Nalgonda, its Animist population is insignificant. On the other hand, judging from the number of married girls at the age-period 5-15, there are several districts which are more addicted to infant and too early marriages, and yet have a higher proportion of women than Karimnagar. Nizamabad in Telingana is the only district in the State which has a preponderance of women, the proportion being 1,003 to 1,000 males. Imperial Table XI on which we have drawn largely in this paragraph, brings out the fact that the excess in its case is due to immigration of females mostly from the neighbouring districts of Karimnagar, Medak, Nandar and Bedar. In the native Nizamabad population, the male element preponderates, the proportion being 993 per 1,000 males.

127. A Probable Explanation for the Low Proportion of Females in Telingana.

The normal proportion of females per 1,000 males is, as we have seen much higher in the Marathwara than the Telingana districts. In Nander it is 998, in Parbhani 993, and in Aurangabad 988. All these districts are in the Aurangabad Division. The other district in the Division, Bhir, has a proportion of 978 and it would have a smaller one but for the considerable immigrant female population in the district. Aurangabad also owes its high proportion, though to a less extent, to a preponderance of females in the immigrant population, but Parbhani and, even more, Nander, have a high natural proportion of females. Osmanabad among Marathwara districts has the smallest proportion of females. The three Kanarese districts have proportions varying from 976 to 979. The re-constitution of almost all the districts during the decade preceding the Census, makes comparisons of the district statistics with those of the previous Censuses at best uncertain. It is well worth enquiring whether the higher proportion of females in Marathwara and the lower proportion in Telingana, are to any extent the results of the prevalence in the Natural Divisions of the two kinds of early marriages to which reference has been made. The proportion of early married women in Marathwara is higher than in Telingana; still the former Division has a larger proportion of women than the latter. Sex proportions have been observed, as remarked above, to be uniform in areas which form more or less uniform blocks. It has been pointed out above that the proportion of females in the Marathwara districts generally approximate to that of the districts which are contiguous to them in Bombay and in the Central Provinces. The Telugu Districts of Madras, which lie alongside of Telingana, have come under special notice as having the lowest proportion of females in that Presidency. Mr. W. Francis discussed them at some length in his report for 1901. In his report of the 1891 Census, Mr. (now Sir Harold) Stuart had hinted at the existence of "Bengal customs of early marriage" in some of the

Telugu districts. Mr. Francis carried the enquiry farther, and concluded that there was "considerable ground for supposing that the deficiency of females in the seven districts (Krishna, Nellore, Cuddapah, Kurnool, Bellary, Anantapur and Chingleput) is to no small extent due to the deaths among young girls which are occasioned by forcing maternity upon them while they are still immature." Now all these districts, with the exception of the last, belong to the Telugu country and form one block with the districts of Telingana. It only remains to add that the features of the Madras statistics on which Mr. Francis laid stress, are repeated in the statistics of Telingana more emphatically than in those of Marathwara.

128. Proportion of Sexes by Religions and Castes.

At the present as in the two previous Censuses, the Mussulmans in this State show a smaller proportion of females than the Hindus. Moreover, while the Hindu proportion has advanced from 965 in 1901 to 971 at this Census, the Mussulman proportion has receded from 958 to 954. The Hindu proportion exceeds the Mussulman at all ages except 5 to 15. The lower ratio at this period may be due to the larger prevalence of too early marriages among Hindus than among Mahomedans. The statistics of the Natural Divisions, however, shows that, in Telingana, the Mussulman proportion is higher than that of the Hindu, at most ages above the age of 5. In Marathwara, on the contrary, the Hindu proportion is 30 per cent. higher. The Mussulman comes midway between the Marathwara and the Telingana Hindu in respect of his proportion of female population. Another noteworthy feature is that the Telingana Mussulman has at certain important age-periods such as 5-10, 10-15, a higher proportion of women not only than Telingana Hindus, but of Marathwara Mahomedans and Hindus as well. In the age-period 15-20 the Mussulman in Telingana has a larger proportion of women than his co-religionists of Marathwara. The inference seems to be justified that the Telingana Mussulman belongs to a more progressive community than his co-religionist of Marathwara, while in the case of the Hindus the reverse would seem to hold good.

129. Sex distribution by Castes.

With the exception of the Animist Lambada, the Mussulman Sayyid and Pathan have the lowest female ratios amongst Hyderabad castes. The lowest Hindu ratio, as will be seen from subsidiary Table IV, is 939 for the Muthrasi. The Mahratta and the Dhangar, with 991 head the list, with the Lingayath 987, the Koli 985, the Munnur 984 and the Mahar 981, close behind. The Brahman and the Komati, the priestly and the commercial castes, have only 961 and 957 females per 1,000 males. The Brahman proportion begins with 969 at the ages period 0-5, and improves to 995 at 5-12. Then it falls to 936, and continue-falling to 774 at 15-20. Between 20-40 it is 911. The lamentable effects of too early marriages are writ large on the face of these figures.

Females per 1,000 Males.

Caste.	0-5.	All ages.
Kapu	818	958
Komati	840	957
Sale	896	950
Munar	944	984
Brahman	969	961
Maratha	978	991
Mahar	984	981
Lingayath	994	987

130. The Brahman and some other castes mentioned in the margin, differ from the general population in having fewer female than male children in the first five years of life. They thus start, so to speak, with a smaller capital of womanhood. The first three castes in the list have less than 900 female per 1,000 males under 5 years and they have also the lowest proportion of males, amongst the selected castes, of all ages. But the latter proportion in all three castes is higher than the former, pointing to a higher rate of mortality among men than women in later age-periods. The Komati and the Sale are but moderately addicted to infant marriages, judging from the proportion of married girls under 12. The Kapu has a much higher proportion, but still considerably lower than several other castes. It is in these castes, if anywhere, should we look for neglect of female children being an operative cause in reducing the

proportion of females to the male population. It is in these and the five other castes in the list, that there is probably a larger number of male than female births. It is, therefore, with reference to these castes that it is least necessary to bring in early marriages as the principal cause of a higher female than male mortality. The Brahman, the Mahar and the Lingayath, however, differ from the rest of this group, in that their proportion of females at all ages is lower than that under 5 years, pointing to a higher proportionate mortality of women than of men in the later age-period. It is also possible that neglect of female children is responsible for the deficiency in the first 5 years. Probably, also, all these castes have a larger proportion of male than female births. It is a remarkable coincidence—to put it no higher—that the Brahman, the Mahar and the Lingayath are much addicted to infant marriages. The Brahman has 31, the Mahar 27, and the Lingayath 23, married girls in every 1,000 females under the age of 5. The Koli (28), the Dhanger (24) and the Maratha (22) are the only other castes having similarly high proportions. In the case of these castes, infant marriage is certainly a factor in lowering the proportion of women at all ages below what it is at the first age-period.

131. We now come to the castes which start with an excess of female children. The marginal table gives their proportions of females under 5 and for all ages. The most remarkable difference between this table and the previous one, is that whereas, in the latter, the proportion of females at all ages was higher or but slightly lower than the proportion for girls under the age of 5, in this table all the castes have very much lower proportions of women at all ages than of girls of 5 years and under. How far this lavish wastage of womanhood, on the part of castes who start with a generous endowment of it at the earliest age-period, is accounted for by an excess of female emigration, cannot be determined in the absence of data bearing on the castes of emigrants. For the same reason, it is impossible to say whether members of these castes from outside the State enter in it in large numbers at the later age-periods. But the aggregate of migration is so small, that it cannot explain the phenomenon we are considering except to a very slight extent. There is no room to doubt that women in these castes are exposed to conditions exceptionally unfavourable to female life. Perhaps, the very surplus of females at the first age-period, is Nature's provision to ensure a working balance of women in the deleterious conditions prevailing in these castes.

Females per 1,000 males.

Caste.	0-5.	All ages.
Dhangar	1,269	991
Golla	1,165	963
Goundla	1,134	957
Koli	1,038	985
Madiga	1,017	970
Muthrasi	1,013	939
Telaga	1,007	967

132. The statement at the margin gives the proportion of married females of all ages and at the age-periods 0-5 and 5-12 in these castes. All the castes, with the exception of the Madiga and the Telugu, have some of the highest proportions of married women in the State and four of them are addicted in a large measure to infant and too early marriages. The sudden fall in the proportion of females to males at 20 and over has a melancholy significance. The Dhangar who has the largest proportion in the state of girls under 5, has the lowest proportion of women past 40. The Golla, the Goundla, the Madiga, the Muthrasi and the Telaga, experience the same fate at an even earlier age-period, 20-40. The Koli, notwithstanding that he tops the list in respect of the proportion of girls married under the age of 12, manages to avoid the worst consequences of the custom, no doubt as the consequence of his strenuous open air life. The statistics point to the other castes in this table as the probable region of most prevalence of the Bengal type of early marriage in these territories. It does not follow, of course, that it is unknown outside these castes.

Married per 1,000.

Caste.	All ages.	0-5	5-12
Dhangar	593	24	355
Golla	571	12	271
Goundla	611	12	273
Koli	585	28	388
Madiga	538	14	254
Muthrasi	571	17	246
Telaga	508	10	245

SUBSIDIARY TABLE I.—General Proportions of the Sexes by Natural Divisions and Districts.

District and Natural Division.	Number of females to 1,000 Males.					
	1911.		1901.		1891.	
	Actual population.	Natural population.	Actual population.	Natural population.	Actual population.	Natural population.
1	2	3	4	5	6	7
State	968	974	964	970	964	971
Telingana	955	......	938	......	958	......
Hyderabad City	937	......	980	......	928	......
Atrafibalda	962	......	966	......	963	......
Warangal	937	......	912	......	936	......
Karimnagar	930	......	917	......	943	......
Adilabad	973	......	989	......	994	......
Medak	972	......	949	......	966	......
Nizamabad	1,003	......	983	......	986	......
Mahbubnagar	968	......	977	......	976	......
Nalgonda	914	......	885	......	957	......
Marathwara	981	......	989	......	969	......
Aurangabad	988	......	998	......	969	......
Bhir	978	......	984	......	956	......
Nander	998	......	1,006	......	981	......
Parbhani	993	......	993	......	961	......
Gulbarga	976	......	975	......	972	......
Osmanabad	957	......	975	......	957	......
Raichur	979	......	993	......	981	......
Bidar	979	......	990	......	951	......

Note.—Figures by districts are not available for columns 3, 5 and 7.

SUBSIDIARY TABLE II.—Number of Females per 1,000 Males at Different Age-periods by Religions at each of the last three Censuses.

AGE.	All religions.			Hindus.			Musalmans.		
	1891.	1901.	1911.	1891.	1901.	1911.	1891.	1901.	1911.
1	2	3	4	5	6	7	8	9	10
0—1	1,071	1,054	1,068	1,075	1,058	1,070	1,081	1,015	1,043
1—2	1,103	1,081	1,106	1,109	1,051	1,109	1,051	1,044	1,082
2—3	1,084	1,075	1,076	1,084	1,078	1,077	1,076	1,034	1,069
3—4	1,103	1,096	1,098	1,115	1,093	1,091	1,118	1,112	1,101
4—5	1,016	1,016	1,009	1,015	1,012	1,007	1,034	1,045	1,008
Total 0—5	1,074	1,058	1,067	1,075	1,057	1,067	1,060	1,051	1,058
5—10	95[illegible]	922	976	958	907	876	964	1,050	992
10—15	796	826	821	796	823	818	765	849	852
15—20	1,038	989	1,009	1,040	996	,014	1,024	926	991
20—25	1,174	1,203	1,168	1,179	1,210	1182	1,175	1,188	1,098
25—30	909	1,008	938	913	1,017	989	896	948	931
Total 0—30	986	981	991	987	979	993	980	998	984
30—40	899	930	948	902	985	948	880	895	927
40—50	852	876	862	854	882	858	844	888	865
50—60	919	926	901	925	980	910	947	899	864
60 and over ...	1,157	1,107	1,054	1,151	1,114	1,088	1,119	1,068	996
Total 30 and over ...	925	986	927	926	941	986	915	900	906
Total all ages actual population	964	964	968	966	965	971	958	958	954
Total all ages natural population	971	970	974	...	...	...	...	...	...

SUBSIDIARY TABLE III—Number of Females per 1,000 Males at Different Age-periods by Religions and Natural Divisions.

AGE.	Telingana.			Marathwara.		
	All religion.	Hindu.	Musalman.	All religion.	Hindu.	Musalman.
1	2	3	4	5	6	7
0—1	1,062	1,066	1,089	1,078	1,074	1,113
1—2	1,116	1,120	1,069	1,097	1,098	1,089
2—3	1,066	1,078	1,046	1,086	1,076	1,084
3—4	1,085	1,082	1,114	1,102	1,101	1,092
4—5	1,018	987	1,002	1,006	1,028	1,013
Total *0—5*	1,064	1,064	1,051	1,070	1,071	1,063
5—10...	970	970	1,017	984	988	971
10—15...	799	793	861	846	846	844
15—20...	997	999	1,027	1,023	1,031	959
20—25...	1,143	1,162	1,055	1,196	1,203	1,138
25—30...	946	950	942	931	929	922
Total *0—30*...	981	983	990	1,002	1,003	980
30—40...	912	911	1,144	972	979	934
40—50...	876	851	848	848	880	860
50—60...	899	915	871	903	904	857
60 and over	1,028	1,042	956	1,112	1,128	1,035
Total 30 and over	905	916	964	949	956	922
Total all ages (Actual population)	955	958	952	981	985	955
Total all ages (Natural population)	......	......	......	......	......	......

SUBSIDIARY TABLE IV—Number of Females per 1,000 Males for Certain Selected Castes.

Caste.	Number of famales per 1,000 Males.						
	All ages.	0–5	5–12	12–15	15–20	20–40	40 and over
1	2	3	4	5	6	7	8
Hindu.							
1. Brahman	961	969	995	936	774	911	1,118
2. Dhangar	991	1,269	926	940	1,279	980	779
3. Golla	963	1,165	808	927	1,178	905	948
4. Goundla	957	1,134	664	1,032	1,489	894	913
5 Kapu	958	818	1,186	793	915	886	1,150
6. Koli	985	1,058	851	853	1,171	1,032	949
7. Komati	957	840	1,145	879	837	987	998
8. Lingayet	987	994	922	781	993	1,103	1,029
9. Madiga or Mang	970	1,017	1,036	888	969	855	1,061
10. Mahar or Mala	981	984	985	934	1,094	1,031	879
11. Mahratta	991	978	1,070	1,028	892	941	1,042
12. Munnur	984	944	936	1,348	588	1,078	1,038
13. Muthrasi	939	1,013	803	1,211	1,365	855	830
14. Sale	950	896	1,060	746	1,002	971	958
15. Telaga	967	1,007	968	938	1,049	910	986
Musalman.							
16. Pathan	899	1,015	900	954	934	867	847
17. Sayyed	912	949	961	1,061	905	906	815
18 Shaikh	972	957	1,005	776	963	1,034	971
Christian.							
19. Indian Christian	942	058	847	982	1,116	923	890
Animist.							
20 Gond	987	801	780	1,110	1,519	1,278	960
21. Lambade	852	848	923	627	857	948	762

SUBSIDIARY TABLE V.—Actual Number of Births and Deaths reported for each Sex during the decades 1901-1910.

(1) HYDERABAD CITY.

Year.	Number of births.			Number of deaths.			Difference between columns 2 and 3. Excess of latter over former (+) defect(—).	Difference between columns 5 and 6. Excess of latter over former (+) defect (—).	Difference between columns 4 and 7. Excess of former over latter (+) defect (—).	Number of female births per 1,000 males births.	Number of female deaths per 1,000 male deaths.
	Males.	Females.	Total.	Males.	Females.	Total.					
1	2	3	4	5	6	7	8	9	10	11	12
Total	41,115	35,920	77,035	41,099	42,272	83,371	— 5,195	+ 1,173	— 6,336	874	1,029
1901 ...	3,864	3,299	7,163	3,529	3,707	7,236	— 565	+ 178	— 73	854	1,050
1902 ...	4,213	3,673	7,886	3,734	3,866	7,600	— 540	+ 132	+ 286	872	1,035
1903 ...	4,293	3,672	7,965	3,869	3,887	7,756	— 621	+ 18	+ 209	855	1,005
1904 ...	4,309	3,784	8,093	3,874	3,842	7,716	— 525	— 32	+ 377	878	992
1905 ...	4,556	3,982	8,538	4,268	4,315	8,583	— 574	+ 47	— 45	874	1,011
1906 ...	4,212	3,696	7,908	4,695	4,873	9,568	— 516	+ 178	— 1,660	877	1,038
1907 ...	4,102	3,708	7,810	4,275	4,538	8,813	— 394	+ 263	— 1,003	904	1,062
1908 ...	4,032	3,478	7,510	4,961	5,076	10,037	— 554	+ 115	— 2,527	863	1,023
1909 ..	3,448	2,999	6,447	3,909	3,919	7,828	— 449	+ 10	— 1,381	870	1,003
1910 ...	4,086	3,629	7,715	3,985	4,249	8,234	— 457	+ 264	— 519	888	1,066

(2) DISTRICTS.

Year.	Number of births.	Number of deaths.	Difference between columns 4 and 7. Excess of former over latter (+) defect (—).
	Both sexes.	Both sexes.	
1	2	3	4
Total	746,949	844,669	— 97,720
1901	60,029	72,118	— 12,089
1902	66,566	70,071	— 3,505
1903	69,422	84,824	— 15,402
1904	73,027	92,199	— 19,172
1905	70,548	80,293	— 9,745
1906	74,415	90,092	— 15,677
1907	76,325	88,954	— 12,629
1908	81,912	84,788	— 2,876
1909	87,350	84,379	+ 2,971
1910	87,355	96,951	— 9,596

Chapter VII.

CIVIL CONDITION.

132. Statistics.

Imperial Table VII gives particulars of the distribution of the population by age, sex and civil condition. Imperial Table XIV furnishes information regarding the civil condition of selected castes. Five subsidiary tables are appended to this chapter giving proportional figures by age, religion and caste.

133. Universality of marriage.

The outstanding feature of the marriage relation in India is its universality. Religious beliefs and social opinion combine to press as many as possible, and as early as possible, into the responsibilities of the married life. Not that there is much sense of responsibility evinced when entering into the marriage relation. In the case of a large proportion of persons, marriage comes at an age when they are incapable of an intelligent appreciation of its import. For the rest, the idea of prudential motives restraining or delaying marriage would be regarded as impious. "He who planted the tree, will see to its being watered properly" expresses the common sentiment as regards matrimony. Malthus would have been regarded as a hopeless lunatic if he had lived in India.

134. Influence of Hinduism in favour of marriage.

Hinduism provides many sacraments for a male human being, covering almost all important events of life from birth to death, but, as it is popularly understood at present, it has only one for women. And that is marriage. An unmarried woman among the higher castes is an outcaste. The example of the higher castes is closely followed and imitated by the other castes. As for men, though there is not the same rigorous obligation imposed on them, public opinion brands protracted bachelorhood as disreputable. An unmarried man is regarded by his neighbours with something of the apprehension with which a mad dog is regarded by the sane of that species. A popular Sanskrit epigram appraises the mischief-making propensities of an unmarried male adult as being equivalent to those of a hundred monkeys. Altogether, the religious and social influence of Hinduism is exerted powerfully in favour of the matrimonial state as being the only honourable state for men and women. "Single blessedness" is appreciated in Sanyasis, or ascetics who have renounced the world, the flesh and the devil, but for the ordinary man or woman, safety in this world and salvation in the next lie in marriage. In the case of a man, the need of having a son to perform his funeral obsequies and, thereafter, the annual *Shradh* to speed his disembodied spirit on its way to *Mukti*, or liberation is, a powerful motive to marriage.

135. The higher status of married women.

In the case of women, a more immediate and potent reason is afforded by the gain in status which follows on the birth of her first child in the domestic circle. In her "Prince of Dreamers," Mrs. F. A. Steel puts into the mouth of her Rajput heroine words which embody the very essence of the Hindu ideal of womanhood. "Motherhood is something, widowhood is something, but wifehood is nescience." The Hindu wife who is not a mother, is the most despised of her sex. "The Fruitful Vine" on the contrary is the autocrat of her household. The periphrasis used by husband and wife in referring to each other shows how much the marriage relation among Hindus is centred on the possession of off-spring. He is "the father of my Krishna," and she, "the mother of my Sita" to each other. So much for the Hindus who form the bulk of the population.

136. Moslem sentiment in regard to marriage.

The sentiments of the Mahomedan masses are nearly the same, except that the metaphysical reasons for them, which seem so necessary to the Hindu, have no place in the Mussulman consciousness. For one thing, the Koranic teaching is entirely on the side of marriage and multiplication of the species. In the second place, Indian Mahomedans have, during the long centuries of their existence in this country, imbibed many of the influences of their Hindu environment. In the case of a large proportion of them, these influences are, indeed, part of the mental heritage which Mahomedanism has left untouched. The same observation applies to Indian Christians.

137. Statistical evidence of the Universal prevalence of marriage.

The universal prevalence of marriage in His Highness the Nizam's Dominions is capable of easy demonstration. Subsidiary Table I shows that there were, in 1911, 445 unmarried males and 295 unmarried females for 1,000 persons of each sex. The corresponding figures at the three previous Censuses were 459, 438 and 448 respectively for males and 312, 293 and 287 for females. The higher proportion of unmarried among males is largely due to infant marriages not being obligatory to the same extent for boys as for girls. Of 3,022,032 unmarried males in the State, 1,744,073 were under 10 years of age and if we take the next five year period, we have accounted for 2,385,596 of them, leaving 636,436 for the remaining age-periods. The smaller number of women in the population as a whole, and in most of the castes, the custom of enforced widowhood which condemns a large number of women often in the prime of life to a celibate life, the prevalence of polygamy, incurable infirmities, and occupations such as soldiering which impose a single life on males, are responsible for the celibacy of this last class. Of a total of 1,941,134 unmarried females 1,612,663 are under 10 years. The number of them under 15 is 1,817,151. The number of unmarried above 15 years of age is 123,983.

138. Infant and Early Marriage.

Another feature, less universal, but equally peculiar to the marriage relation in this country, is the very early ages at which it is instituted in many castes and sects. There has been for many years a great deal of controversy as to the origin of infant and early marriages in India. The common opinion at one time among educated Hindus was that such marriages came into vogue in the unsettled conditions of early Mahomedan rule when marriage was regarded as affording some protection against the violence of the conquering race. But this view is no longer held, as it has been conclusively shown from the evidence of writers on pre-Mahomedan India that early marriages were prevalent long before the banner of Islam was unfurled in Hindustan. Another theory propounded by some Hindu scholars is that at some unknown period of the history of Hindu society, the growing influence of the priesthood was, from selfish reasons, exerted against the education and freedom of Hindu women, with the result that infant marriage and enforced widowhood became normal features of Hindu social life. This is to mistake effect for cause. The illiteracy of Indian women did not precede the institution of early marriage, but followed it.

139. Probable origin of the custom.

In enquiries of this kind, it is well to bear in mind the late Sir Henry Maine's profound aphorism that no ancient institution ever came into existence except under the stress of some practical necessity. Everybody admits that the women of the Vedic period occupied a position of absolute equality with men in respect of education and freedom of movement. There was no *purdah* and no infant marriage. The very *Mantras*, or verses from the Vedas, which form part of the marriage rite of the caste Hindus to-day, proclaim the fact that the marriages for which they were originally intended, were marriages between men and women with their sex consciousness fully developed. It is inconceivable that women brought up under the Vedic system would have submitted to the mummery of infant marriage. It is evident that the later degenerate system was devised in contact with a class of women accustomed to less exalted notions of their position in relation to men. The Indo-Aryans at an early stage of their expansion to the east and south of India freely intermarried with the women of indigenous tribes. It was a necessity forced upon them by the conditions of their existence in this country. Now, it is well-known that several of these tribes tolerate a good deal of pre-marital license in young men and women. If the Indo-Aryan husband wished to ensure that his indigenous bride was free from pre-marital contamination, the only course open to him was to marry her as early as possible before the age of puberty. This seems to be the only satisfactory explanation of the origin of a custom so entirely at variance with the marriage system of the Vedic religion. Once the custom came into vogue, it was bound to spread rapidly in a community which elevated purity of blood to the level of a fetich. When the morality of a community declines, it has resort to mechanical means of protecting the honour of its women. When once suspicion takes the place of confidence in women, when faith in its womankind no longer beats with the blood of a community, it ceases to educate them, lest they might abuse their literacy to carry on love intrigues by means of letters. This theory of the origin of early marriage as a safeguard against pre-marital unchastity on the part of brides taken from indigenous tribes, squares so well with all the subsequent history of Hindu society that it may be unhesitatingly accepted in preference to any other.

140. Some facts in confirmation of the above theory.

Attention may be called in this connection to the fact that the so-called marriage is, in several parts of the country, but a formal adoption of the girl to the *gotra* or sept of the bridegroom and that the real wedding is the consummation ceremony which takes place when the girl has attained the age of puberty. It is also significant that while women in ancient times were freely allowed to study the Vedas, in later times "women and Sudras" were linked together in a common disability as regards the study of the Hindu sacred books. A further fact which goes to confirm this theory of the origin of infant marriages is that the largest proportion of child-marriages is to be found amongst the Animists and the lowest Hindu castes as well as amongst the highest. This point will be further noticed when we come to deal with marriage by castes.

141. Extent of the prevalence of early marriages in the State.

Imperial Table VII shows that there were 9,592 married males and 27,913 married females under 5 years of age. To these numbers should be added those of the widowed under that age, 318 males and 1,258 females. Between the ages of 5 and 10, 32,646 males and 183,093 females are married, and the number of widowed is 1,590 and 5,534 respectively. These figures work out to a proportion of 10 persons married and widowed for every 1,000 males under 5 years of age, the corresponding figure for females being 29. Between 5 and 10, the proportions are 40 for males and 225 for females. About 5 per cent. of the married and widowed males and about 14 per cent. of the married and widowed females are under 15 years of age. As compared with the previous Censuses, there seems to be a very slight decrease in the proportion of infant marriages in these dominions. There is nothing to show that this is due to increased enlightenment or the spread of social reform ideas. Economic pressure, accentuated by the heavy mortality from plague, is probably the real cause. The number of married persons per 1,000 of each sex below 10 years of age at the four Censuses is given in the margin.

Married persons per 1,000 of each sex.

Census.	Males.	Females.
1881	27	129
1891	20	118
1901	25	100
1911	24	115

142. Enforced widowhood.

A third peculiar feature of Indian marriage customs, as observed by certain castes of Hindus, is the custom of enforced widowhood. When the husband dies, remarriage is prohibited to the widow, however young she may happen to be. (There is no corresponding disability imposed on the husband). Owing to the fact that the castes which prohibit the remarriage of widows are almost invariably addicted to infant and too early marriages, it not seldom happens that a young girl is often doomed to widowhood before she has been a wife except in a technical sense. The number of widows under 10, according to Imperial Table VII, is 6,792; that under 15 is 17,979. Sir Ramakrishna Bhandarkar, than whom there is no higher authority on a point like this, is of opinion that this custom is not sanctioned by the usage of the ancient Hindus. "Widow-marriage," he says, "was a thing by no means unknown even at such a late period as the beginning of the twelfth century of the Christian era, for, in a work written by a Jaina in 1170 of the Vikram era, corresponding to 1114 of the Christian era, a story is told of a certain ascetic sitting down to a dinner along with other ascetics. The other ascetics rose up when he sat down and left their seats. He asked them why they had done so, upon which they told him that he had committed an irreligious deed in having taken the vow of an ascetic, before going through the previous condition of a married life. They then directed him to go away and marry a wife. He went away and demanded the daughter of men belonging to his caste in marriage. But as he had become an old man, nobody would give his daughter to him, whereupon he went back to the ascetics, and told them of what had occurred. They then advised him to marry a widow and he went away and did accordingly. But in still later times the practice became entirely obsolete."* The same distinguished Sanskritist and leader of the Hindu social reform movement is also of opinion that the custom of *Sati* or the burning of widows on the funeral pyres of their dead husbands, though it prevailed in pre-historic times, had been given up in the Vedic period, and was revived later, probably at about the same time as the custom of enforced widowhood was introduced.

143. Enforced widowhood generally found in combination with early marriage.

The close affinity which exists between the customs of infant marriage and enforced widowhood suggests that both might have had a common origin. The marginal table, abstracted from sub-table III, shows that the communities which have the largest proportion of child-wives tend, other conditions being similar, to have also the largest proportion of widows. The high proportion of Mahomedan widows is obviously an illustration of the influence of environment and is also, probably, evidence of the prevalence of polygamy among them to a larger extent than among other communities. The Jains are really a caste like the Brahmans, for social purposes, and their figures ought, strictly speaking, to be compared with those of Brahmans. It has been pointed out above that the theory that the practice of infant marriages was originally adopted as a means of ensuring purity in wives taken from indigenous tribes given to pre-marital license, is more satisfactory than any other that has yet been put forward. Might it not be that enforced widowhood, and the even more drastic device of *Sati*, were also brought into vogue, as means of preventing wives taken from indigenous tribes from returning on the death of their husbands to their original practices? These strange wives would have had to be impressed in all possible ways that they belonged body and soul to their husbands, in order that they might be entirely weaned away from any thought of their old surroundings, and completely broken to the monandrous system of marriage.

Per 10,000.

Religion.	Married females under 10.	Widows, al ages.
Jain	903	2,037
Hindu	1,272	1,794
Musulman	266	1,715
Animist	684	1,034
Christian	207	1,094

144. Comparison with previous Censuses.

A comparison of the statistics of widowhood of this and the previous Censuses reveals a small but gratifying decline in the proportion of widows in

* Address to the Madras Hindu Social Reform Association, December 27th, 1894.

communities other than the Hindu and the Jain. The high proportion of both widows and widowers in 1901, extending as it did to all ages and every caste and creed, was the sign-manual of the dread scourges of famine and plague which left such a sinister mark on almost every phase of the Census of that year. The proportion of widowers at the present Census remains what it was in 1891. But the statistics of widowers has no special significance, as widowhood for males is merely a temporary condition, except in the case of those far past their prime. They simply mean that so many or such a proportion of widowers were not able to secure successors to their deceased spouses when the Census caught them on its schedules. The very high proportion of widows to widowers in the total population, shows that widowhood, though not enforced as a custom except by certain Hindu castes, is still in considerable vogue amongst non-Hindus. The position is best explained by saying that while, as regards widowers, the prevailing sentiment favours remarriage, as regards widows it deprecates remarriage even in communities which do not prohibit it.*

Widowed per 1,000.

Census.	Males.	Females.
1881	47	192
1891	41	180
1901	52	189
1911	41	177

145. Polygamy.

In the whole State there are, according to the present Census, 21,937 more married males than females. These are either married men who have immigrated to the State more or less temporarily leaving their wives behind them in their Native Province or the husbands of women who have gone to other provinces. The number of emigrants, male and female, as observed in Chapter III, is in excess of that of immigrants, that of women far more so than that of the men. There are 42,847 more female emigrants than immigrants of that sex. A considerable proportion of them probably found husbands outside these Dominions, but doubtless there were also a certain proportion of married women among them. What that proportion is, it is impossible to say with any degree of exactness in the absence of entries relating to civil condition or age in the Table for birthplace. But supposing that the proportion of married women among them is the same as among the female population in the State, namely, 528 per 1,000, the number of married women emigrants would be 22,623. From this number we have to deduct the probable number of the wives left behind by the married men among the net surplus of male emigrants. Taking 514 per 1,000 males, the proportion in the State, as the proportion of married men among the latter, we get for 3,433 male emigrants, which is the number in excess of that of male immigrants, 1,764 as the number of married men. Deducting this number from the estimated number of married women who left these territories, we get 20,859 as the net exodus of married women from the State, which is very near the excess of married men enumerated in it, namely, 21,937. We get very nearly the same result if we deduce the proportions from the excess of male immigrants and female emigrants over the immigrants and emigrants of the opposite sex. The male immigrants exceeded the females by 3,035, and the female emigrants exceeded the males by 36,379. The proportionate numbers of married among both classes, deduced as above, are 1,612 married male

*Her Highness the Begum of Bhopal in "An Account of My Life" ascribes the repugnance to the remarriage of widows prevalent among the higher classes of Musulmans to Afghan tradition. She writes :— "One of the chief causes of this estrangement was my mother's remarriage. This was an act contrary to the customs of the Afghan race, and the offence was aggravated by the fact that she had chosen to marry a man of an alien family. As a matter of fact, second marriages and the remarriage of widows are contrary neither to Muhammadan custom nor to the Muhammadan religion. For a considerable number of years, however, the Muhammadans of India had rigidly adhered to the custom of the Afghans and this had now taken such a hold on society that any breach of it was regarded as a heinous sin. This feeling was shared by men and women alike. Even those whose ideas had been modified by Western education never permitted second marriages in their own families, and up to the present day the practice is viewed with disfavour by nearly all Muhammadans of Afghan descent." An Account of My Life (John Murray, London, 1912) page 77. A striking instance of the insidious influence of the sentiment against the re-marriage of widows, is that of the Lingayats. The founder of the sect, Basava, expressly sanctioned remarriages. Nevertheless, though they are not actually prohibited, the community as a whole does not regard them with favour at the present day. See Edgar Thursten's Castes and Tribes of Southern India (Government Press, Madras, 1909), Vol. IV, p. 252.

immigrants who did not bring their wives with them and 19,210 married females emigrants who left their husbands behind them. The total of married men in the State who had left their wives or whose wives had left them is, in this case, 20,823, which also is very near the enumerated number, namely, 21,937. Whichever way we look at the matter, it is evident that the excess of married men in the State is closely related to the statistics of migration. As a married man is the possessor of at least one wife who was alive at the time of enumeration, an equation between the number of married males and females in the State, is possible only on the basis of practical monogamy.

146. Relative numbers of married males and females.

The statistics of married persons in the districts show an excess of married females in about one-half of the districts and a deficiency of them in the other half. The marginal table gives the names of the districts in which there is an excess of married females. In the other 9 districts, and in Hyderabad City, there is a deficiency of married females as compared with that of married males. If we take the excess of married females in the seven districts noted in the margin to be the result of the prevalence of polygamy in them, we shall be forced to infer from the excess of married males in others the existence of polyandry in those districts. But polyandry is not known to exist anywhere in these Dominions and it must exist on a large scale if the excess of married males in the majority of districts is to bear this interpretation. The real significance of the excess of married females noted in some districts and that of married males in others, is that either the married females had been enumerated in their parents' homes or that the married males had been enumerated in neighbouring districts to which they had gone on business or pleasure. The excess of married females in the seven districts is greatest at ages below 20, showing that they were either tender girls who were too young to be sent to their husbands or young women come home from their husbands' places in the neighbouring districts, it may be, for their first confinement. Moreover, as territorial contiguity plays but a subordinate part in Indian marriages in which caste is the main consideration, the district figures are not of much importance in forming a judgment as to the prevalence of polygamy in the State. For the same reason as that given in the case of districts, the statistics of married persons in each religion cannot throw much light on the point in question. Although, no doubt, caste is supreme only among the Hindus, persons of other religions are also more or less influenced by the sentiment and are averse from contracting marriages out of the groups to which they belong. Even Indian Christians are not altogether free from the sentiment. Still the statistics of religion have more value than those of districts in a question of the kind we are discussing. Subsidiary Table IV gives the number of females per 1,000 males, unmarried, married, widowed. Only among the Animists and the the Jains does the number of married females exceed that of married males. The former have 1,049 married females and the latter 1,003 for every 1,000 married males. Next after the Animists and the Jains, the Hindus have the largest number of married females, namely, 996 per 1,000 married males. The Musulman proportion is 969 and that of the Christians, 960. The Animists, it is clear, are addicted to polygamy. Imperial Table XIV shows that the Gond has more married females than males, and the Lambada, too, at all ages below 40. There are only 16 married females more than married males in over 5,009 married persons of each sex among Jains, and that too, wholly in Marathwara. Hindu married females, too, exceed the number of married males of the same religion in this Division. Imperial Table XIV deals with the civil condition of selected castes. We find that 13 out of 38 Hindu castes have more married females than males, and that this is the case with Shaiks, among Musulmans, and also with Indian Christians. The presence of Indian Christians in this list warns us against

Districts where there is an excess of married females.

District.	Number of married males.	Number of married females.
Medak	176,817	179,609
Nizamabad	156,521	157,977
Nalgonda	248,266	250,986
Aurangabad	230,631	232,886
Bhir	169,728	171,605
Osmanabad	169,455	171,172
Bidar	245,138	246,339

placing implicit reliance on the excess of married females in these castes as evidence of the prevalence of polygamy among them. If it is to be assumed that for all the other castes which show a deficiency of married females, the missing wives are to be found outside the State, it is equally probable that the excess of married women in the above-mentioned castes had there husbands somewhere beyond the borders. The Hindu and Musulman castes which have a conspicuously larger number of married females than males may be addicted to polygamy, but it is impossible to say that the other castes are entirely free from it.

147. Probable omission of polygamous wives.

In the previous Census Reports the prevalence of polygamy in this State has been admitted. Mr. Mirza Mehdi Khan, the Officer in charge of the Census operations in this State in 1891 and 1901, writing in the plenitude of his local knowledge, declared in both his reports that polygamy obtained in these territories and obtained, too, to a great extent. He expressed surprise that, notwithstanding that the City containing the largest number of cases of polygamy, as also many married women engaged as menial servants in the zenanas of the better classes, the proportion of wives to 100 husbands was only 97*. It is even less at this Census. In view of the uniformly low proportions of wives exhibited by the State it is impossible to think that there has been no omission in the enumeration of married women. It is probable that a man with many wives, even though he may not think that there is any reason to be ashamed of it, may yet not feel obliged to enumerate each of his spouses for the information of the Census official. The enormous disproportion between the number of widowers and widows, especially in communities where infant marriage and child-mothers are uncommon, is in all probability to be attributed partly at any rate to the fact that, while the death of the husband in a polygamous marriage, widows at one fell stroke several females, the death of one of his wives does not make him a widower.

148. Polygamy among Hindus.

Among the higher Hindu castes, a second wife is usually taken only when the first wife is believed to be incapable of fulfilling the principal function, according to Hindu ideas, of wifehood, that is, of becoming a mother. The only other justifying reasons are those which would procure a divorce in communities where divorce is allowed. In either case, the first wife suffers a sort of civil death. She ceases to count in the affairs of life, and it may well be that she ceases to be counted on the Census schedule also. Very often the Hindu who has more than one wife marries a second wife, when his first wife is alive, against his own better and more humane judgment, under pressure from aged parents or the importunity of would-be parents-in-law with daughters verging on the perilous age of puberty.

149. Civil condition by Religions—Hinduism.

The statistics of the total population of the State, which have been reviewed in the preceding paragraphs, are but the statistics of the Hindu community slightly tempered by those of other communities, especially the Mussalman. Not only does Hinduism claim a numerically overwhelming majority of His Highness the Nizam's subjects, but the ideas of social and family life which are in the air, so to speak, and insensibly permeate the consciousness of almost every community, are those distinctively associated with the Hindu social system. The observations made on the general statistics are, therefore, largely those suggested by those of the Hindu section of the population.

150. Influence of caste in propagating certain ideas bearing on marriage.

In the chapter on Caste, it will be necessary to explain how that system has become the medium for the propagation of certain social and personal habits. Among these are, universality of marriage, and infant and early marriages. Negative aspects of this propagandism are the rooted Hindu antipathy to remarriage of widows and to divorce. In view of the fact that the Hindu law does not recognise such a thing as divorce—though the Sudra castes have judicially

* Census Report of Hyderabad, 1891, Part I, page 317.

recognised customs permitting it—a strictly qualified right to take a second wife is accorded to married men who have no children by their first wives. The extent and the degree to which these ideas are found to inspire the custom of a Hindu caste, is a safe index of its position in the social scale. One of the most interesting facts brought out by the Censuses in several parts of the country, is the gradual assimilation of these ideas by castes which at one time were wholly untouched by them. Nor is the insidious influence of these Hindu ideas confined to the classes within the pale of the Hindu caste system. Mussulmans and Christians are also largely affected by them. Rather is it more correct to say that Mahomedanism and Christianity have been powerless to root out these ideas from the large section of their adherents who represent in themselves or through their ancestors, near or remote, the success of their proselytising propaganda.

151. Civil condition by castes.

The Hindus as a whole have, as might be expected, the largest proportion of married males and females of all the religious communities of Hyderabad. The actual proportions are 523 and 537 per 1,000 persons of each of the two sexes, those for the whole State being 514 and 528, respectively. But the above ratios high as they are, are the mean of those of several castes some of which have much higher ratios still. The palm in respect of married males is carried off by the Koli caste with 592 per 1,000 persons. Next to it comes the Dhangar, 577, Lingayath, 566, the Maratha, 545, the Brahman, 542, the Kapu, 538, the Golla, 530, the Komati, 527 and the Mahar and the Munnur, 524. Such is the order of precedence in regard to the proportion of married males in each caste, as set forth in Subsidiary Table V. This order is not preserved when we come to consider the statistics of the other sex. Then, the Koli yields his palm to the Goundla who has 611 married females to every 1,000 of that sex, to the Munnur, 607, and to the Dhangar, 593, and has to be content with the fourth place with 585. The Golla and the Muttrasi follow with 571 each, the Kapu has 565, next comes the Brahman with 556. Barring the effects of migration and polygamy, a higher proportion of married females than of married males, means that the total female population is less than the total male population. Only two of the selected castes have a lower proportion of married females than the average for the whole Hindu population.

Proportion of Married per 1,000 persons.

Caste.	Males.	Females.
Koli	592	585
Dhangar	577	593
Lingayath	566	550
Maratha...	545	542
Brahman...	542	556
Kapu	538	565
Golla	530	571
Komati	527	523
Munnur	524	607
Mahar	524	548
Goundla	508	611
Muttrasi	498	571

152. The extent of the prevalence of marriage in a caste can be better judged by looking at the proportion of the unmarried than at the proportion of the married. For the latter does not include the "widowed" who form a considerable proportion of the females in most Hindu castes. The Munnur has the smallest proportion of unmarried females, and the Madiga, the Mahar, the Sale and the Telaga, the highest, among Hindu castes. The Brahman is pre-eminent in respect of the marriage of girls under the age of 5 years. In the next age-period, 5-12, the Munnar proportion of unmarried girls is reduced to 385 per 1,000 females. The nearest approach to this figure is that of the Koli who has 596 unmarried girls of this age in 1,000 females. The Lingayath has the next lowest proportion, 603, and the Brahmin comes fourth with 633. The Munnur and the Koli may thus be said to be the two castes most addicted to early marriage in the State, with the Lingayath and the Brahman following close behind. The Telaga, the Mahar and the Maratha have the largest number of unmarried females in the age-period 20-40, namely 22 and 21 respectively in 1,000 of the sex. The Telaga has the largest proportion of spinsters at the age of 40 and over. A peculiar feature of the statistics of the civil condition of the Munnur caste, is worth notice. The proportions of unmarried, married and widowed, for both males and females, remain the same at 20-40 and at 40 years and over. There is no other instance of this kind in Subsidiary Table V. It is

as if there was a rule that no one, male or female, who was not married before the twentieth year of age, should be married ever after. Even such a rule, however, can not account for the constancy of the number of widowers and widows at the last two age-periods.

153. Infant and early marriage by castes.

The castes which show the largest proportion of early-married males are not invariably those which have the largest proportions of females, as is evident from the marginal statement. The Brahmans have the largest proportion of young girls married under the age of 5 but they do not marry their male children at that age to the same extent as five other castes. The Census Commissioner of India has suggested that a comparison of the relative ages of husband and wife as disclosed by the statistics of marriage by caste, would throw light on the practice, said to prevail in some parts of the country, of union of young boys with adult women, the father or some other relation assuming the procreating function on his behalf. Such a practice can be looked for only where the number of married males of tender years is in considerable excess of the number of married females at the same age-period. The only castes which offer this opening are the Bhoi, the Dhobi, the Mangala, and the Munnur. Of these the Bhoi figures of married males are in excess of those of married females not only at the age-period of 0–5, but also from 5–12. It is obvious that in these four castes the child-husbands would be often younger than their wives. Whether the practice referred to by the Census Commissioner prevails among them is not known.

Per 1,000 persons under 5 years.

Caste.	Males.	Females.
Dhangar...	25	24
Munnur	23	20
Maratha	16	22
Lingayath	14	23
Mahar	13	27
Brahman	11	31
Golla	10	12
Koli	6	23

154. That child marriages have come to be practically regarded as an essential feature of popular Hinduism, is clear from the fact that every one of the selected castes, in Subsidiary Table V, has a larger or smaller number of males and females married in the age-period 0-5. The Brahmin, the Koli, the Mahar, the Dhangar, the Lingayat, the Maratha, and the Munnur, have each more than 20 females in every 1,000 married in this age-period. The extent to which the prohibition against the remarriage of widows, prevails in each caste, must be judged not by the proportion of girl widows, or old widows but by that of the widows in the productive period of life. The Lingayath has a larger proportion of widows at every age-period up to 20 then the Brahman, but from 20 to 40 and upwards his proportion of widows is very much lower than the Brahman's. The Koli who has about the same low proportion of widows at ages from 20 to 40 as the Lingayath, has the largest number of widows of any Hindu caste at 40 and over. The sentimental or sacramental reasons which lead to the marriage of female children at tender years, do not apply to the remarriage of child widows. Widows past their 40th year have few chances of remarriage even in communities where it is not looked down upon. A man who marries a widow is actuated by practical reasons, and generally chooses a bride who is neither too young nor too old. For this reason, the proportion of widows at the age-period 20-40 is the only safe test as regards the prevalence of the remarriage of widows in any caste. The two castes which have the highest proportion of widows at this age-period are the Brahman and the Komati. It is evident that the restriction against the remarriage of widows, is far less common among Hindu castes than the custom of child marriage.

155. Civil condition of Musalmans.

Owing to the fact that child marriages are far less common amongst Musulmans than among Hindus, the proportion of married persons among the former is lower than among the latter. Subsidiary Table III shows that only 96 males and 266 females in 10,000 persons of each sex under the age of 10 are married among Musulmans as against 255 and 1,272 respectively among Hindus, and that at 10-15, the Hindu proportion of married is 1,704 males and 7,114 females as against 606 and 3,246 for Musulmans. Child marriages, to the extent to which they are practised in the Musulman community, are not, it is evident, an established custom as among Hindus, but are rather the outcome of the fancy of fond parents and grand parents to enjoy the spectacle of their little ones playing the part of husband and wife. In the adult ages, however, the Musulman proportion of married females is notably higher than that of the Hindus. In the age-period 15-40, the number of married Hindu females in 10,000 of that sex and age, is 6,810; the Musulman proportion is 8,415. Only the Jains have a larger proportion of married females than the latter in this age-period. At 40 and over, again, the Musulman proportion of married females is higher than that of the Hindus. But the most remarkable feature of the Musulman statistics of civil condition, is the comparatively large proportion of widows. The marginal table gives the proportion of married and widowed females, for All Religions, for Hindus and for Musulmans. It shows that the Musulman proportion of widows to married females was higher than that of Hindus, and of All Religions taken together, not only at this but at all previous Censuses with the exception of that of 1901. This seems to show that widowhood is a more common incident of marriage among Musulmans than among the Hindus. There is only one community with a larger proportion of widows to married women, namely, the Jains. An analysis of the proportionate figures at the several age-periods, shows that this relatively higher proportion of widows to married woman, prevails up to the age of 40. At 5-10, the Hindu has 242 married females and 7 widows for every one thousand of the sex; the Musulman has only 51 of the former, but he has 4 of the latter. At the latter rate, the Hindu should have 20 widows at the same age-period. At the next age-periods up to 40 years there is the same disproportionately large number of widows among Musulmans. Subsidiary Table IV affords further proof of this phenomenon. It shows that for every 1,000 widowers, there are 4,154 widows among Hindus and 4,436 widows mong Musulmans. The latter have, relatively to widowers, the largest number of widows of any community in the State. The Musulmans, as a class, are physically and materially better off than the Hindus, as shown by the fact that they suffered less from famine than the latter, and this excessive proportion of widows as compared with wives and widowers, seems to confirm the surmise that there has been some omission of wives of polygamous marriages at the Census enumeration.

Married and widowed per 1,000 females.

Denomination.	1881.		1891.		1901.		1911.	
	Married.	Widowed.	Married.	Widowed.	Married.	Widowed.	Married.	Widowed.
All Religions	521	192	527	180	499	189	528	177
Hindus	526	193	533	179	504	190	537	179
Mussulmans	466	193	476	184	457	178	472	171

156. Civil condition of Jains.

For the largest proportions of widowhood, however, we have to turn to the statistics of the Jain community. The Hindu community embraces many castes with varying customs of marriage. The Jains are a caste rigidly adhering to the customs of infant marriage and enforced widowhood in their most exaggerated form. They have by far the largest proportion of widowers as well as widows of any religious community in the State, 84 in 1,000 males and 204 in 1,000 females as against 41 and 177 respectively for all religions. The large proportion of widowhood points to an exceptionally high mortality at all ages and among both sexes.

157. Christians.

The proportion of married persons in the community of Christians has steadily increased since 1881, except for a set-back at the last Census, the cause of which is sufficiently obvious from the fact that the proportion of widowed at that Census was higher than that of the three other Censuses of this State. As the converts become consolidated into a community, they naturally reproduce the customs of the community from which they are drawn. Child marriages are not unknown among Christians, though, of course, they do not prevail amongst them to the same extent as among Hindus. The Hindus have 11 males and 31 females in every 1,000 persons under the age of 5 in the married state; the Christian proportions are 5 and 8. In the next age-period, 5-10, 13 males and 36 females in 1,000 of each sex are married. That the marriage state is not quite so universal among Christians as among other communities, is evident from the fact that 72 females in 1,000 at between the 20th and 40th year are unmarried, the corresponding figure for All Religions being 27. The number of married females for 1,000 married males amongst Christians is the lowest of that for any community in the State, which shows that this community has a large proportion of immigrant males than the others. This is especially the case in Marathwara.

158. Animists and Marriage.

The proportion of married persons amongst Animists, unlike that among Christians, has steadily and largely decreased during the last 20 years. In 1891, there were 538 married males and 550 married females respectively, in 1,000 persons of each sex. In 1901, they fell to 483 and 496, and at the present Census they are 409 and 467. The fall at some of the age-periods is most remarkable. Thus at 15-20 the number of married males in 1891 was 601, in 1901 it was 408; in 1911 it is 180. Only in the age-periods, 40-60 and 60 and over, do the proportions show increases over those at the 1901 Census. The proportion of married females is higher than in 1901 at the two preceding age-periods also. It seems improbable that there has been any sudden change in the notions regarding marriage prevalent among the Animists. It is likely that with the younger generations of married men especially, it is becoming the fashion to adopt Hindu ideas of marriage and to pass as Hindus. The married Animist is under a strange temptation to pass for a Hindu than the unmarried one. His wife or wives would, by adopting the Hindu name and gods, appreciably advance in the estimation of village womanhood. When her child is ill she could have the services of the local magic-man. In several other ways the advantages of belonging to an ancient established religion would be more apparent to women than to men. And the transition is so easy. No recantation of old beliefs or customs is demanded. The woman has merely to put on the red *Kunkum* symbol of Hindu womanhood on her forehead and, if not a widow, a few glass or other cheap bangles on her wrists. Child marriages are fairly common in the community. There is evidently no restriction on the remarriage of widows. The Animists have the smallest proportion of widows in the population.

SUBSIDIARY TABLE I.—Distribution by Civil Condition of 1,000 of each Sex, Religion and Main Age-period at each of the last four Censuses.

Religion, Sex and Age.	Unmarried.				Married.				Widowed.			
	1911.	1901.	1891.	1881.	1911.	1901.	1891.	1881.	1911.	1901.	1891.	1881.
1	2	3	4	5	6	7	8	9	10	11	12	13
All religions.												
Males	445	459	438	448	514	489	521	505	41	52	41	47
0—5	990	988	993	972	10	12	7	27	...	...	...	1
5—10	960	959	964		38	38	35		2	3	1	
10—15	839	857	815	823	156	183	180	170	5	10	5	7
15—20	593	631	536	568	398	350	454	420	9	19	10	17
20—40	136	149	113	134	835	805	857	822	29	46	30	44
40—60	31	44	23	32	874	833	876	855	95	123	101	113
60 and over	27	36	21	25	734	703	723	737	239	261	256	238
Females	295	312	293	287	528	499	527	521	177	189	180	192
0—5	971	977	977	867	28	21	22	129	1	2	1	4
5—10	775	810	761		219	179	234		6	11	5	
10—15	326	403	281	297	656	564	699	675	18	33	20	26
15—20	75	117	56	71	896	831	915	880	29	52	29	49
20—40	27	73	20	23	859	779	858	818	114	148	122	159
40—60	19	28	15	12	470	456	384	447	511	516	601	541
60 and over	18	21	12	9	132	171	111	140	850	808	877	851
Hindu.												
Males	436	453	432	443	523	494	526	510	41	53	42	47
0—5	989	987	993	973	11	13	7	27	...	...	...	1
5—10	957	959	962		41	38	36		2	3	2	
10—15	824	848	803	815	170	141	191	178	6	11	6	7
15—20	558	607	506	541	432	373	483	442	10	20	11	17
20—40	117	134	98	121	853	819	872	835	30	47	30	44
40—60	29	43	21	29	873	832	877	857	98	125	102	114
60 and over	26	34	19	23	730	699	722	736	244	267	259	241
Females	284	306	288	281	537	504	533	526	179	190	179	193
0—5	968	976	976	862	31	22	23	134	1	2	1	4
5—10	751	795	743		242	193	252		7	12	5	
10—15	270	367	223	273	711	598	758	698	19	35	19	29
15—20	54	102	43	63	915	843	927	887	31	55	30	50
20—40	25	75	18	21	858	775	859	819	117	150	123	160
40—60	19	28	15	12	464	455	523	447	517	517	462	541
60 and over	17	20	11	8	129	166	110	138	854	814	879	854
Musalman.												
Males	499	507	489	488	464	448	472	467	37	45	39	45
0—5	997	998	992	973	3	2	6	26	...	...	2	1
5—10	982	963	981		16	35	17		2	2	2	
10—15	935	937	930	908	61	60	67	88	4	3	3	4
15—20	821	829	789	758	175	163	206	232	4	8	5	10
20—40	248	262	228	244	727	700	747	715	25	38	25	41
40—60	41	53	38	56	881	843	874	843	78	104	88	101
60 and over	31	45	29	41	758	734	736	746	211	221	235	213
Females	357	365	340	342	472	457	476	466	171	178	184	192
0—5	996	996	987	940	4	4	11	57	...	...	2	3
5—10	945	918	924		51	74	72		4	8	4	
10—15	664	693	590	584	325	289	402	399	11	18	8	17
15—20	214	228	157	171	768	785	820	788	18	37	23	41
20—40	41	63	36	44	859	816	847	801	100	121	117	155
40—60	20	30	18	20	496	459	452	450	484	511	530	530
60 and over	18	21	15	23	144	207	119	158	838	772	866	819

SUBSIDIARY TABLE I.—Distribution by Civil Condition of 1,000 of each Sex, Religion and Main Age-period at each of the last four Censuses.

Religion, Sex and Age.	Unmarried. 1911.	1901.	1891.	1881.	Married. 1911.	1901.	1891.	1881.	Widowed. 1911.	1901.	1891.	1881.
1	2	3	4	5	6	7	8	9	10	11	12	13
Animist.												
Males	564	474	427	...	409	488	538	...	27	48	35	...
0—5	991	981	981	...	8	18	16	...	1	1	3	...
5—10	978	960	931	...	21	38	62	...	1	2	7	...
10—15	932	808	746	...	62	186	246	...	6	6	8	...
15—20	814	564	385	...	180	408	601	...	6	28	14	...
20—40	272	132	74	...	704	824	898	...	24	44	28	...
40—60	36	29	13	...	901	876	915	...	63	95	72	...
60 and over	34	42	12	...	788	694	760	...	178	264	228	...
Females	430	370	344	...	467	496	550	...	103	134	106	...
0—5	982	967	979	...	17	30	20	...	1	3	1	...
5—10	878	858	941	...	119	133	57	...	3	9	2	...
10—15	750	508	399	...	241	471	588	...	9	21	13	...
15—20	217	223	70	...	767	740	916	...	16	37	14	...
20—40	35	34	14	...	911	852	939	...	54	114	47	...
40—60	18	37	8	...	624	550	649	...	358	413	343	...
60 and over	26	18	10	...	201	205	201	...	773	777	789	...
Christian.												
Males	584	636	648	673	392	310	325	295	24	54	27	32
0—5	995	998	995	991	5	2	4	9	...	...	1	...
5—10	986	990	981		13	9	18		1	1	1	
10—15	964	969	968	960	35	28	34	40	1	3	3	...
15—20	859	898	879	901	139	101	106	97	2	1	15	2
20—40	434	552	592	655	553	414	392	337	13	34	16	18
40—60	46	104	60	116	890	716	851	776	64	180	89	108
60 and over	35	41	34	58	749	584	739	659	216	375	227	283
Females	443	480	464	482	448	394	418	393	109	126	118	125
0—5	992	996	989	985	8	4	10	14	...	...	1	1
5—10	962	958	971		36	43	26		2	...	3	
10—15	777	917	831	890	220	81	168	108	3	2	1	2
15—20	331	413	423	424	655	562	556	559	14	25	21	17
20—40	72	119	105	118	856	760	800	794	72	121	95	88
40—60	45	62	38	51	548	491	531	466	407	447	436	483
60 and over	29	15	48	64	171	214	151	163	800	771	806	773
Jain.												
Males	448	442	418	382	468	487	508	524	84	71	74	94
0—5	964	980	988	955	35	17	9	43	1	3	3	2
5—10	947	961	965		50	36	33		3	3	2	
10—15	860	848	809	777	131	139	179	206	9	13	12	17
15—20	582	598	572	618	409	384	407	353	9	18	21	29
20—40	236	214	188	164	705	735	761	776	59	51	51	60
40—60	85	78	71	46	719	761	752	762	196	161	177	192
60 and over	78	57	47	15	554	589	584	470	368	354	369	515
Females	278	259	262	230	518	541	543	557	204	200	195	213
0—5	973	969	977	817	20	26	21	175	7	5	2	8
5—10	832	791	783		170	198	208		8	11	9	
10—15	556	359	812	250	630	620	675	716	14	21	13	34
15—20	40	18	26	60	923	931	936	897	37	51	38	43
20—40	20	21	11	48	829	830	859	830	151	149	130	122
40—60	13	9	5	9	431	437	453	512	556	554	542	479
60 and over	10	22	13	8	116	143	122	76	874	835	865	921

Note.—Figures for Animists for 1881 are not available.

SUBSIDIARY TABLE II.—Distribution by Civil Condition of 1,000 of each Sex at certain ages in each Religion and Natural Division.

Natural Division and Religion.	MALES.																	
	All ages.			0—5			5—10			10—15			15—40			40 and over.		
	Unmarried.	Married.	Widowed.	Unmarried.	Married.	Widowed.	Unmarried.	Married.	Widowed.	Unmarried.	Married.	Widowed.	Unmarried.	Married.	Widowed.	Unmarried.	Married.	Widowed.
1	2	3	4	5	6	7	8	9	10	11	12	13	14	15	16	17	18	19
State.																		
All religions	445	514	41	990	10	...	960	38	2	839	156	5	222	752	26	30	841	129
Hindu	436	523	41	989	11	...	957	41	2	824	170	6	200	774	26	28	840	132
Musalman	499	464	37	997	3	...	982	16	2	935	61	4	358	621	21	39	843	118
Animist	564	409	27	991	8	1	978	21	1	932	62	6	373	606	21	35	873	92
Christian	584	392	24	995	5	...	986	13	1	964	35	1	50	488	11	43	857	100
Jain	448	468	84	964	35	1	947	50	3	860	131	9	301	649	50	83	679	238
Telingana.																		
All religions	469	496	35	993	7	...	972	27	1	892	106	2	247	734	19	26	855	119
Hindu	458	506	36	992	8	...	970	29	1	881	117	2	219	761	20	24	854	122
Musalman	521	445	35	997	3	...	990	9	1	969	29	2	411	570	19	38	858	104
Animist	570	404	26	992	7	1	979	20	1	938	57	5	383	597	20	34	878	88
Christian	611	366	23	998	2	...	990	10	...	981	19	...	554	435	11	44	856	100
Jain	393	515	92	966	34	...	984	16	...	907	93	...	309	648	43	16	713	271
Marathwara.																		
All religions	419	534	47	986	14	...	946	51	3	780	211	9	198	771	31	33	827	140
Hindu	410	542	48	985	15	...	942	55	3	761	229	10	181	786	33	32	826	142
Musalman	484	477	39	997	3	...	976	22	2	907	87	6	313	664	23	39	841	120
Animist	508	453	39	983	17	...	961	32	7	867	124	9	289	682	29	43	835	122
Christian	462	510	28	984	13	3	971	27	2	885	111	4	235	749	16	41	863	96
Jain	451	466	83	964	35	1	945	52	3	859	132	9	301	649	50	86	677	237

Natural Division and Religion.	FEMALES.																	
	All ages.			0—5			5—10			10—15			15—40			40 and over.		
	Unmarried.	Married.	Widowed.	Unmarried.	Married.	Widowed.	Unmarried.	Married.	Widowed.	Unmarried.	Married.	Widowed.	Unmarried.	Married.	Widowed.	Unmarried.	Married.	Widowed.
1	20	21	22	23	24	25	26	27	28	29	30	31	32	33	34	35	36	37
State.																		
All religions	295	528	177	971	28	1	775	219	6	326	656	18	36	866	98	19	377	604
Hindu	284	537	179	968	31	1	751	242	7	270	711	19	31	868	101	18	373	609
Musalman	357	472	171	996	4	...	945	51	4	664	325	11	75	841	84	20	393	587
Animist	430	467	103	982	17	1	878	119	3	750	241	9	67	886	47	21	502	477
Christian	443	448	109	992	8	...	962	36	2	777	220	3	130	811	59	40	468	492
Jain	278	518	204	973	20	7	822	170	8	356	630	14	24	847	129	12	346	642
Telingana.																		
All religions	311	509	180	981	18	1	828	167	5	356	630	14	37	864	99	17	383	600
Hindu	301	523	176	979	20	1	809	185	6	285	699	16	[illegible]	867	108	17	378	605
Musalman	366	459	175	997	3	...	972	26	2	778	215	17	81	[illegible]	83	15	387	598
Animist	433	465	102	982	17	1	873	124	3	773	218	9	66	888	46	20	506	474
Christian	455	433	112	995	5	...	974	26	...	818	179	3	139	8[illegible]1	60	39	451	510
Jain	252	527	221	891	...	109	441	559	...	370	593	37	28	864	108	23	284	693
Marathwara.																		
All religions	279	547	174	960	38	2	716	276	8	294	685	21	36	867	97	20	371	609
Hindu	267	550	183	955	43	2	688	304	8	254	724	22	31	870	99	20	367	613
Musalman	349	482	169	996	4	...	922	74	4	567	418	15	79	835	86	28	399	573
Animist	402	485	113	978	17	5	924	71	5	509	480	11	77	864	59	22	466	512
Christian	393	506	101	982	18	...	912	79	9	584	414	2	95	851	54	48	475	477
Jain	279	518	203	977	20	3	841	150	9	355	632	13	24	846	130	11	349	640

SUBSIDIARY TABLE III.—Distribution by Main Age-periods and Civil Condition of 10,000 of each Sex and Religion.

Religion and age.	Males.			Females.		
	Unmarried.	Married.	Widowed.	Unmarried.	Married.	Widowed.
1	2	3	4	5	6	7
All religions	4,446	5,143	411	2,951	5,281	1,768
0—10	9,753	236	11	8,810	1,153	37
10—15	8,888	1,558	54	3,256	6,565	179
15—40	2,219	7,525	256	363	8,657	980
40 and over	297	8,409	1,294	139	3,770	6,041
Hindu	4,344	5,236	420	2,840	5,366	1,794
0—10	9,734	255	11	8,688	1,272	40
10—15	8,240	1,704	56	2,696	7,114	190
15—40	2,000	7,738	262	2,399	6,810	791
40 and over	282	8,396	1,322	187	3,725	6,088
Musalman	4,987	4,644	369	3,568	4,717	1,715
0—10	9,897	96	7	9,717	266	17
10—15	9,353	606	41	6,642	3,246	112
15—40	3,583	6,207	210	750	8,415	835
40 and over	386	8,484	1,130	199	3,938	5,868
Animist	5,643	4,084	273	4,296	4,670	1,034
0—10	9,858	136	6	9,822	659	19
10—15	9,322	619	59	7,499	2,412	89
15—40	8,144	1,801	55	2,165	7,673	162
40 and over	353	8,733	914	208	5,018	4,774
Christian	5,837	3,921	242	4,431	4,475	1,094
0—10	9,903	89	6	9,784	207	9
10—15	9,642	348	10	7,772	2,200	28
15—40	5,006	4,879	115	1,398	8,111	591
40 and over	483	8,572	995	409	4,549	5,042
Jain	4,286	4,913	801	2,779	5,184	2,037
0—10	9,557	426	17	9,023	903	74
10—15	8,604	1,307	89	3,559	6,306	135
15—40	3,011	6,491	498	238	8,468	1,294
40 and over	330	6,790	2,380	119	3,465	6,416

SUBSIDIARY TABLE IV.—Proportion of the Sexes by Civil Condition at certain ages for Religions and Natural Divisions.

Natural Division and Religion.	Number of Females per 1,000 Males.														
	All ages.			0—10			10—15			15—40			40 and over.		
	Unmarried.	Married.	Widowed.	Unmarried.	Married.	Widowed.	Unmarried.	Married.	Widowed.	Unmarried.	Married.	Widowed.	Unmarried.	Married.	Widowed.
1	2	3	4	5	6	7	8	9	10	11	12	13	14	15	16
State.															
All religions...	642	994	4,161	925	4,996	3,560	319	3,462	2,692	164	1,150	3,835	587	418	4,305
Hindu...	635	996	4,154	914	5,109	3,658	268	3 416	2,772	154	1,128	3,868	616	411	4,282
Musalman	682	969	4,436	1,006	2,838	2,525	605	4,558	2,383	204	1,324	3,885	460	415	4,646
Animist	698	1,049	3,481	951	4,892	3,077	622	3,018	1,163	287	3,805	2,618	463	452	4,109
Christian	688	960	3,806	1,022	2,406	1,750	724	5,679	2,667	197	1,268	3,917	707	398	3,796
Jain	562	1,003	2,208	1,018	2,287	4,750	321	3,741	1,182	73	1,208	2,892	113	405	2,142
Tellingana.															
All religions...	638	990	4,938	943	5,384	5,375	318	4,753	5,679	146	1,161	5,017	603	407	4,580
Hindu...	630	990	4,712	934	5,448	5,713	257	4,747	6,325	133	1,129	5,246	656	406	4,550
Musalman	676	998	4,884	1,024	2,437	2,583	691	6,329	3,981	193	1,434	4,208	363	397	5,029
Animist...	693	1,053	3,597	951	4,892	3,077	636	3,008	1,200	163	1,416	2,172	472	455	4,260
Christian	617	981	3,945	1,036	2,514	1,000	750	3,667	7,000	183	1,341	4,167	684	402	3,889
Jain	588	851	2,000	753	16,500	...	256	4,000	...	70	1,020	1,900	1,000	287	1,848
Marathwara.															
All religions...	647	997	3,569	905	4,802	2,894	319	2,740	1,955	185	1,140	3,113	574	420	4,073
Hindu...	641	1,001	3,787	893	4,918	2,936	282	2,667	1,965	177	1,138	3,070	587	418	4,059
Musalman	688	966	4,145	993	2,991	2,500	528	4,058	2,015	217	1,244	3,662	542	430	4,357
Animist	749	1,016	2,771	991	1,686	1,571	464	3,059	929	275	1,310	2,094	402	422	3,161
Christian	762	893	3,282	966	2,272	2,000	590	3,328	500	377	1,058	3,108	800	377	3,406
Jain	563	1,011	2,218	1,018	2,287	4,750	323	3,734	1,091	73	1,212	2,415	106	411	2,003

SUBSIDIARY TABLE V.—Distribution by Civil Condition of 1,000 of each Sex at certain ages for Selected Castes.

Caste.	Distribution of 1,000 males of each age by civil condition.																	
	All ages.			0-5.			5-12.			12—20			20—40			40 and over.		
	Unmarried.	Married.	Widowed.	Unmarried.	Married.	Widowed.	Unmarried.	Married.	Widowed.	Unmarried.	Married.	Widowed.	Unmarried.	Married.	Widowed.	Unmarried.	Married.	Widowed.
1	2	3	4	5	6	7	8	9	10	11	12	13	14	15	16	17	18	19
Hindu.																		
Brahman	410	542	48	988	11	1	912	85	3	445	548	7	129	851	20	25	800	175
Dhangar	382	577	41	975	25	—	889	111	—	455	543	2	53	907	40	9	864	137
Golla	447	530	23	989	10	1	937	59	4	597	388	15	84	899	17	28	908	69
Goundla	470	508	22	993	6	1	951	47	2	661	325	14	94	897	9	32	895	73
Kapu	489	538	23	992	7	1	906	92	2	610	388	2	81	895	24	9	916	75
Koli	382	592	26	992	6	2	866	131	3	415	579	6	81	946	25	10	904	86
Komati	432	527	41	993	6	1	900	95	5	606	373	21	66	895	39	24	865	108
Lingayeth	380	566	54	985	14	1	851	138	11	420	565	15	24	904	72	19	852	129
Madiga, Mang	456	511	33	991	7	2	953	43	4	615	373	2	92	877	31	11	896	93
Mahar, Mala	436	524	40	986	13	1	905	91	4	609	375	16	55	902	43	22	869	109
Maratha	406	545	49	983	16	1	872	123	5	581	441	28	109	837	54	37	846	117
Munnur	416	524	60	976	23	1	850	145	5	491	480	29	70	884	46	70	884	46
Mutrasi	454	498	48	995	5	—	974	25	1	704	283	13	106	856	38	15	843	142
Sale	454	507	39	993	7	—	935	64	1	624	354	22	38	928	34	13	870	117
Telaga	461	489	50	991	9	—	966	33	1	698	281	21	112	844	44	11	844	145
Musalman.																		
Pathan	472	483	45	1,000	—	—	976	23	1	786	207	7	185	781	34	47	816	137
Sayyed	476	475	49	1,000	—	—	974	25	1	802	186	12	226	734	40	42	824	134
Shaik	502	456	39	1,000	—	—	985	14	1	877	115	8	205	766	29	26	855	119
Christian.																		
Indian Christian	527	427	46	1,000	—	—	998	2	—	845	144	11	224	735	41	36	815	149
Animist.																		
Gond	523	458	19	997	3	—	944	55	1	478	519	3	17	955	28	1	930	69
Lambada	559	373	68	991	4	5	957	32	1	661	129	210	240	726	34	4	862	134

Caste.	Distribution of 1,000 females of each age by civil condition.																	
	All ages.			0-5.			5-12.			12-20.			20-40.			40 and over.		
	Unmarried.	Married.	Widowed.	Unmarried.	Married.	Widowed.	Unmarried.	Married.	Widowed.	Unmarried.	Married.	Widowed.	Unmarried.	Married.	Widowed.	Unmarried.	Married.	Widowed.
1	20	21	22	23	24	25	26	27	28	29	30	31	32	33	34	35	36	37
Hindu.																		
1 Brahman	246	556	198	968	31	1	633	355	12	41	886	73	8	780	212	3	515	482
2 Dhangar	287	593	120	975	24	1	637	355	8	31	915	54	2	874	124	1	600	399
3 Golla	280	571	149	988	12	...	723	271	6	18	950	32	2	855	143	1	507	492
4 Goundla	260	611	129	987	12	1	722	273	5	5	969	26	1	870	129	3	568	429
5 Kapu	270	565	165	985	14	1	646	347	7	120	849	31	2	850	148	2	501	497
6 Koli	254	585	161	971	28	1	596	388	16	49	896	55	3	864	133	3	458	539
7 Komati	294	523	183	982	17	1	684	308	8	221	726	53	14	791	195	9	503	488
8 Lingayeth	284	550	166	975	23	2	603	382	15	198	705	97	16	850	134	10	569	421
9 Madiga, Mang	332	538	130	985	14	1	740	254	6	110	847	43	13	857	130	3	620	377
10 Mahar, Mala	324	543	133	972	27	1	713	275	12	223	726	51	21	872	107	5	547	448
11 Maratha	290	542	168	976	22	2	688	288	24	213	700	87	21	842	137	2	546	452
12 Munnur	233	607	160	978	20	2	385	604	11	63	896	41	10	866	124	10	866	124
13 Mutrasi	295	571	134	980	17	3	743	246	11	112	864	24	4	880	116	2	545	453
14 Sale	330	546	124	988	11	1	732	263	5	147	819	34	13	881	106	9	595	396
15 Telaga	336	503	161	989	10	1	750	245	5	153	713	34	22	843	135	16	485	499
Musalman.																		
16 Pathan	373	492	135	1,000	...	...	930	67	3	507	570	23	49	852	99	26	528	446
17 Sayyed	355	482	163	1,000	...	...	935	63	2	384	585	32	33	846	116	17	474	509
18 Shaik	354	485	161	1,000	...	...	932	64	4	433	535	32	45	862	93	10	478	512
Christian.																		
19 Indian Christian	412	470	118	1,000	...	...	997	3	...	444	514	42	30	878	92	19	568	413
Animist.																		
20 Gond	397	498	105	999	1	...	842	153	5	112	827	61	3	944	53	1	513	486
21 Lambada	469	419	112	988	12	...	949	50	1	382	474	144	25	916	59	4	570	426

Chapter VIII.

EDUCATION.

159. Statistical Tables.

The statistics with which this Chapter deals are contained in Imperial Tables VIII and IX, and the nine subsidiary tables appended to it. Imperial Table VIII gives the distribution of Education by religion and age, while table IX gives the figures for selected castes. Subsidiary Tables I to VI are abstracted from the Imperial Tables. Subsidiary Tables VII to X are compiled from figures supplied by the Educational Department. Provincial Table II gives the population of Talukas by religion and education.

160. Changes in method of enumeration.

The following extract from the Instructions of the Imperial Census Commissioner relates to the method of enumeration at the present and the three previous Censuses:—

" In 1881 and 1891 the population was divided in respect of Education into three categories—Learning, Literate and Illiterate. It was found, however, that the return of the Learning was vitiated by the omission at the one end, of children who had not long been at school, who were entered as Illiterate, and at the other, of the more advanced students, who were classed as Literate. There were thus great discrepancies between the Census Return of the number of Learning, or children under instruction, and the corresponding Statistics of the Education Department. It was, therefore, decided in 1901 to confine the entry in the enumeration schedules to the two main categories of Literate and Illiterate. The same system has been maintained on the present occasion. The instructions to the enumerators have been slightly altered in the hope of making them clearer, but their purport is the same, persons who could " both read and write any language " were to be entered as Literate. In 1901, no general indication was given as to the standard to be taken in applying the rule. On the present occasion it was laid down in the instructions for the superior Census Staff that a person should be regarded as Literate if he could write a letter to a friend and read the answer to it, but not otherwise."

In view of this change in the method of enumeration, it is thought difficult to institute a precise comparison with the results of Censuses taken prior to 1901. It has been suggested that the best plan would be to exclude from the comparison persons under 15 years of age, and to add to the number shown as Literate in 1891 all persons over that age who were then classed as Learning.

161. Application of the above to Hyderabad.

So far as this State is concerned, the observations of the Census Commissioner of India do not seem to have force. The Census figures under " Learning " both in 1881 and 1891 were far in excess of the figures, supplied by the Educational Department, of pupils under instruction, showing that there was no omission at either end of those who should have been included in that category. On the other hand the figures of the Educational Department at the first two Censuses, would seem to have been underestimates. The large majority of elementary schools in and before 1891 was, as shown in Subsidiary Table VII, "private" institutions not under the control or supervision of the Department, and it is not improbable that it had no accurate information regarding the numbers attending them. Since 1891, there has been a steady diminution in the number of private schools, and an even more marked decrease in the number of scholars on their rolls. There were in 1911 about 30 per cent. more private than public elementary schools ; but the total of scholars in the latter were over 72 per cent. higher. Owing to this fact, as well as to the increasing supervision exercised over private schools by the Department, the number of scholars as given in subsidiary Table VII may be accepted as accurate.

162. Comparison with previous Censuses.

For these reasons, a comparison of the actual figures of literacy (including Learning) recorded at the present and previous Hyderabad Censuses is not open to the objections urged by the Census Commissioner. The marginal table gives the population, the total number classed otherwise than as Illiterates, and the proportion of such to the population at each Census. The figures for Learning and Literate are lumped together for 1881 and 1891. The table shows a striking decrease in the population classed otherwise than as Illiterate since 1891. There was a sudden rise in the number at the 1891 Census. The population increased by 17·1 per cent., but the increase in Learning and Literate during the preceding decade was 36·1 per cent. In the period between 1891 and 1901, the population decreased by 3·5 per cent., but the decrease in the number of other than Illiterates was no less than 24·1 per cent. At the present Census an increase of population, since 1901, of 20·04 per cent., is accompanied by an increase in the number of Literates, during the same interval, of only 11·9 per cent. As compared with 1891, the figures for 1911 represent an increase of population amounting to 15·9 per cent., but there has been in the same period an actual decrease of persons classed otherwise than as Illiterate of 15·2 per cent. The conclusions to be drawn are clear. As compared with 1901 there has been an increase in the number of Literates, but at a rate less than that of the increase of population. Educational expansion has not kept pace with the growth of population. As compared with 1891, the position is still worse: absolutely as well as relatively, the Nizam's Dominions are worse off to-day than they were twenty years ago, and, curiously enough, the population during the period has increased by about the same ratio as the Literates have decreased. It would appear that at a time of good seasons and general well-being the education tends to expand faster than population; that at a time of distress and calamity, it shows its extreme sensitiveness to environment by outstripping the rate at which population diminishes; and that when once it has suffered a check, it takes more time to rehabilitate itself than the population does to make up for lost numbers. The loss of population through famine and pestilence is made good sooner than the setback experienced in the educational progress of the country. The map printed below shows the number of Literate males per mille in each District of the State.

Census.	Population.	Not Illiterates.	Number per mille.
1881	9,845,594	318,880	32·5
1891	11,537,040	434,240	37·6
1901	11,141,142	329,169	29·55
1911	13,374,676	368,166	28·

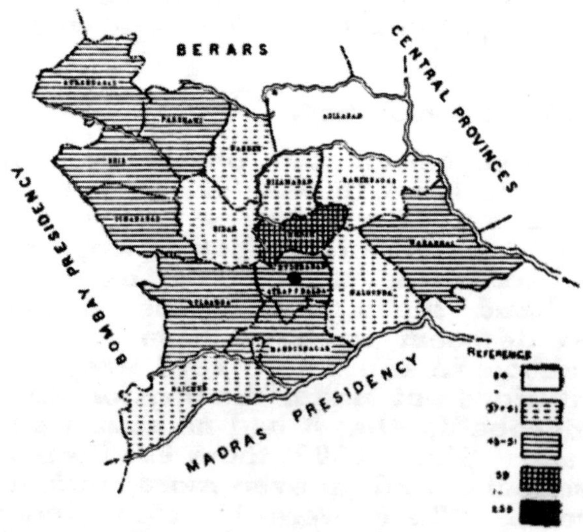

163. Progress of Education according to Age.

It is obvious from the totals of scholars given in Subsidiary Table VII for the years 1911, 1901 and 1891, that though the figure for 1911 shows a decrease of about 2 per cent. as compared with that for 1901, it is nearly 29 per cent. in excess of that for 1891. The marginal table compares the total number of scholars under instruction in the elementary schools in the State with the number of Literates under 15 in the four Census years. The figure in the second column for 1881 and 1891 is the total returned as "Learning." All the Literates below the age of 15 in the present and in the previous Censuses, are accounted for by the return furnished by the Educational Department which indeed shows a considerable excess. In 1881 and 1891, the position is reversed, and the number of "Learning" was in excess of the number of pupils in the elementary schools. It is obvious that the effect of the change made in the schedule at the Census of 1901, was to place about 37 per cent. of children in the Elementary Schools in the category of Illiterate. The percentage so displaced at the present Census is nearly 43 per cent., the larger proportion being no doubt due to the more precise definition of Literacy as the ability to read and reply to a letter from a friend suggested by the Census Commissioner of India. At the present Census, to a larger extent than at the previous one, scholars in the lowest standards have been classed as Illiterate.

Census.	Learning or Literate under 15.	Scholars in Elementary Schools.
1881...	67,825	8,320
1891...	79,736	63,514
1901...	51,129	80,743
1911...	43,663	76,065

164. Proportion of children of school-going age under instruction.

Taking the population of school-going age, as usual, at 15 per cent. of the total population, less than 5 per cent. of them were under instruction in 1911. The corresponding proportion in 1901 was nearly 6 per cent.

165. Elementary Education.

There were in 1901, 80,743 scholars in the elementary schools whereas in 1911, there were only 76,065. This decrease is faithfully reflected in the Census Statistics of Literates under ten, showing that the loss has been largely in the earliest stages of instruction. The youngest generation, it is clear, is being practically kept away from schools to a far larger extent than was the case 10 years ago. The very foundations of the educational system appear to be shaken. The old system which, whatever its defects, imparted the rudiments of Literacy, is fast collapsing, and there is as yet no adequate substitute for it. The public schools have been increasing far too slowly, while the old private schools have been rapidly diminishing. Moreover, the public school, judging from the larger attendance, is far too concentrated and inelastic to meet the needs of the community. These tendencies are brought out by the Statistics of public and private schools. The problem before the State is how to combine the cheapness and elasticity of the old private elementary schools with the advantages associated with the stricter discipline and the better regulated working of the departmental schools. This problem, though more frequently pressing in the Nizam's Dominions than elsewhere, is at the root of the educational expansion in the whole of India.

Census.	Population under 10.	Literate under 10.
1901	2,808,521	14,937
1911	3,613,680	9,493

166. Secondary Education.

While the state of elementary education as disclosed by the Census Statistics of Literacy at the age-period 0—15, and confirmed by those contained in the Educational returns, is unsatisfactory ; the decade was one of conspicuous advance as regards secondary education. The number of scholars attending secondary schools in the State was 13,826 in 1901 and 16,326 in 1911. The number of Literates in the age-period 15—20 in the same two years was 35,807 and 38,249 respectively. The close correspondence in the difference between the two sets of figures, about 2,500 in each case, is convincing evidence that 15—20 is pre-eminently the age for secondary education in the State.

167. Literacy of the Younger Generations in 1911 and 1901.

The marginal table gives an idea of how far the younger generations are equipped for the struggle of life in respect of literacy as compared with the corresponding generations of 10 years ago. It is extremely unlikely that any appreciable proportion of those returned as literates under ten is under the age of five years. The population under 5 years has, therefore, been left out, though the number of literates under age 10 is given as in Imperial Table VIII. It is once again clear that the educational position is worse than what it was ten years ago. The same conclusion emerges from a comparison of the statistics of literacy for the age-period of 10—20 or of 15—20 at the present and the previous Censuses. Subsidiary Table V gives the proportion of literates at the age-period 15—20 in 1901 and 1911; in the former year it was 42 and in the latter 38 per mille.

Persons at 5—20 years of age.

Census.	Population.	Literate.	People per 1000.
1901	3,655,564	86,936	......
1911	4,091,945	81,932	......

168. Proportion of Adult Literates.

The proportion of literates above the age of 20 has remained almost stationary since 1901 at between 37 and 38 per one thousand persons. This is what might have been expected. Having regard to the fact that the Census knows nothing of grades of literacy, and that the most accomplished scholar in the realm and the petty trader who barely escapes being illiterate by his ability to trace the characters of the alphabet on paper, are alike literates and nothing more to the enumerator, the statistics of literates above 20 are without any means of expansion, except immigration or emigration, or an exceptional number of deaths of literates. The statistics of literacy which are of most significance are those relating to the young and adolescent.

169. Comparison with other Provinces.

The proportions of literates per one thousand persons in Hyderabad is 28, which compares very unfavourably with the figures for the Central Provinces and Berar and the Bombay and the Madras Presidencies and the Baroda and Mysore States.

Hyderabad	28
Bombay	70
Madras	75
Baroda	101
Mysore	63
C. P. and Berar	33

170. Education of Women.

The proportion of literates in India and more especially in the Nizam's Dominions is considerably lowered by the almost total illiteracy of the female population. Exclusive of women, the proportion of literates in this State is 51 per thousand. The women's ratio 4 per thousand pulls it down to 28. Low as is the proportion of literate women, it is noteworthy that it has been steadily increasing during the last twenty years. In 1891 the ratio was 2 per thousand; in 1901 3 and in the current Census 4. The number of female literates increased by 5,194 during the decade. No less than 3,758 or over 70 per cent. of this number was among women of 20 years and over. There was a falling off in the number under 10, but it was more than made up by the increase in the following age-periods. As between the two great religions of the State, the Musalmans have a much larger proportion of women as of men literates than the Hindus, the proportion being 13 and 2 per mille respectively. The Parsis have the highest proportion

586, followed by Buddhists 583, Jews 500, Brahmo-Samaj 222, Christians 163, and Arya Samaj 108. Among the Hindus, the Brahmin has the highest proportion of female literates, 25 for every 1,000 women, the Rajput, the Komati and the Sathani following with 13, 12 and 10 respectively. All these castes stand high also in the scale of male literacy, so that the relation, though a rather indeterminate one, between male and female literacy is unmistakable. Among the Mussulmans the Moghal and the Sayyid have the highest proportion of female literates, 30 and 27 respectively per 1,000 women, and they stand also at the top of their creed in respect of literate males. Of the 24,077 female literates no less than 10,550 are inhabitants of Hyderabad City, the proportion for the City being 44 per 1,000 women. Atrafabilda and Aurangabad have the next highest proportion, 4 per 1,000. In point of women's education, Telingana is far ahead of Marathwara, the proportions being 5 and 2 respectively. As in other respects, the presence of the capital within its area gives Telingana an advantage over Marathwara. The number of female literates in English is 3,561 ; of this number 1,912 or 53·7 per cent. are Europeans and Anglo-Indians, 738 are Indian Christians, 355 Hindus and 328 Musalmans. The figures are of no significance.

171. Literacy by Religion.

Glancing down the first column of Subsidiary Table I, the high ratio of literacy of the Syrian Christian arrests attention. It is one thousand per mille, and all the one thousand are females. This phenomenon ceases to be extraordinary when it is found that the Syrian Christian population of the State consists of one person of the female sex. The Jew has 833 literates per mille, the Parsi 723, the Buddhist 600. The Arya Samaj with 266 is much behind the Brahmo Samaj with 417 literates per thousand persons. The Jain has 204 and the Sikh 173 literate persons for every thousand of his creed in the State. The proportion for the Christian faith, including all sects, is 247. Animism is the least literate creed, the ratio of Literates to total population being 1 to 1,000.

172. Literacy among Hindus and Mahomedans.

Coming to the two principal religions of the State, the Musalman proportion is much higher than that of the Hindus, the respective proportions being 59 and 23 per one thousand persons of each creed. The marginal table throws some interesting light on the relative proportions of Hindu and Mahomedan literacy in the Bombay and Madras Presidencies, and the Central Provinces and Berar and in the three premier Native States of India. The marked predominance of Mahomedans over Hindus in point of literacy in the Madras Presidency, the Central Provinces and Berar and the three principal Native States, is in striking contrast to their relative position in the Bombay Presidency, where there are proportionately more Mussalmans than in any of the other Provinces or of the Native States. The stimulus to education among Mahomedans seems to be in inverse ratio to their numerical strength in these provinces. It is worthy of note that, contrary to the general tendency, the superiority of the Musalman proportion becomes slightly less marked if the statistics of female literacy is excluded, the proportion of male literates in the two religions being 103 and 43 respectively.

Literate per 1,000.

Province.	Hindus.	Mahomedans.
Hyderabad	23	59
Bombay	66	43
Madras	72	87
Baroda	94	128
Mysore	56	125
C. P. and Berar	33	69

173. Hindu and Musalman Literacy Compared.

The disproportion between Hindu and Musalman literacy is visible at every age-period under 20. Three Hindu boys out of one thousand under 10 are in school, the corresponding figure for Musalmans being 10. In the next age-period 10-15, the proportions are 35 and 78 respectively per one thousand boys of each creed. Between 15 and 20, 142 Musalman youths per mille are counted as literates, while only 59 Hindu young men of that age are included in the category. The proportion of male literates above 20 and upwards is among Mahomedans 143 and among Hindus 62 per one thousand of the population of each religion. The proportion of female literates, however, is much higher at this age-period as in all preceding ones for Musalmans than for Hindus, the figures being 14 and 2 per one thousand females of each religion respectively. It is evident that as between Hindu and Mahomedan literacy, the relative position was less unequal ten years ago than it is now. The marginal table compares the ratios for the two religions at the present and the two previous Censuses. For 1891, the figures of "Literates" and "Learning" have been lumped together for the purpose of this comparison. The improvement in the proportion of Musalman literates is far from being commensurate with the growth of the Mahomedan population, but the proportion of Hindu literates has actually receded notwithstanding that the Hindu population has increased by 17·7 per cent. during the decade. The Hindu proportion determines the proportion of the whole State, and Hyderabad cannot continue to remain on the present low plane of literacy when all the rest of India is being swayed powerfully by a great tidal wave of educational advance.

Ratio per 1,000.

Census.	Hindu.	Musalman.
1891	35	60
1901	25·36	54·64
1911	23	59

174. Literacy by Castes.

It should not be overlooked, however, that the Hindu population is made up of very heterogeneous elements. Subsidiary Table VI gives details of distribution of literacy by castes. The Brahmin caste with a proportion of 262 literates per mille and the Chambhar and the Madiga with 1 per mille, are component parts of the Hindu population. Between these extremes, we have every grade of literacy, the Komati with 176 per mille, the Sathani, 115 per mille, the Rajput, 73 per mille, the Sunar 66, the Lingayat 42, and the Dewang and the Kapu 25, at the one end, and the Chakala and the Waddar 2, the Dhangar, the Dhobi and the Bhoi 3, the Kumbhar and the Mahar 4, and the Golla, the Koli and the Nahvi 5, at the other. As compared with the Hindu castes, the limits of variation in Mussalman literacy are very narrow. The Mughal at the top has 109 literates (of both sexes) per 1,000 persons, while the Shaik at the bottom has 49. Female literacy within each of the two great religious communities as a rule follows at a considerable distance the proportion of male literacy. The only notable exception is the Rajput who with 131 male literates per 1,000 male persons has 13 female literates, that is a larger proportion of the latter than the Sathani and the Komati whose rates of male literates are 211 and 332 respectively per mille. On the whole, however, it is safe to say that the education of men exerts a recognisable influence in favour of the education of women. The social and economic position of a caste has a definite relation to female literacy. The better placed classes naturally incline to give some education to their women.

Caste.	Male literates per 1,000.	Female literates per 1,000.
Brahmin	469	25
Komati	332	12
Sathani	211	10
Rajput	131	13
Mughal	180	30
Shaik	88	9

175. English education by castes.

The statistics bearing on distribution of literacy in English by caste, present some strange anomalies. The Brahmin is indisputably at the head of all Hindu and Mahomedan castes and sects in point of English literacy as of literacy in his own vernaculars, among the Musalmans, the Mughal similarly is first in both respects. But the surprising feature of the statistics is the relatively high proportion of English literacy in some castes which are low in the scale of literacy in their vernaculars. Some of the more conspicuous cases of this kind are given in the marginal table. The Mahar, one of the lowest Hindu castes in the scale of literacy, has more English-knowing members than the Rajput who is far above him in general literacy as in social position. The explanation, no doubt, is that Mahars are largely employed in domestic service by Englishmen and they find a knowledge of that language useful in their avocations. The town-dwelling castes have a higher proportion of English literates, than those which live chiefly in rural areas.

Caste.	English literates per 10,000.	Literates per 1,000.
Sathani	19	115
Telugu	14	18
Komati	18	176
Mahar	11	4
Kurma	7	7
Rajput	6	73
Munnur	5	16
Sonar	4	66

176. Literacy among Animists.

The low position which the Animists occupy in the scale of literacy among the subject of His Highness the Nizam, is the reflex of their low position in all other respects. They number 285,722 and are next to the Hindu and Mahomedans, numerically the most important section of the population. There are only 247 literates among them or less than one in a thousand of the population.

177. Distribution by natural Divisions and Districts.

The situation of the capital City in it gives Telingana an aspect of superiority in literacy over Marathwara, which is not borne out by the statistics furnished by the districts. Imperial Table Part III is devoted to the statistics relating to the City. Nearly 20 per cent. of the literates, over 70 per cent. of the literates in English and nearly 81 per cent. of female literates, in the State, are found within the limits of the Capital City though its population is less than four per cent. of that of the State. No wonder that under all heads, Hyderabad City exhibits proportions of literacy which can only be described as phenomenal in comparison with those of the districts. Although much ahead of the rest of the dominions, Hyderabad City comes off poorly in comparison with the other important capitals of the Indian Peninsula.

178. Telingana.

If Hyderabad City is excluded from the Telingana figures, the proportion of literates in the two great natural divisions are about equal. Medak and Atraf-i-balda are the only two districts which have an average of literates equal to or higher than that for the whole State. The capital is situated in the latter district which with Medak occupies a central position in the State. Adilabad, also in Telingana, is the only district with a proportion of less than 20 literates per 1,000 of the population. Its actual proportion is only 13. The district is an isolated tract with a considerable population of Animistic tribes. Warangal has an even larger Animistic population, but five of its eight talukas are traversed by a railway. It is of some significance, though there is no need to exaggerate it, that these five talukas have a much higher proportion of literates than the three other talukas of the district. In five out of the eight Marathwara districts, the proportion of literates is 25 and above per 1,000 inhabitants, while only four districts in Telingana including Medak and Atraf-i-balda have so high a proportion.

179. Literacy in Jagir Talukas.

This seems to be the proper place to call attention to the extremely low proportion of literacy shown by several of the Jagir talukas. Provincial Table II gives particulars of the population of talukas by education. Several of the Jagir talukas, in Marathwara particularly, have a considerable population, but the number of literates in them is much below that of the other talukas.

180. Distribution by Vernaculars.

The statistical tables this year do not furnish particulars regarding the prevalence of literacy in each of the principal Vernaculars of the State. By literacy is understood literacy in one's own vernaculars. At the last Census the proportion of literates in each of the four principal vernaculars, Marathi, Canarese, Urdu and Telugu were included in the Subsidiary Tables. The marginal table is abstracted from them. It is not possible to find out the exact proportion of literacy in each of the vernaculars this year owing to the omission of the corresponding columns in the Tables, but in view of the importance of such information to the Administration, an attempt is made to give a rough idea of it by reference to the divisional and district figures. The principal areas where such of the Vernaculars is spoken are indicated in the marginal statement. The bulk of the population of Adilabad is Telugu speaking. The proportion for Marathwara excluding the districts of Gulburga, Raichur and Bidar may, therefore, be accepted as a sufficiently correct estimate of the extent to which literacy prevails among the Marathi-speaking people of the Nizam's Dominions. This will be about 25 per 1,000 persons, which is higher than the proportion of the whole of Marathwara, Raichur and Bidar are two of the three best literate districts of Marathwara, and their elimination has the effect of raising the average of the rest of the division—Marathwara proper. The districts of Gulburga, Raichur and Bidar, where Canarese is the principal Vernacular, have also a considerable Telugu-speaking population. But for the purpose of a rough estimate, a fairly accurate result is obtained by combining the proportions given for the three districts in Subsidiary Table II and dividing it by 3, to get the ratio per 1,000 persons. This comes to 22. Urdu is spoken all over the State, so that district ratios are no clue to the extent of literacy in that Vernacular. But the number of Urdu-speaking persons is nearly equal to that of Mussalmans,—Urdu-speakers 1,341,622, Mussalmans 1,380,990. The ratio of Mussalman literates to the total Mussalman population is 58 in 1,000 persons. The Telingana proportion of literacy would not be a precisely correct estimate for the Telugu-speaking population owing to the exceptional position of Hyderabad City which is situated therein. But it may be regarded as a broadly correct proportion. It is 32 per mille. It appears, therefore, that the Urdu-speaking population has the highest proportion of literates in the State, that the Telugus come in next, the Marathas third, and the Canarese last of all. The proportion of literates in each of the languages to the total population will roughly be as stated in the marginal table.

Literates in each Vernacular per 1,000 persons, 1901.

Marathi	1·13
Canarese	·45
Urdu	·79
Telugu	1·76

Marathi	...Marathwara, Adilabad.
Canarese	...Gulburga, Raichur and Bidar.
Urdu	...Throughout the State.
Telugu	...Telingana, Raichur, Bidar & Gulburga.

Literates in each Vernacular per 1,000 persons, 1911.

Marathi	1·5
Canarese	0·40
Urdu	0·58
Telugu	1·6

181. Literacy in English.

It is worthy of note that though there has been a recession in respect of literacy in the Vernaculars during the last decade, that literacy in English has made remarkable progress. The proportion of literates in English rose from 13 to 20 per 10,000 persons of both sexes. For men alone the proportions were

21 and 34 respectively. Reference has already been made to the fact that the great majority of English literates are concentrated in Hyderabad City. Exclusive of these, the natural division of Telingana is less advanced than Marathwara, Atraf-i-balda and Warangal and Medak in Telingana and Aurangabad and Parbhuni and Bhir, Gulburga and Raichur in Marathwara have proportions of male literates in English exceeding 10 per 10,000 persons. The largest proportion of English literates are found as might be expected between the ages of 15 and 20. Though as the marginal figures show the Nizam's Dominions are behind the principal British Provinces and Native States in Peninsular India, still the rapid rise during the last 10 years shows that the working knowledge of the English language is coming to be regarded in Hyderabad as elsewhere in this country as a valuable asset in the battle of life.

Male literates in English per 10,000 persons.

Madras ...	121
Bombay	145
Mysore ...	117
Baroda ...	90
Central Provinces and Berar	54
Hyderabad	34

182. Higher Education.

The statistics of University examinations given in Subsidiary Table VIII shows a considerable falling off in the number of candidates who matriculated in the year 1911. Out of 26 candidates only 2 passed, the corresponding figures for 1901 being 112 and 18 respectively. This large decrease in the number of students entering the University courses of study is but the reflex of the general retrogression in the lowest stages during the decade. There is no change in the figures relating to the Intermediate examination. The number of candidates for the B.A. examination also showed a considerable decline. Altogether higher education must be said to be languishing.

183. Books published in the State.

The ten years ending 1910 show a very remarkable increase in the number of books published in the State. As against 3 and 169 respectively in the two previous decades there were 933 books issued. 883 of them were in Urdu and were all published during the last three years of the decade. Arabic claimed the next largest number of publications, namely, 25, and Telugu came third with 14 books; 6 books in Persian, 2 each in English and in Marathi and one in Canarese make up the rest.

184. Prospects of Educational Progress.

The position of the population in respect of literacy and education generally, as disclosed by the statistics compiled at the Census as well as those supplied by the Educational Department, has been set forth in the foregoing paragraphs. It is necessary to add that the Government of His Highness the Nizam are fully alive to the significance of these figures and have in contemplation measures which, it is expected, will lead to substantial improvements during the next few years. It may, therefore, be confidently hoped that the task of the writer of the next Census Report of the State will be a far more pleasant one so far as the statistics of literacy are concerned.

SUBSIDIARY TABLE I.—Education by Age, Sex and Religion.

Religion.	Number per Mille who are Literate: All ages. Total.	All ages. Males.	All ages. Females.	0—10 Males.	0—10 Females.	10—15 Males.	10—15 Females.	15—20 Males.	15—20 Females.	20 and over. Males.	20 and over. Females.	Number per Mille who are Illiterate. Total.	Males.	Females.	Number per Mille who are Literate in English. Total.	Males.	Females.
1	2	3	4	5	6	7	8	9	10	11	12	13	14	15	16	17	18
All Religions ..	28	51	4	4	1	40	6	69	7	72	4	972	949	996	2	3	1
Hindu	23	43	2	3	1	35	3	59	4	62	2	977	957	998	1	1	..
Musalman ..	59	103	13	10	3	78	18	142	26	143	14	941	897	987	5	9	..
Animist	1	1	....	....	....	3	1	3	....	2	....	999	999	1,000	..	..	..
Christian.. ..	247	317	163	65	45	264	216	345	278	341	202	753	683	837	181	242	107
Indian Christian.	126	154	96	....	....	....	....	....	....	....	....	874	846	904	47	60	33
Roman Catholic.	115	144	83	....	....	....	....	....	....	....	....	885	856	917	..	..	..
Syrian	1,000	....	1,000	....	....	....	....	....	....	....	....	....	..	....	..	..	..
Other Christian	132	159	102	....	....	....	....	....	....	....	....	868	841	898	..	..	..
Jain	204	375	14	39	7	303	17	465	16	498	17	796	625	986	3	5	1
Sikh	173	280	37	27	11	211	32	317	37	372	45	827	720	963	9	11	8
Parsi	723	842	586	390	196	746	659	891	754	923	698	277	158	414	475	642	280
Arya Samaj ..	266	411	108	56	43	357	222	250	200	556	109	734	589	892	121	200	36
Brahmo Samaj ..	417	611	222	....	....	....	500	....	667	786	143	583	389	778	139	278	..
Buddhist	600	625	583	250	....	....	....	....	1,000	1,000	667	400	375	417	100	250	..
Jew	833	1,000	500	....	500	1,000	....	1,000	....	1,000	500	167	..	500	500	750	..

Details by age for the four sub-heads under "Christians" have not been abstracted.

SUBSIDIARY TABLE II.—Education by Age, Sex and Locality.

District and Natural Division.	Number per Mille who are Literate: All ages. Total.	All ages. Males.	All ages. Females.	0—10 Males.	0—10 Females.	10—15 Males.	10—15 Females.	15—20 Males.	15—20 Females.	20 and over. Males.	20 and over. Females.
1	2	3	4	5	6	7	8	9	10	11	12
State	28	51	4	4	1	40	6	69	7	72	4
Telingana	32	57	5	5	1	44	8	77	10	83	6
Hyderabad City	145	239	44	30	13	186	67	308	74	306	46
Atraf-i-balda	28	51	4	5	1	41	5	60	7	73	4
Warangal	25	45	3	4	1	37	4	68	5	66	3
Karimnagar	20	37	2	2	....	29	2	48	3	56	2
Adilabad	13	24	1	1	....	20	1	33	2	38	1
Medak .. .. - ..	31	59	3	6	1	53	6	84	6	81	4
Nizamabad..	20	38	1	3	....	26	2	50	2	56	2
Mahbubnagar	25	47	2	3	1	36	3	58	4	68	3
Nalgonda	21	39	2	3	1	32	4	53	4	59	3
Marathwara	23	44	2	4	1	36	6	61	4	62	2
Aurangabad	25	45	4	4	2	38	9	64	9	65	4
Bhir	25	49	1	4	....	46	1	69	2	68	2
Nander	21	41	1	4	....	34	1	63	3	57	1
Parbhani	25	47	2	4	1	40	3	62	2	66	2
Gulburga	25	47	2	5	....	41	2	68	3	65	2
Osmanabad	26	50	2	5	....	39	3	66	3	70	2
Raichur	20	38	3	4	1	23	4	49	5	54	3
Bidar	21	40	1	3	...	31	2	58	3	56	2

SUBSIDIARY TABLE III.—Education by Religion, Sex and Locality.

District and Natural Division.	Number per mille who are Literate.									
	Hindu.		Musalman.		Animist.		Christian.		Jain.	
	Males.	Females.	Males.	Females.	Males.	Females.	Males.	Females.	Males.	Females.
1	2	3	4	5	6	7	8	9	10	11
State	43	2	103	13	1	......	317	163	375	14
Telingana	45	2	156	22	1	......	343	175	515	62
Hyderabad City	189	19	259	49	......	... ..	672	373	695	122
Atraf-i-balda	46	2	86	8	6	1	488	258	224	......
Warangal	46	2	121	18	1	......	97	50	476	......
Karimnagar	34	1	108	5	1	......	297	197	514	34
Adilabad	24	1	81	8	1	......	947	222	169	29
Medak	53	2	112	9	6	......	245	197	439	......
Nizamabad	36	1	69	3	15	4	147	96	615	......
Mahbubnagar	48	2	90	4	4	......	448	374	......	......
Nalgonda	36	1	122	12	......	......	60	37	1,000	1,000
Marathwara	42	1	59	5	2	1	204	113	369	12
Aurangabad...	40	2	59	11	5	1	168	92	382	14
Bhir	46	1	59	3	......	......	1,000	1,000	422	4
Nander	36	1	71	3	... .	......	625	310	363	6
Parbhani	43	1	68	3	......	......	672	396	282	7
Gulburga	45	1	53	3	......	......	231	144	425	19
Osmanabad	47	2	52	3	......	... ..	188	25	378	21
Raichur	38	2	75	6	......	......	199	143	361	16
Bidar	58	1	48	3	......	......	162	67	297	11

SUBSIDIARY TABLE IV.—English Education by Age, Sex and Locality.

District and Natural Division.	Literate in English per 10,000.													
	1911.										1901.		1891.	
	0—10		10—15		15—20.		20 and over.		All ages.		All ages.		All ages.	
	Males.	Females.	Males.	Females.	Males.	Females.	Males.	Females.	Males.	Females.	Males.	Females.	Males.	Females.
1	2	3	4	5	6	7	8	9	10	11	12	13	14	15
State	3	2	24	7	56	10	48	6	34	5	21	5	14	3
Telingana	5	3	39	13	90	18	79	11	55	10	35	8	25	...
Hyderabad City	66	48	515	161	962	170	788	117	682	110	389	84	284	56
Atraf-i-balda	7	1	80	4	43	12	28	7	21	5	14	2	3	...
Warangal	1	...	6	4	28	8	31	5	19	4	6	3	4	1
Karimnagar	...	...	1	...	1	1	3	1	2	...	...	...	2	...
Adilabad	...	...	1	...	2	2	6	2	3	1	...	...	1	...
Medak	1	...	9	...	28	3	13	2	11	1	1	1	4	...
Nizamabad	1	...	4	1	8	3	10	1	7	1	2	...	1	...
Mahbubnagar	1	1	1	5	2	2	6	1	4	1	5	2	2	...
Nalgonda	...	...	1	...	3	1	6	...	4	...	1	2	3	...
Marathwara	1	...	7	1	19	2	17	2	12	1	5	1	3	...
Aurangabad	1	...	13	2	40	2	30	4	21	2	16	2	9	1
Bhir	...	...	3	...	15	...	24	...	15	...	5	...	1	...
Nander	...	...	3	...	10	1	12	...	8	...	1	...	...	...
Parbhani	1	1	9	3	23	3	25	2	17	2	5	...	1	...
Gulburga	1	...	12	1	27	3	19	2	14	2	2	...	7	1
Osmanabad	...	...	4	...	6	...	9	...	6	...	...	...	...	...
Raichur	2	...	6	2	12	5	14	3	10	2	7	8	7	2
Bidar	...	...	3	...	10	1	4	...	4	...	...	...	...	...

SUBSIDIARY TABLE V.—Progress of Education Since 1881.

District and Natural Division.	Number of Literate per mille.															
	All Ages.								15—20				20 and over.			
	Males.				Females.				Males.		Females.		Males.		Females.	
	1911	1901	1891	1881	1911	1901	1891	1881	1911	1901	1911	1901	1911	1901	1911	1901
1	2	3	4	5	6	7	8	9	10	11	12	13	14	15	16	17
State	51	55	60	...	4	3	2	...	69	77	7	6	72	75	4	4
Telingana	57	60	66	...	5	6	3	...	77	93	10	10	83	76	6	6
Hyderabad City ...	289	251	211	...	44	36	21	...	308	318	74	60	306	309	46	35
Atraf-i-balda	51	63	67	...	4	6	1	...	60	83	7	10	73	83	4	7
Warangal	45	52	52	...	3	2	1	...	63	72	5	3	66	72	3	3
Karimnagar	37	33	47	...	2	1	1	...	48	49	3	1	56	50	2	1
Adilabad	24	15	23	...	1	2	...	...	33	25	2	4	38	22	1	2
Medak	59	47	77	...	3	4	1	...	84	64	6	6	81	62	4	4
Nizamabad	38	41	50	...	1	2	1	...	50	55	2	3	56	55	2	2
Mahbubnagar	47	60	60	...	2	7	2	...	58	84	4	12	68	75	3	7
Nalgonda	89	32	48	...	2	3	1	...	53	65	4	5	59	41	3	4
Marathwara... ...	44	41	48	...	2	1	1	...	61	66	4	2	62	66	2	1
Aurangabad	45	61	54	...	4	3	1	...	64	75	9	5	65	85	4	3
Bhir	49	59	47	...	1	1	1	...	69	69	2	1	68	84	2	1
Nander	41	43	39	...	1	...	1	...	62	55	3	1	57	59	1	...
Parbhani	47	49	41	...	2	1	...	...	62	62	2	1	66	70	2	1
Gulbarga	47	38	52	...	2	1	1	...	63	67	3	2	65	50	2	1
Osmanabad	50	60	49	...	2	1	...	...	66	79	3	2	70	83	2	1
Raichur	88	41	60	...	3	2	1	...	49	76	5	4	54	52	3	1
Bidar	40	37	45	...	1	1	...	...	58	50	3	1	56	50	2	1

Note.—(1). Columns 4 and 8 include persons over 15 who were shown in the 1891 Census returns as 'Learning.'

(2). Proportional figures for 1881 are not given as persons subsumed under 'Learning' for that year are not detailed by age-periods

SUBSIDIARY TABLE VI.—Education by Caste.

Caste.	Number per 1,000 who are literate.						Number per 10,000 who are literate in English.					
	1911.			1901.			1911.			1901.		
	Persons.	Males.	Females.	Persons.	Males.	Females.	Persons.	Males.	Females.	Persons.	Males.	Females.
1	2	3	4	5	6	7	8	9	10	11	12	13
Hindu.												
1. Bhoi	3	5	...	...	...	...	...	1	...	...	...	...
2. Brahman	262	489	25	...	...	...	116	221	6	...	...	...
3. Chakala...	2	3	...	...	...	...	...	1	...	...	...	...
4. Chambhar	1	2	...	...	...	...	...		...	...	...	...
5. Dewang or Koshti ...	25	48	1	...	...	...	...	1	...	...	...	...
6. Dhangar	3	6	...	...	...	...	...	1	...	...	...	...
7. Dhobi	3	6	...	...	...	...	...	...	..	...	...	...
8. Golla	5	9	...	...	...	...	5	9	1	...	...	...
9. Goundla...	8	16	...	...	...	...	...	1	...	...	...	...
10. Hatkar	12	23	1	...	...	...	7	13	...	...	...	...
11. Kalal	17	32	1	...	...	...	6	11	...	...	...	...
12. Kapu	25	48	1	...	...	...	5	10	...	...	...	...
13. Koli	5	10	...	...	...	...	...	1	...	...	...	...
14. Komati	176	332	12	...	-	...	13	24	1	...	...	...
15. Kummara, Kumbhar ...	4	7	...	...	...	...	3	6	...	..	...	...
16. Kurma	7	14	...	...	...	...	7	13	...	...	...	...
17. Lingayet	42	82	2	...	...	...	2	5	...	...	...	...
18. Lohar	15	29	1	...	...	...	...	...	...	...	...	...
19. Madiga, Mang... ...	1	1	...	...	...	..	...	1	...	...	...	...
20. Mahar, Mala	4	6	1	...	...	...	11	20	1	...	...	...
21. Mali	5	9	...	...	...	...	...	...	...	...	...	...
22. Mangala	7	14	...	...	...	...	3	6	...	...	..	...
23. Maratha...	12	23	1	...	...	...	3	5	...	...	...	...
24. Munnur...	16	31	1	...	...	...	5	10	...	...	...	...
25. Mutrasi	12	22	1	...	...	...	3	5	...	...	...	...
26. Nahvi (Warik)... ...	5	9	...	...	...	...	1	1	...	...	...	...
27. Panchal...	39	75	1	...	...	...	2	3	...	...	...	...
28. Rajput	73	131	13	...	...	-	6	10	1	...	...	...
29. Sale	13	25	...	...	...	...	1	2	...	...	...	...
30. Satani	115	211	10	...	...	...	19	36	1	...	...	...
31. Sunar	66	125	3	...	...	...	4	7	...	...	...	...
32. Sutar	16	31	1	...	...	...	1	3	...	...	...	...
33. Telaga	13	24	2	...	...	...	14	26	2	...	...	...
34. Teli	22	43	1	...	...	...	1	2	...	...	...	...
35. Uppara	9	16	1	...	...	...	...	...	...	...	...	...
36. Velama	32	60	1	...	...	...	1	2	...	...	...	...
37. Waddar...	2	4	...	...	...	.	...	...	...	...	...	...
38. Wanjari	8	15	...	...	...	..	...	...	...	...	...	...
Musalman.												
39. Mughal	109	180	30	...	...	...	111	195	17	...	...	...
40. Pathan	77	132	15	...	...	...	69	126	4	...	...	...
41. Sayyed	97	160	27	...	...	...	108	196	12	...	...	...
42. Shaik	49	88	9	...	...	...	37	70	3	...	...	...
Christian.												
43. Indian Christian ...	126	154	96	...	...	...	471	602	331	...	...	...
Animist.												
44. Gond	...	1	...	...	...	...	...	...	...	...	...	...
45. Lambada	1	2	...	...	...	...	...	...	...	...	...	...

Note.—Figures for 1901 are not available as Imperial Table IX for that year was not prepared.

SUBSIDIARY TABLE VII.—Number of Institutions and Pupils according to the Returns of the Education Department.

Class of Institution.	1911. Number of		1901. Number of		1891. Number of	
	Institutions.	Scholars.	Institutions.	Scholars.	Institutions	Scholars.
1	2	3	4	5	6	7
Total	2,295	94,959	2,687	97,526	3,140	73,973
Public	1,036	66,484	847	57,972	580	40,979
Arts Colleges	1	84	2	52	3	83
Oriental Colleges	1	42	1	127	... ..	......
Secondary Schools	88	16,326	70	13,826	58	8,533
Primary Schools	921	48,113	766	43,149	519	32,209
Special Training Schools ...	2	362	2	376	3	97
Other Schools	23	1,557	6	442	2	57
Private	1,259	28,475	1,840	39,554	2,560	32,994
Advanced	15	523	20	1,960	25	1,689
Elementary	1,244	27,952	1,820	37,594	2,535	31,305

SUBSIDIARY TABLE VIII.—Main Results of University Examinations.

Examination.	1911.		1901.		1891.	
	Candidates.	Passed.	Candidates.	Passed.	Candidates.	Passed.
1	2	3	4	5	6	7
Matriculation	26	2	112	18	151	42
First Examination in Arts or Intermediate Examination in Arts	13	6	13	4	8	3
B. A. Degree Examination.						
English language division	7	5	13	7	3	1
Second language division	6	4	13	10		
Science division	6	5	12	3		
Oriental Examinations.						
Munshi	...	...	44	18	9	4
Munshi Alum	...	...	7	4	4	3
Munshi Fazil	...	...	2	2	...	...
Moulvi	...	...	16	13	7	4
Moulvi Alum	...	...	8	6	3	3
Moulvi Fazil	...	...	2	2	...	...

Note:—The Punjab University having severed its connection with the Oriental Colle e, the Oriental examinations are from 1911 held by the State and the results for that year have not therefore been shown.

SUBSIDIARY TABLE IX.—Number and Circulation of Newspapers, etc.

Language.	Class of Newspapers (Daily, Weekly, etc.)	1911.		1901.	
		No.	Circulation.	No.	Circulation.
Urdu	A.—Daily	2	1,300	1	800
	B.—Bi-Weekly	...	......	1	50
	C.—Weekly	1	500	7	1,950
	D.—Monthly	8	4,600	4	1,700
	Total ...	11	6,400	13	4,500
Urdu and Mahratti	A.—Weekly	...	......	2	170
	Grand Total ...	11	6,400	15	4,670

SUBSIDIARY TABLE X.—Number of Books Published in each Language.

Language.	Number of Books published in										Total of decade.
	1901	1902	1903	1904	1905	1906	1907	1908	1909	1910	1901-1910
Urdu	25	17	9	84	66	63	43	94	153	356	164
Persian	...	...	...	12	2	...	...	1	3	10	......
Arabic	...	..	...	28	5	2	...	11	6	20	.....
Telugu	1	4	4	3	1	3	...	1	6	11	3
Marathi	...	...	...	...	...	...	1	...	3	...	1
Canarese	...	...	...	...	...	...	...	...	...	8	1

Chapter IX.

LANGUAGE.

185. Statistics.

Imperial Table X contains particulars as to the number of persons in the State as well as in the several districts, who speak each of the languages spoken in these Dominions. The enumerators were instructed to enter under language the language which each person ordinarily used in his own home. In the case of infants and deaf-mutes, the language of their mother was to be entered. The entries in the Census schedules were found generally to be correct. In certain cases synonyms were used, for instance, Musalmani for Urdu, but they have been classified under the ordinary name in the table. Three Subsidiary Tables are appended to this chapter showing the distribution of the total population by language according to the Census, according to the classification adopted by the Linguistic Survey, the proportion of the population in each district and of the principal castes speaking each of the languages.

186. Vernaculars of the State.

Of the total population of 13,374,676, the number of persons who speak the languages, which are grouped together in Imperial Table X as Vernaculars of the State, is 13,219,118. That is to say, over 98 per cent. of the population speak one or other of the 12 languages regarded as being indigenous in the State. The marginal table gives the actual number of persons who returned themselves as speaking one of the four principal languages of the State. Telugu, Marathi, Canarese and Urdu are the only languages, each of which, is spoken by over one million persons. These four together account for more than 96 per cent. of the population of these Dominions. The 8 remaining languages of the group, (Vernaculars of the State) are, as their names denote, spoken by particular tribes. Bhili is the speech of the Bhils, Gondi of the Gonds and Lambadis of the Lambadas. Six out of these languages, namely, Bhili, Kaikadi, Kolhati, Lambadi, Pardhi and Wadari are classed, according to the Linguistic survey, as dialects of Gujarati. Of the remaining two languages, Yerakula is a dialect of Tamil, and Gondi is said to belong to the stage intermediate between Dravida and Andhra. Of the Gujarati dialects, Lambadi is the mother tougue of the largest number of persons. In fact, it is evident from Subsidiary Table III that the speakers of Lambadi number nearly 100,000 more persons than the caste of that name. In contradistinction to this, it is noteworthy that the speakers of Bhili number less than the tribe of Bhils and that a large proportion of Gonds have not returned themselves as speaking the Gondi language. Yerkula, on the other hand, would seem to be spoken by many outside the tribe of that name.

Language	Speakers
Telugu	6,367,578
Marathi	3,498,758
Canarese	1,680,005
Urdu	1,341,622

187. Other Languages spoken in the State.

Languages spoken in the State, not included in the group of Vernaculars of the State, are classified in three other groups, namely, Vernaculars of India foreign to the State, languages spoken in Asia outside of India, and European languages. Of Vernaculars of India foreign to the State, Rajasthani has the

Rajasthani	50,208
Western Hindi	37,814
Tamil	25,027
Gujarati	14,984
Eastern Hindi	6,609
Arabic	5,683
English	3,843

largest number of speakers. Next to it comes Western Hindi, followed by Tamil and Gujarati and Eastern Hindi. The bulk of those who speak an Asiatic language foreign to India, claim Arabic for their mother tongue, while all but a negligible fraction of speakers of European languages in the State have English for their vernacular. The marginal Table gives the actual numbers of those who speak these languages.

188. The four principal Languages of the State.

It is evident from the above that the languages which are of special importance, as being those spoken by the largest numbers of the population, are Telugu, Marathi, Canarese and Urdu. The marginal Table compares the actual number of persons speaking each of these four languages since the 1881 Census. The number of Telugu speakers has increased by almost 50 per cent. during the last 30 years and that of Canarese speakers by 35 per cent. As regards Urdu, the figure for the 1881 Census includes Hindi. The Marathi-speaking population has increased the least. The proportion of persons speaking each of these four languages has varied since 1891 as shown in the marginal Table. It is clear that while the proportion of Marathi speakers is considerably less than what it was twenty years ago, and while Canarese has lost some ground during the last decade, Telugu has steadily continued to advance. As regards Urdu, the figures in the marginal Table show that the proportion of Urdu speakers has declined somewhat during the last ten years.

Language.	1881.	1891.	1901.	1911.
Telugu ...	4,266,470	5,031,069	5,148,056	6,367,578
Marathi ...	3,147,745	3,493,858	2,895,864	3,498,758
Canarese ...	1,238,519	1,451,046	1,562,018	1,680,005
Urdu ...	1,035,305	1,193,382	1,158,490	1,341,622

Number of persons in 1,000 of population			
Speaking	1891.	1901.	1911.
Telugu	430	462	476
Marathi	303	260	261
Canarese	126	140	126
Urdu	104	104	100

189. Distribution of the Telugu-speaking population.

The population of Telingana has increased by 52·3 per cent. since 1881. The increase in the number of Telugu-speaking persons during the same period is very nearly 50 per cent., and it is easy to see that there is a close connection between the increase in the population of Telingana and in the number of Telugu-speakers in these Dominions. The reason is obvious. Over 80 per cent. of the people of Telingana own Telugu as their mother-tongue and more than seven-eighth of the Telugu-speaking population of the State is found in that Natural Division. As compared with 1891, there is a decrease of 78 in 10,000 in the number of Telugu-speakers in Telingana. The Telugu-speaking population of Marathwara also shows a set-back since 1891. In that year, the number of Telugus in the Marathwara and Karnatic linguistic divisions averaged 1,635 in 10,000 of the population, whereas at the present Census the proportion of Telugu-speakers in Marathwara (which includes the Karnatic division of 1891) is only 1,215. These two facts would seem to show that the expansion of the Telugu-speaking population has reached its zenith. It is interesting to note that while the number of the Telugu-speaking population of the Marathwara districts is 807,547, the number of persons in Marathwara who returned some locality in Telingana as their birth-place, is only 40,906. It follows that the bulk of the Telugus in Marathwara are not immigrants but have been settled there for more than a generation. The largest proportion of them are found in the Kanarese districts of Raichur, Gulbarga and Bidar, and in Nander which belongs as much to Telingana as to Marathwara in respect of its natural characteristics. Owing to the general reconstitution of the districts, a comparison of the statistics obtained at previous Censuses are not likely to be fruitful. In Karimnagar, Medak and Nalgonda, over 90 per cent. of the population is Telugu-speaking.

190. Distribution of the Marathi-speaking population.

Although the name of Marathwara has been applied to all the districts which are not included in Telingana, the Marathi-speaking population does not absolutely or relatively, occupy the same numerical position there as the Telugus do in Telingana. Marathwara consists of two clearly-marked linguistic divisions, namely, Marathwara proper and the Karnatic districts where Canarese is the dominant vernacular. In Gulbarga, for instance, there are only 37,749 persons speaking Marathi, as against 680,617 speaking Canarese and 229,669 speaking Telugu. The instance of Raichur is even more anomalous. The number of Marathi-speakers in the district is only 3,311, while the number of persons speaking Telugu and Canarese is respectively 282,451 and 625,706. There is no particular reason why these two districts should be included in Marathwara rather than in Telingana, and there is at least one good reason against it. It is a common complaint in the Canarese districts of the Bombay Presidency that their educational interests have suffered owing to their being treated as part and parcel of the districts of Maharashtra even to the extent of Marathi being taught, instead of Canarese, in many of their elementary schools. The inclusion of the Canarese districts in Marathwara is calculated to obscure the special administrative and educational interests of the people who speak Canarese—a Dravidian language. The distinctively Marathwara districts are Aurangabad, Bhir and Parbhani in the Aurangabad division, and Osmanabad in the Gulbarga division. In Bidar, the Canarese and the Telugu speakers together outnumber the Marathas, and Nander, as observed above, partakes of the character of both natural divisions. Speaking generally, the Aurangabad division, with Osmanabad thrown in, would exactly cover Marathwara, properly so called, and would form a homogeneous administrative unit, with a common vernacular language and a people inheriting the historical and cultural developments associated with it. The Marathi-speaking population numbers less than 50 per cent. of the total population of Marathwara, as the term is used in this report, but it would comprise over 80 per cent. of the population of the Aurangabad division together with the district of Osmanabad.

191. Variations in the Marathi-speaking population.

The number of Marathi speakers in the population has increased by about 350,000 in the last thirty years, but others have increased much more, and the result is that the former occupy a proportionately less conspicuous position now than in 1881. The heavy decrease, shown in the number of Marathas in 1901, is due to the loss of population sustained by the Marathwara districts owing to the famines of the preceding decade. They have recovered their lost numbers during the subsequent decade, but they have done little more. Owing to the different connotations in which Marathwara is used, it is not easy to institute a comparison between the Marathi-speaking population of the natural division at this and the previous Censuses. Such a comparison on the basis of districts is impossible owing to the reconstitution of the latter. But Telingana has throughout remained a more or less constant and recognisable unit of territory, and it is of interest to see how the Marathi-speakers in that division stand to-day as compared with a generation back. At the Census of 1891, there were reckoned 217 Marathi-speaking persons in 10,000 of the population of Telingana, at the present Census, their proportion is 324. They constitute more than one-fifth of the population of Adilabad. In other Telingana districts, their position is one of numerical insignificance. In Marathwara itself, their principal strongholds are Bhir, Parbhani and Osmanabad.

192. Distribution of Canarese Speakers.

The Canarese speakers show an increase about 120,000 during the decade but their proportion per 10,000 of the population has fallen from 140 in 1901 to 126, reducing them to the position which they occupied in 1891. They have, in fact, receded in the same proportion as the Telugus have advanced. One reason of this small increase in their actual numbers accompanied by a retrogression in their proportional figure, is that they have not increased as much as the speakers of the other languages during the decade. But, on the other hand, it has to be remembered that the Marathi speakers suffered heavily in the decade previous to 1901, while the Canarese actually increased in number and in proportion. Since 1881, the population of the typically Canarese districts of Gulbarga and Raichur has increased by 53 and 43 per cent. respectively. But the number of Canarese speakers has increased in the same period by only a little over 35 per cent. The district of Bidar suffered, no doubt, heavily in the famines which ushered in the twentieth century, but Bidar has a larger Maratha than Canarese population, and it is by no means certain that the latter suffered as much as the former. Then, again, in 1891, there were 113 Canarese-speaking persons in every 10,000 of the population of Telingana. At the present, there are only 55. Altogether, it would seem that between the Telugus on one side and the Marathas on the other, the Canarese-speaking population is being hard pressed. There is no evidence to show, and it is extremely improbable, that any appreciable number of them is giving up Canarese in favour of Marathi or Telugu as their mother-tongue. Such a change would presuppose the prevalence of inter-marriage between Telugu or Marathi speakers and Canarese speakers, to an extent inconceivable in the present state of Indian social life. Parbhani is the only district outside the Karnatic districts, where there are over 500 Canarese speakers for 10,000 of the population.

193. Distribution of the Urdu-speaking Population.

The Urdu-speaking population is not confined to any particular district. The number of persons who returned Urdu as their mother-tongue at the present Census is 1,341,622 or 39,368 less than the Musalman population of the State. Whatever the languages returned by these 40,000 persons might be, it is certain that all those who returned Urdu as their mother-tongue are Musalmans. In the first two Censuses held in this State, Urdu was classified as a dialect of Hindi and included Hindustani: since 1901, Urdu is treated as a main language, and the figures for Hindustani are separately given. "The name 'Hindustani' when denoting any particular form of speech," according to Dr. Grierson, "is properly reserved for a language whose vocabulary is neither excessively Persianized nor excessively Sanskritized."* It is extremely doubtful whether those who returned their mother-tongue as Hindustani had an accurate idea of what they meant. In popular language, the two words seem to be used practically as being synonymous with each other, and in any case, the addition of the 24,280 persons who returned Hindustani to those who returned Urdu as their mother-tongues, will appreciably reduce the number of Musalmans whose mother-tongue is not indicated by the Census figures. It also enables a suggestive comparison of the state of things in 1891 with that at the present day. Writing of the Urdu (including Hindustani)† speaking population of this State in 1891, the Census Superintendent observed :—

> "The total Musalman population of this Province is 1,138,666; and the number returned as speaking Urdu is 1,198,382. Thus, it would at first sight appear that nearly 60,000 persons who ought to have been returned as speaking dialects of Hindi have returned themselves as speaking Urdu. But this is not so, as the Kayasths, Lodhas, Rajputs, Khatries and many others from the north, though not Musalmans, have returned their parent tongue as Urdu."

He added that the term 'Hindi' was popularly applied in the Hyderabad State to the dialects of the Hindus who use the Devnagari character, and to whom belonged the Pardesis, Purbhaiyas, &c., who, having immigrated into the State, earned a living either by military service or by serving as cooks and *pandyas*.‡ The

* *Imperial Gazetteer*, Vol. I, page 366.
† Census Report of 1901, page 165.
‡ Census Report of Hyderabad, 1891 Part II, pages 81, 82.

number of persons who returned Hindi in that year was 77,558. Separate figures were not given for Hindustani in 1891. In 1901, Hindi, Urdu and Hindustani were distinguished in the returns. The Hindi speakers had largely decreased, their number being 28,767. The number of Hindustani speakers was 3,166. The number of Urdu speakers was 1,158,490, as against 1,155,750, the number of the Musalman population. There were thus, more Urdu speakers than Musalmans in 1901 also. In 1911, however, things have changed. Even with the help of over 24,000 Hindustanis, we are unable to account for the mother-tongue of the whole Musalman population. Even after laying under contribution Arabic, Persian and Pashto, there are over 8,000 Musalmans left without a distinctively Musalman vernacular. Two conclusions follow. The first is that, under the influence of the Hindi-Urdu controversy in Upper India, Hindus have altogether given up returning Urdu as their mother-tongue. The second is, that for the first time at the present Census, some thousands of Musalmans in these Dominions returned a mother-tongue which was an Indian vernacular other than Urdu. The Musalman population has increased during the last decade by 19·4 per cent., the Urdu-speaking population has increased only by 15·8 per cent. Excluding Hyderabad City, where nearly half the population are Urdu speakers, the largest proportions of them are found in Gulbarga, Bidar, Aurangabad and Nander, which are associated with the history of the ancient Mahomedan Kingdoms of the Deccan.

194. Minor Vernaculars of the State.

Eight other languages are included in Group A of Imperial Table X among vernaculars of the State. The names and number of persons returned against each of them are shown in the marginal Table. Seven of these languages are classed as Gipsy Dialects in Sub-Table I (*a*), and, according to the Linguistic survey, as dialects of Gujarati in Subsidiary Table I (*b*). Dr. Grierson dismisses the so-called Gipsy languages of India in his article in the new edition of the *Imperial Gazetteer*, with the remark that some of them are mere thieves' jargons, others are hybrids developed in journeys from place to place, and some real dialects of well-known languages. But he speaks of Labhani, spoken by the Labhanas or Banjaras, the great carrying tribe of Central and Western India as an offshoot of Rajasthani.* The number of persons speaking Lambadi has increased nearly 100 per cent. since 1901 when it was according to Subsidiary Table I, a little over 120,000. The Lambadi speakers are found in Warangal, Nalgonda and Gulbarga. The word Lambadi, as used at the present Census, includes Lamani or Banjari, which was returned as their mother-tongue at the 1901 Census by 92,209 persons. At that Census, speakers of Lambadi were enumerated in Warangal, Medak and Mahbubnagar—all Telingana districts—while the speakers of Lamani or Banjari, in the Marthwara districts, numbered several thousands. At the present Census Lambadi speakers were enumerated in all districts. Subsidiary Table III gives the strength of the Lambadi tribe as 142,044. The difference between that number and the number of speakers of the Lambadi language, is probably due to the fact that the Lambadis are practically a sub-tribe of a large tribe, called Korvas in the last Census Report, and that the language is spoken by other sub-tribes also. At the 1901 Census, the number of Lambadis and Lamanas together exceeded the number of persons speaking the languages bearing these names. Next to Lambadi in importance, among the minor vernaculars of the State, is Gondi which is spoken by over 70,000 persons. Here, again, we find a lack of correspondence between the strength of the Gond tribe and the number of persons speaking the Gondi language. Here, however, the difference is in favour of the

Bhili	7,012
Gondi	73,939
Kaikadi	2,763
Kolhati	262
Lambadi	237,899
Pardhi	834
Wadarai	1,048
Yerukala	7,398

* *Imperial Gazetteer*, Vol. I, page 368.

tribe. Over 50,000 Gonds speak some language which is not Gondi. At the last Census, on the other hand, there were more speakers of Gondi than Gonds. The Gonds have, like other Animistic tribes, been adopting Hindu gods, but it would be interesting to know whether they change their language also. Gondi is officially classified as a language intermediate between Malayalam and Telugu It has one dialect, Koya, spoken by about 8,000 persons principally in Warangal The case of Bhili, in respect of the relation of the number of the tribe to the number of speakers of the language, is similar to that of Gondi. Yerukala or Erkala, which is a dialect of Tamil, is spoken by over 7,000 persons though the tribe of that name numbers only 2,013. There are very few persons who speak this language in Marathwara, and in Telingana there are only three districts in which their number exceeds 1,000. These are Warangal, Atrafibalda and Nalgonda. The other minor vernaculars of the State do not call for notice.

195. Vernaculars of India Foreign to the States.

The twelve major and minor vernaculars of the State, referred to in the last paragraph, comprise 13,219,118 inhabitants of these territories, leaving 155,558 to be accounted for otherwise. Of this latter, 140,592 speak vernaculars of India. The main distribution of this group—Group A (II) of Imperial Table X—is outlined in the marginal Table. The other vernaculars have less than 1,000 speakers each. Considerably more than a third of the total number of persons who speak vernaculars of India foreign to the State, speak Rajasthani.

Rajasthani	50,208
Western Hindi	37,814
Tamil	25,027
Gujarati	14,984
Eastern Hindi	6,609
Punjabi	3,414

The dialect of Rajasthani which practically all of them speak, is Marwari. Only about 600 persons returned some other dialect of Rajasthani, such as Rajputi, Rangri and Bikaneri, as their mother-tongue. The speakers of Marwari are found in the largest numbers in the City and in the Marathwara districts, especially in Aurangabad, Parbhani and Bhir. They do not seem to have acquired a hold on the Telingana districts. Western Hindi figures in Imperial Table X, both as a vernacular of the State and as an Indian vernacular foreign to the State. Through its dialect, Urdu, it is a vernacular of the State. Its other dialects are not among the languages recognised as indigenous to these Dominions. Of these latter Hindustani and Hindi spoken by 24,270 and 12,261 persons respectively are the most important. Urdu is the Persianised form of Hindustani and Hindi is a Sanskritised form of the same language. Hindustani itself is that dialect of Western Hindi whose home is the Upper Gangetic Doab, in the country round Meerut. The number of persons who returned Hindustani as their vernacular at the present Census, is about eight times as many as those in 1901. Hindi speakers on the other hand have decreased considerably during the decade. The Hindustanis are found principally in Aurangabad and the speakers of Hindi in Hyderabad City. The Tamil-speaking population in the State has received a set-back during the decade. Their total number at the 1901 Census was 27,475. At the present Census, they number 25,027. They have rather improved their position in Hyderabad City, where their number has increased from 17,718 in 1901 to 18,885. But they have lost ground in the districts. The number of those who have Gujarati for their mother-tongue is 14,984. In Subsidiary Table I many of the minor languages spoken in the State, including Lambadi, are classed as dialects of Gujarati, which is thus made to show an aggregate of over 260,000 speakers. There has been some decrease in the number of the Gujarati-speaking population during the decade, but it is probably temporary. Eastern Hindi, which is another name for Pardesi, had only 136 speakers in 1901 but at the present Census it has been returned by 6,609 persons, mostly residents of the Aurangabad district. It is hard to believe that some of these variations represent anything more than differences of nomenclature.

196. Non-Indian Languages.

The total number of persons in the State, who speak non-Indian languages is 14,966. Arabic and English account for 14,526 of them. Arabic is spoken by 5,683 persons, about 50 per cent. of them being residents of Hyderabad City. English is spoken by 8,843 persons, of whom 7,219 were enumerated in the Capital City. Of the other languages, Persian is spoken by 256 persons. There has been a considerable falling off in the number of speakers of non-Indian Asiatic languages since 1901.

197. General Observations.

There is no evidence that, as amongst the four main languages of the State, any one is displacing any other. Languages like Telugu, Marathi, Canarese and Urdu are not merely convenient means of communicating with one's neighbours, but embody the religious, historical and æsthetic traditions of large communities. A Marathi-speaking man might learn Telugu or Kanarese, Urdu or English, as a convenience but it is extremely unlikely that he will adopt any of them as his mother-tongue. Mother-tongue literally is the language of the mother. And in India, and specially among Hindus, intermarriages between persons speaking different languages are extremely infrequent. If there is any interchange of languages in the State, it can only be among the tribes speaking rude dialects which vary from district to district. On the whole, all the available evidence shows that the number of persons speaking one of the main languages tends to increase or decrease with the ethnic group to which they belong. Although in the past, many aboriginal tribes adopted Aryan languages, no such movement is perceptible, at the present day, except perhaps among the Animistic tribes.

198. Hyderabad City.

The marginal table gives the distribution according to language of the population of Hyderabad City. The Urdu and Telugu elements have steadily increased, and are the principal components of the city population. Of the rest, the Tamils have steadily improved their position, but the Marathi-speaking section has decreased. As regards Rajasthani and Hindi, it is unsafe to draw any conclusion as their connotation has varied from time to time. The variations in the number of persons speaking English as their vernacular call for no remark.

Language.	1911.	1901.	1891.
Urdu	244,709	213,092	194,930
Telugu	185,318	169,680	158,889
Tamil	18,885	17,718	15,426
Marathi	15,699	18,563	16,587
Rajasthani ...	9,583	9,482	...
Western Hindi ...	8,281	2,360	8,808
English	7,219	6,562	7,378

SUBSIDIARY TABLE I.—Distribution of Total Population by Language.

(a)—*According to Census.*

Language.	Total Number of Speakers. 1911.	1912	Number per mille of Population of State in 1911.	Where chiefly spoken (District or Natural Division).
1	2	3	4	5
Bhili	7,012	2,836	1	Aurangabad.
Kanarese	1,680,005	1,562,022	126	Gulbarga, Raichur, Bidar.
Eastern Hindi	6,609	136	......	
Pardesi	6,609	136	......	Aurangabad.
Gipsy Languages	248,299	124,822	18	
Lambadi	237,899	120,894	18	Warangal, Nalgonda, Gulbarga.
Kaikadi	2,763	2,380	......	Adilabad, Bhir.
Waddari	1,048	940	......	Atrafibalda, Bhir.
Minor Gipsy Dialects	1,589	608	......	
Gondi	73,939	75,564	6	
Gondi	65,896	59,669	5	Adilabad, Warangal.
Koya	8,043	15,895	1	Warangal.
Gujarati	15,060	16,253	1	
Gujarati	13,661	15,064	1	Hyderabad City, Aurangabad, Gulbarga, Parbhani.
Minor Gujarati Dialects	1,399	1,189	......	Hyderabad City, Warangal, Gulbarga.
Marathi	3,498,763	2,898,738	261	
Marathi	3,496,200	2,895,864	261	Marathwara, Adilabad.
Are	2,378	1,464	......	Karimnagar.
Minor Marathi Dialects	185	1,410	......	
Panjabi	3,414	2,659	......	Hyderabad City.
Rajasthani	50,208	59,620	4	
Marwari	49,547	57,777	4	Hyderabad City, Aurangabad, Parbhani.
Minor Rajasthani Dialects... ...	661	1,843	......	
Tamil	32,425	34,396	3	
Tamil	25,027	27,475	2	Hyderabad City.
Yerkala	7,398	6,921	1	Warangal, Atrafibalda, Nalgonda.
Telugu	6,367,578	5,148,056	476	Telingana, Raichur, Bidar, Gulbarga.
Western Hindi	1,379,436	1,191,047	108	
Urdu	1,341,622	1,158,490	100	Throughout the State.
Hindustani	24,280	3,166	2	Aurangabad.
Hindi	12,261	28,767	1	Hyderabad City.
Minor Dialects	1,273	624	......	
Other Indian Languages	1,962	4,492	......	
Pashto	786	1,565	......	Hyderabad City.
Minor Indian Languages	1,176	2,927	......	Do.
Asiatic Languages	5,975	10,367	......	
Arabic	5,683	9,937	......	Do
Minor Asiatic Languages	292	450	......	Do.
European Languages	3,989	8,051	1	
English	3,843	7,907	1	Do.
Minor European Languages ...	146	144	......	Do.
African Languages (Somali) ...	2	......	......	Do.

SUBSIDIARY TABLE I.—Distribution of Total Population by Language.

(b)—*According to Linguistic Survey.*

Family.	Sub-Family.	Branch.	Sub-Branch.	Group.	Language.	Dialect.	Total Number of Speakers.	Number per mille of Population of State.	Where chiefly spoken (District or Natural Division.)
1	2	3	4	5	6	7	8	9	10
Tibeto-Chinese.	Tibeto-Burman	Assam Burmese	....	Burma	Burmese ..	....	1	..	
Dravidian ..	....	....	....	Dravida	Tamil ..	....	32,495	3	
					Tamil ..	....	25,027	2	Hyderabad City.
						Yerukala ..	7,398	1	Warangal, Atrafi-balda, Nalgonda.
					Kanarese ..	....	1,680,005	126	Gulbarga, Raichur Bidar.
					Malayalam ..	....	243	..	Hyderabad City.
				Intermediate	Gondi ..	....	73,939	6	
					Gondi ..	....	65,896	5	Adilabad, Warangal.
						Koya ..	8,043	1	Warangal.
				Andhra	Telugu ..	....	6,267,578	476	Telingana, Raichur Bidar, Gulbarga.
Indo-European.	Aryan ..	Indian ..	Non-Sanskritic.	Shina Khowa ..	Kashmiri ..	....	4	..	
			Sanskritic ..	Sanskrit ..	Sanskrit ..	....	5	..	
				North-Western.	Sindhi ..	....	307	..	
						Kachchi ..	307	..	
				Southern	Marathi ..	....	3,498,763	261	
					Marathi ..	....	3,496,200	261	Marathawara, Adilabad.
						Agari ..	2	..	
						Are ..	2,878	..	Karimnagar.
						Dhangari ..	11	..	
						Goanese ..	86	..	
						Kathodi ..	42	..	
						Koli ..	3	..	
						Konkani ..	29	..	
						Panchali ..	12	..	
				Eastern	Oriya ..	....	265	..	
					Bengali ..	....	194	..	
					Bihari ..	....	142	..	
				Mediate	Eastern-Hindi..	....	6,609	..	
						Pardesi ..	6,609	..	Aurangabad.
				Western	Western Hindi.	....	1,279,436	108	
						Bondili ..	103	..	
						Brajbhasha ..	287	..	
						Hindi ..	12,261	1	Hyderabad City.
						Hindustani ..	24,270	2	Aurangabad.
						Lodhi ..	49	..	
						Rathora ..	884	..	
						Urdu ..	1,341,622	100	Throughout the State.
Indo-European.	Aryan ..	Indian ..	Sanskritic ..	Western ..	Rajasthani ..	....	50,206	..	
						Bikaneri ..	18	..	
						Marwari ..	49,547	4	Hyderabad City, Aurangabad, Parbhan.
						Rajputi ..	393	..	
						Rangri ..	255	..	
					Gujarati ..	....	265,871	20	
					Do. ..	....	13,661	1	Hyderabad City, Aurangabad, Parbhani.
						Bhili ..	7,012	1	Aurangabad.
						Beldari ..	30	..	
						Bohari ..	17	..	
						Ghisadi ..	371	..	
						Jain ..	85	..	
						Kotari ..	42	..	
						Kaikadi ..	2,768	..	
						Kathiawadi ..	9	..	
						Kayashti ..	76	..	
						Khatri ..	396	..	
						Kolhati ..	262	..	
						Lambadi ..	237,899	18	Warangal, Nalgonda, Gulbarga.
						Nagari ..	288	..	
						Pardhi ..	384	..	
						Parsi ..	75	..	
						Patkari ..	142	..	
						Rangri ..	48	..	
						Sorathi ..	289	..	
						Thakori ..	79	..	
						Waddari ..	1,048	..	
					Panjabi ..	....	3,414	..	Hyderabad City.
				Western Sub...	Western Punjabi.	....	15	..	
						Multani ..	4	..	
						Peshwari ..	11	..	
		Erasian ..	....	Eastern ..	Pashto ..	....	786	..	Hyderabad City.
				Western ..	Persian ..	....	256	..	Do.
Semitic ..	....	....	....	....	Arabic ..	....	5,688	..	Do.
Hamitic ..	....	....	....	....	Somali ..	....	2	..	Do.
Mongolian ..	....	....	....	Japanese ..	Japanese ..	....	3	..	
				Ural, Altaic ..	Turkish ..	....	28	..	
Indo-European.	....	....	....	Teutonic ..	English ..	....	6,848	1	Hyderabad City.
					Dutch ..	....	1	..	
					German ..	....	18	..	Do.
				Celtic ..	Irish ..	....	1	..	Do.
				Romanic ..	Portuguese ..	....	70	..	Do.
					French ..	....	18	..	Do.
					Italian ..	....	36	..	Do.
				Balto Slavonic.	Russian ..	....	2	..	Do.

SUBSIDIARY TABLE II.—Distribution by language of the Population of each District.

District and Natural Division.	Number per 10,000 of population speaking							
	Urdu.	Telugu.	Marathi.	Canarese.	Goudi.	Lambadi.	Other State languages.	All other languages.
1	2	3	4	5	6	7	8	9
State ...	1,003	4,761	2,616	1,256	55	178	14	117
Telingana ...	892	8,268	324	55	110	244	12	95
Hyderabad City ...	4,888	3,702	318	46	...	2	8	1,041
Atrafibalda ...	1,167	7,716	642	192	...	204	29	50
Warangal ...	459	8,632	76	...	175	619	23	26
Karimnagar ...	338	9,490	86	...	4	70	6	6
Adilabad ...	457	6,134	2,172	25	924	225	13	50
Medak ...	776	9,089	39	20	2	61	5	18
Nizamabad ...	725	8,752	147	168	...	190	4	19
Mahbubnagar ...	666	8,861	56	165	...	232	18	7
Nalgonda ...	410	9,188	19	...	...	414	11	8
Marathwara ...	1,115	1,215	4,934	2,471	...	111	17	137
Aurangabad ...	1,818	44	7,948	8	...	138	77	467
Bhir ...	713	29	8,990	20	...	69	18	161
Nander ...	1,058	1,880	6,287	541	3	135	6	90
Parbhani...	927	119	8,636	11	...	100	8	199
Gulbarga ...	1,460	1,996	328	5,918	...	232	5	60
Osmanabad ...	941	61	8,580	354	...	24	10	80
Raichur ...	780	2,834	38	6,278	...	50	2	28
Bidar ...	1,456	1,621	3,718	3,073	...	78	10	49

SUBSIDIARY TABLE III.—Comparison of Caste and Language Tables.

Tribe.	Strength of tribe (Table XIII).	Number speaking tribal language (Table X).
Bhili ...	9,921	7,012
Gondi ...	124,341	73,939
Lambadi ...	142,044	237,899
Erkala ...	2,013	7,398

Chapter X.

INFIRMITIES.

199. Comparison with previous Censuses.

The marginal Table gives a comparative view of the statistics of the four infirmities for which they have been collected since 1881. There was a decrease in the total for all infirmities in 1891, but the figures for 1901 showed a phenomenal fall from those of the previous Census. This time the figures bear a more intelligible relation to those of 1881 and 1891 than to those of 1901. Taking the State as a whole, the total number of persons afflicted shows a very remarkable increase over the figures of the last Census. In 1901 the total of afflicted was 2,635, whereas the number at this Census is 26,831 (exclusive of those enumerated under more than one head) or over ten times as many as in 1901. The increase occurs in respect not only of one infirmity but of all infirmities. The number of insanes and deaf-mutes is more than seven times, that of blind over twelve times, and that of lepers over eleven times as many as in 1901. Some increase in the number of persons afflicted was to be expected in sympathy with the growth of population during the last decade. But a 20 per cent. increase of population cannot be held to account sufficiently for an one thousand per cent. increase in the number of persons suffering from the infirmities included in the Census. The number of the immigrant population in 1911 was less by about 10 per cent. than in 1901, and there is otherwise no reason to refer the extraordinary rise in the number of the afflicted to that source. There has been no change in the instructions issued to enumerators which may account for it. Some part of the increase is doubtless due to the wearing away of the shyness of the people in giving the information sought for by the enumerators. The fact that the increase in the number of female figures is strikingly larger than in the case of the male, is conclusive testimony to the gradual disappearance of the attitude of suspicion of the objects of the Census. The number of males afflicted was nine times and that of the females, twelve times higher than at the previous Census. Other causes too might have contributed to the increase to some extent, such as the relatively smaller mortality, owing to more favourable seasons. The use of the special infirmity slip in place of the ordinary one used on previous occasions, may have also facilitated the compilation of statistics. When all is said, however, the increase is too considerable to be regarded as satisfactorily explained by all the abovementioned causes put together. It seems less rash to assume that the statistics of the Census of 1901, so far as infirmities were concerned, were much below the mark than to seek to find an explanation for a miraculous increase on the basis of those figures.

Total afflicted.

Infirmity.	1881.	1891.	1901.	1911.
Insane ...	2,295	1,584	334	2,560
Deaf-mute ...	3,873	4,419	627	4,431
Blind	11,723	10,632	1,344	16,263
Leper	2,989	2,977	330	3,785
Total ...	20,880	19,612	2,635	27,002

200. Infirmities by Natural Division.

Subsidiary Table I gives the number of persons afflicted per 100,000 of the population at each of the last four Censuses in each Natural Division and district. The marginal Table abstracted therefrom shows the relative incidence of the afflictions in the two Natural Divisions. Taking all four infirmities together, there is little to choose between the two Natural Divisions. In both of them the incidence is about 50 for every 10,000 persons. The strikingly lower proportion of insanes in Marathwara is

Infirmities.	Telingana.	Marathwara.
Insane	30	9
Deaf-mute	38	29
Blind	109	134
Lepers	28	27
Total ...	50	50

made up by the higher proportion of the blind, so that in one way or another Nature would seem to deal with the population of each of the two Divisions with even-handed severity.

201. Infirmities by Race and Religion.

There are only two communities in the State, whose aggregates warrant a statistical comparison, namely, the Hindu and the Mahomedan. Animists are numerically the next most important. Imperial Table XII-A gives the statistics for selected castes, tribes or races. The figures in the marginal table are taken from it. The Hindu population is about eight times as large as the Moslem and over forty times as large as the Animists. Examining the figures in the light of these ratios, the Mahomedans are better off than the Hindus in respect of all infirmities except insanity. This is also true of the Animists, though the reasons for the superiority of these two communities are of a radically opposite character. The Mahomedan in Hyderabad enjoys a material and social position higher than the Hindu's. The Animist, on the other hand, leads a life of primitive simplicity and does not require to toil in the fields or at the forge to supply himself with his few elementary needs. He lives in the open air and is free from all worrying cares about rains and crops, the Sowcar and the Sircar. The term, Hindu, includes some higher castes who enjoy the some social advantages as the Mahomedans and also some castes which are not far removed from the natural simplicity of the Animist. But the mass of the Hindu population consists of toilers, and as such is more exposed than others to infirmities which find their victims most readily among those enervated by excessive toil.

Infirmities.	Hindu.	Musalman.	Animists.
Insanes	2,180	332	41
Deaf-Mute... ...	3,931	382	94
Blind	14,226	1,165	207
Lepers	3,378	311	56

202. Distribution by Sex.

The proportion of females to males under all heads excepting leprosy, is over 60 per cent. The only infirmity whose incidence is nearly equal on both the sexes is blindness. In respect of the other three, making allowance for the greater tendency to concealment, women seem to enjoy a certain appreciable amount of natural immunity as compared with men, owing, it may be, to their more protected lives or even to greater powers of resistance inherent in their constitution. The proportion of female sufferers is lowest in the case of leprosy, clearly due to a considerable extent to greater motives for concealment. In regard to deaf-mutism, where there is no difficulty of diagnosis and which is not easily concealed, the proportion between the sexes is less considerable. The test of insanity necessarily varies according to the standard of sanity in a given community, and where women are held to be naturally of a lower order of intelligence than men, only extreme cases of deviation from the normal are likely to be reported as definitely coming under the category of insanity. It should also be borne in mind that there is always a greater likelihood in India of mental afflictions in the case of women being attributed to "possession" rather than to insanity.

Infirmities.	Males.	Females.	Females per 1,000 males.
Insane	1,547	1,013	655
Deaf-Mute ...	2,522	1,899	752
Blind	8,287	7,976	962
Lepers	2,762	996	361

203. Distribution by Age.

Imperial Table XXII, Part I, gives details of distribution by age of the afflicted population and for each infirmity. There are some general features of these figures which call for remark. Up to the age of 10 the numbers always tend to be smaller than they may be expected to be. The explanation is that parents will not give up the hope and expectation of finding a cure for the infirmities of their offspring until the failure of years leaves them absolutely without an excuse wherewith to satisfy even their own minds. In the case of girls the marriageable age marks the limit up to which parents will continue to exercise their own, and to impose upon, the credulity of others. Another noteworthy feature of these statistics is that the figures rise and fall with amusing regularity in the first half and the second half of each successive decade. It would almost seem as if there was a feeling of obligation in the popular mind to observe a strict veracity to the decade while it was permissible to exercise some discretion as to units. Men and women prefer to be on the wrong side of forty, for instance, to being on the right side of fifty, so long as the claims of conscience are satisfied by their admitting the number of actual decades that they have spent on earth. This point has been discussed in the Chapter on the age distribution of the population. The largest number of afflicted persons in one age-period occurs between 30 and 35 for both sexes. The next worst period is 40-45 for men and 60-65 for women.

204. Insanity.

Imperial Table XII, Part II, gives the distributon by administrative Divisions and districts, while Subsidiary Table I gives the proportions of people afflicted for every 100,000 of the population by Natural Divisions and districts. Blindness claims over 60 per-cent. of the total afflicted in the Nizam's Dominions. The largest proportion of insanes is found in Hyderabad City which has 56 for every 10,000 inhabitants. This figure, however, includes 81 inmates of the Lunatic Asylum attached to the Central Jail who are not natives of the City and whose sojourn within its limits is wholly involuntary. If these are excluded, as is but fair, the City's actual proportien falls to 41 per 100,000 inhabitants. The map of these Dominions printed below indicates the proportion of insanes to the total population of each district.

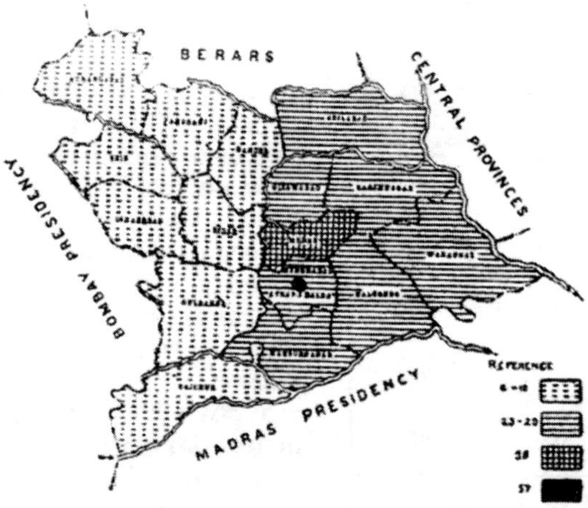

Medak district shows the next highest proportion 43. The lowest afflicted among Telingana districts is Adilabad, which has 23 insanes to each 10,000 of its population, while the highest in Marathwara is only 12·5 for Gulbarga. In fact, insanity is very much at a discount in the Marathwara districts. The use of narcotic drugs and spirits is the principal cause of insanity in the Nizam's Dominions and it may be that they are less in fashion in Marathwara than in Telingana.

Another fact worthy of note is the high proportion of female to male insanes in Telingana as compared with Marathwara. In Marathwara the proportion of female usually is 50 per cent., while in Telingana it is over 71 per cent. of that of male lunatics. More than one district in Telingana has proportionately more female insanes than males. Warangal has 25 male and 27 female insanes, and Mahbubnagar 23 male and 24 female insanes for every 100,000 of their populations. It is unprofitable to speculate as to the causes of these variations. The statistics recorded in the Tables pertaining to this Chapter are the least reliable of those compiled in respect of infirmities, owing partly to the difficulties in the way of accurate diagnosis, and partly to intentional concealment. Both these causes affect the statistics of insanes more than those of any other infirmity included in the Census returns.

205. Distribution by Age.

Subsidiary Table II, gives the distribution of the afflicted population, the statistics of which are to be found in Imperial Table XII, Part I, according to age-periods. The real significance of this distribution can be gathered only in the light of the observations offered in the Chapter on Age. Here it is sufficient to mention that the age-periods 10-15 shows the largest number of lunatics of both sexes. With the exception of a brief interval between the ages of 35 and 40, the proportion is maintained at a high figure till the age of 45 when there is a sudden drop to less than 50 per cent. of the figure for the immediately preceding age-period. Though there is a rather noticeable rise in the age-period 50-55, very few lunatics would seem to live beyond the age of 50. The largest proportion of male insanes occurs between the ages of 25 and 30, and indeed the period between 20 and 35 would seem to be fraught with much peril for the male intellect. This is perhaps due to the fact that it is about the most stressful period of a man's life. It is significant that, for women, the period of greatest risk from insanity is between 10 and 20. The strain of early marriage and maternity is clearly visible in these figures.

206. Distribution by Caste.

Subsidiary Table IV gives the proportion of the afflicted in selected castes, the actual figures are to be found in Imperial Table XII-A. The Sayyeds among Mahomedans and the Telagas and the Komatis among Hindus have the largest proportion of female insanes, namely 25, 26 and 25 respectively for every 100,000 persons of each caste, while the Animistic Lambaba, the Hindu Maratha, Koly, Dhangar and Lingayat have the least, their proportions being 3, 4, 5, 7 and 9 respectively. The Mahar and the Brahman at either end of the social scale, have the same number, 17, of female insanes, though as regards male insanes, the Brahman with 50 per 100,000 persons is second only to the Komati with his 57 per 100,000, while the Mahar, with 17, is fifth best in the list being preceded by the Animistic Gond with 6, the Hindu Maratha with 7, the Hindu Dhangar with 9, and the Lingayat with 15 respectively. Taking men and women together the Maratha and the Dhangar would seem to be the least liable to have their mental equilibrium upset. The Brahman's excessive ceremonialism, the Komati's abnormal concentration on his Cash-box and the Sayyed's "scroll and sanctities" may be held to account for their high proportion of male and female insanes, but there is no such pre-occupation to explain the same phenomenon as regards the Goundla, the Kapu, the Madiga and the Mang. The truth seems to be that accidental causes, such as the zeal and capacity of enumerators, have much to do with the high or low proportion of the afflicted in any area or caste in the present state of public sentiment in regard to the treatment of the insane.

207. Deaf-Mutism.

The reasons adduced for distrusting the figures of the Census of 1901 for the totals of all the four infirmities, apply to each of them. They apply with special force to deaf-mutism which is a congenital defect. Persons suffering from it are short-lived. The proportion of such persons to the total number living at each age-period should, therefore, show a steady decline. The number of deaf-mutes, male and female enumerated in the present Census, is 4,421. In the 1901 Census it was only 627. The number of deaf-mutes under the age of 10 in the present Census is 856 so that we have 3,565 additional afflicted to be accounted for otherwise than by birth in the State. The actual number of deaf-mutes under 10 is very probably much higher, owing to the reluctance, already alluded to, of parents to return young children as afflicted with an incurable malady. Even assuming that all the 627 deaf-mutes enumerated at the 1901 Census were still living, where did the remaining 2,938 over 10 years come from? There is nothing to show that the larger number of them were immigrants. It follows that the increase in the numbers is to a great extent due to the figures for 1901 being much below the then actual deaf-mute population of the State. In any case, there is good reason to think that the enumeration at the present Census of this class of afflicted persons, as of other classes, has been more satisfactory than at any previous Census.

208. Distribution by Natural Divisions and Districts.

The subjoined map shows the proportion of deaf-mutes to the total population of each district. Telingana has a larger proportion of deaf-mutes than Marathwara, the figures being 38 and 29 per 10,000 of the population respectively. Mahbubnagar has 56, Warangal 51, Nalgonda 43 and Medak 37. In Marathwara, Nander shows the highest proportion of deaf-mutism (38) and is followed by Bidar (36) and Gulbarga (35). Hyderabad City in Telingana and Aurangabad in Marathwara have the least number of deaf-mutes, 16 and 15 per 10,000 persons:—

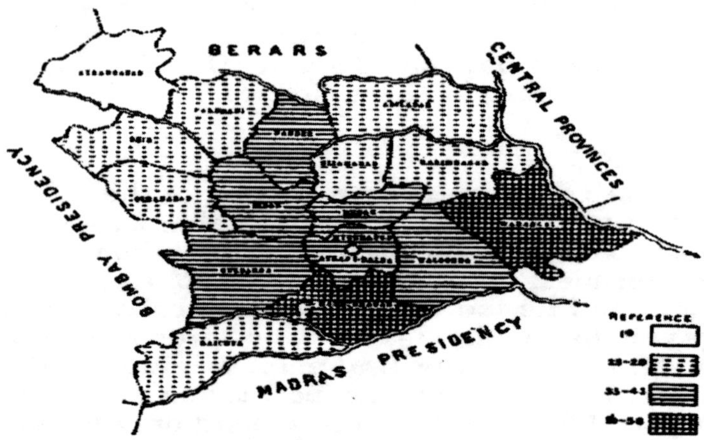

209. Distribution by Creeds and Castes and Sex.

Mahomedans are somewhat less afflicted with this infirmity than Hindus, the actual numbers being 382 and 3,931 respectively, whereas the ratio of Mahomedans to Hindus is less than 1 : 9. The Komatis are, again, unenviably prominent, the proportion of deaf-mutes among them, 58 to 100,000 persons, being the highest in the Nizam's Dominions. The Telagas come next with 42. Amongst Mahomedans, the Shaiks show the highest proportion, 30 per 100,000 persons. If the female figures are excluded, the melancholy predominance of these castes in respect of this infirmity, is still further emphasized. The Komati has 67, the Telagas 53, and the Shaiks 37 deaf-mutes to every 100,000 males.

210. Insanity and Deaf-mutism.

The Komati amongst the Hindus and the Shaik amongst the Mahomedans have also the largest number of male insanes. The coincidence is noteworthy as lending support to the fact that cretinism and deaf-mutism have often been found in close association. In the All-India Census Report for 1901, the suggestion was thrown out that deaf-mutism, cretinism and goitre may be due to the injurious properties of the water of certain rivers, and that their distribution was perhaps more a matter of locality than of class. The figures for Hyderabad do not support such exclusive reliance on locality as the sole-cause of the infirmity. We have seen above that the Komatis head the list among the castes of Hyderabad, both as regards insanity and deaf-mutism. The districts of Mahbubnagar and Warangal which have the largest porportion of deaf-mutes, have by no means the largest proportion of insanes.

211. Blindness.

Blindness is by far the most common of the four infirmities. It is responsible for more than 60 per cent. of the total afflicted from all causes. For one thing, total blindness is not an infirmity which admits of doubt or concealment. Then,again,it appeals to the sympathy of neighbours and does not excite feelings of loathing. Many persons who would be most reluctant to state that their children or the women of their family were afflicted with insanity or leprosy, would readily admit that they were blind, either wholly or partially. In fact, the tendency often is to exaggerate any markedly defective eye-sight into total blindness. As a matter of actual fact also, blindness is far more common than any of the other infirmities. The glare of the summer sun, the use of smoky wood-fuel in ill-ventilated kitchens, and general carelessness and neglect arising from the ignorance and poverty of the mass of the population, have a most injurious effect on its eye-sight. The fact that this is the one infirmity where the number of women sufferers are nearly equal with, and in some districts and castes actually more than, that of men, points to the main causes being insanitary dwellings and ignorance. The subjoined map shows the proportion of the blind in each district:—

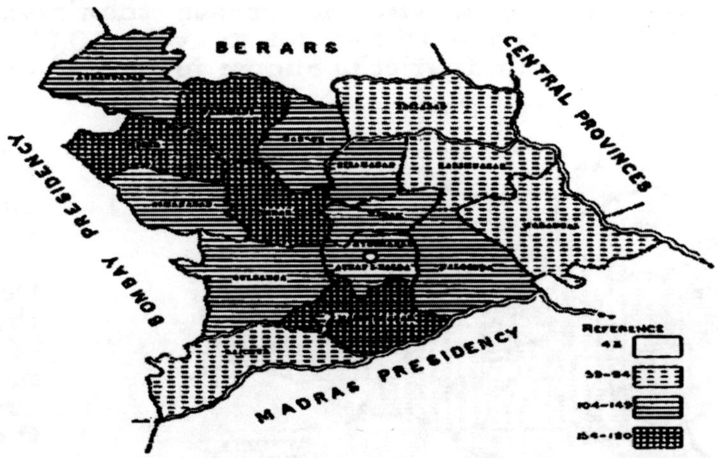

As observed already, Marathwara suffers more from blindness than Telingana, though the two districts which have the highest proportion of the blind in the Nizam's Dominions lie in either Natural Division. Parbhani, in Marathwara, has 190 and Mahbubnagar, in Telingana, 180 blind per 10,000 persons. It is remarkable that in both these districts the proportion of blind females is in excess of that of blind males. In Parbhani, the figures are 191 and 188, and in Mahbubnagar, 181 and 186 respectively for 10,000 of each sex. Bidar in Marathwara comes third with 178 for both sexes, 179 for males and 177 for females. The fourth place is taken by Bhir, also in Marathwara. Hyderabad City has the fewest blind in the State, the proportion being 43 per 10,000 persons. Perhaps, the restful prospect afforded by the forest covered tracts of Telingana are more favourable to the preservation of the people's eye-sight than the bleak open spaces of Marathwara. Raichur, in Marathwara, has a remarkably low proportion of blind, next only to that of Hyderabad City.

212. Distribution by Caste.

The Komati caste heads the list in respect of this infirmity also. Its proportion is 264 males and 202 females per 100,000 persons. The next most afflicted class is the Golla, with 145 males and 160 females, and the third on the list is the Brahmin, with 152 males and 123 females. The Maratha, who is but little affected by insanity and deaf-mutism, has a high proportion of persons whose eye-sight is more or less badly affected. The proportion is 137 for males and 160 for females. The Koli has 116 blind males and 137 females per 100,000. Among the poorer castes women suffer more than men from this infirmity, a clear proof that it is closely connected with hard toil. All the three Mahomedan sects for which statistics are given, have a very low incidence of blindness.

213. Comparison with previous Censuses.

According to the figures given in the Census Report, the proportions of blind to every 100,000 persons in the State were, in 1881, 119, in 1891, 92, in 1901, 12 as against 122 in 1911. As already remarked, however, the figures for 1901, are palpably unreliable. The figures for Hyderabad City alone afford a somewhat firm basis of comparison, and they show that there has been a notable improvement due no doubt to the growing popularity of modern methods of treatment. This is also brought out by a comparison of the figures for 1881, which would seem to be fairly reliable, with those of the current Census. The increase of population in the thirty years has been 35 per cent. but the number of blind is only 38 per cent. more than that in 1881. The almost rhythmic regularity with which the figures rise at the age periods of 30-35, 40-45, 50-55, and 60-65, and fall in the second half of each of the decades, has already been noticed. After the age of 30 the number of blind women tends at almost every age-period to exceed the number of blind men. One reason, no doubt, is that eyesight is more neglected in the case of women than in that of men.

214. Lepers.

The first thing which attracts attention in the statistics of leprosy is that there are far fewer women afflicted with the disease than men. The proportion for the whole State is 41 males and 15 females to every 10,000 of the population. The proportion of lepers in each district is shown in the following map :—

This disparity in the liability of the two sexes to this disease is borne out by the figures of the previous Hyderabad Censuses as also by those of other parts of India. Concealment may account to some extent for it, but there would seem to be some intrinsic cause making the gentler sex more resistant to this disease.

215. Distribution by Natural Divisions and Districts.

The average for Telingana is higher than for Marathwara, the proportions being 30 and 27 in every 10,000 of the population respectively. Osmanabad in Marathwara, Medak and Nizamabad in Telingana have the highest averages in the Dominions, Nizamabad having the additional distinction of having the largest proportion of women lepers.

216. Distribution by Castes.

Amongst Hindu castes the Mutrasi comes first with 75 male and 20 female lepers, though the Komati is an easy second with 70 male lepers and 19 female lepers, to every 10,000 of the population. This caste would seem to merit the attention of students of pathology as well as of sociology for its unenviable predominance in every department of infirmity. The Munnur caste has 65 male and 18 female lepers to every 10,000 persons, and is second in order of precedence. The Madiga and the Mang, the Mahar, the Telaga, the Koli and the Goundla have also high averages. The Shaik, among Mahomedans, has the highest average, but it is much lower than that of the above mentioned Hindu castes. Among the Hindus, the Lingayath has the lowest proportion of persons suffering from this infirmity, and next to him comes the Brahmin. The largest proportion of lepers occurs at the age-period 40-45, and the majority are persons past 30.

SUBSIDIARY TABLE I.—Number afflicted per 100,000 of the Population at each of the last four Censuses.

District and Natural Division.	Insane.								Deaf-Mute.							
	Male.				Female.				Male.				Female.			
	1911	1901	1891	1881	1911	1901	1891	1881	1911	1901	1891	1881	1911	1901	1891	1881
1	2	3	4	5	6	7	8	9	10	11	12	13	14	15	16	17
State	23	4	18	30	15	2	10	16	37	7	46	49	29	4	30	29
Telingana	34	6	24	36	25	2	15	19	43	6	59	52	32	3	37	31
Hyderabad City...	82	49	43	84	30	13	11	9	18	14	38	59	15	6	30	32
Atrafibalda	26	1	25	33	21	...	18	17	35	...	62	57	36	2	40	29
Warangal	25	5	24	41	27	...	17	20	55	7	71	58	47	5	48	34
Karimnagar	34	2	20	40	24	1	13	28	35	2	52	58	21	2	35	30
Adilabad	27	2	25	7	19	2	14	8	35	8	33	25	24	3	29	19
Medak	48	3	32	38	33	3	16	25	45	6	78	59	29	2	61	25
Nizamabad	27	4	24	32	22	3	16	12	31	4	27	31	27	4	16	16
Mahbubnagar	23	1	13	38	24	1	12	21	68	12	69	89	48	...	44	69
Nalgonda	30	...	24	40	33	...	14	19	51	1	64	32	35	1	38	15
Marathwara	12	2	12	27	6	1	6	15	31	10	36	50	26	5	24	30
Aurangabad	7	2	17	36	4	1	5	19	15	1	42	93	16	4	23	53
Bhir	12	2	10	37	6	1	7	22	28	1	48	119	20	7	25	69
Nander	13	3	13	28	7	3	7	14	40	1	40	41	35	6	31	23
Parbhani	10	4	13	32	4	...	5	22	30	12	32	26	23	4	22	13
Gulbarga	15	2	9	22	10	2	5	18	36	7	34	39	34	5	22	18
Osmanabad	9	2	24	22	3	...	4	11	32	13	33	35	26	5	22	22
Raichur	9	...	10	7	4	...	6	6	29	13	33	18	21	14	24	12
Bidar	16	1	16	25	8	...	9	9	42	5	49	45	29	4	25	22

District and Natural Division.	Blind.								Leper.							
	Male.				Female.				Male.				Female.			
	1911	1901	1891	1881	1911	1901	1891	1881	1911	1901	1891	1881	1911	1901	1891	1881
	18	19	20	21	22	23	24	25	26	27	28	29	30	31	32	33
State	122	15	100	128	121	9	84	110	41	4	39	42	15	2	13	18
Telingana	109	9	84	105	109	6	70	86	42	4	34	32	17	1	12	14
Hyderabad City...	48	21	69	93	88	17	57	67	13	5	33	25	7	2	17	16
Atrafibalda	132	7	116	145	135	2	105	128	42	...	45	40	14	...	8	14
Warangal...	82	10	27	88	76	5	64	71	30	4	24	24	16	1	13	13
Karimnagar	91	5	63	99	79	3	46	88	39	3	27	34	14	...	9	12
Adilabad	86	12	64	76	103	4	57	94	19	4	38	30	14	2	11	26
Medak	135	10	166	144	151	5	124	106	9	7	99	62	22	...	22	22
Nizamabad	108	8	51	76	100	8	38	56	87	4	39	38	35	5	15	17
Mahbubnagar	181	11	109	175	186	9	99	121	35	6	22	26	15	2	10	12
Nalgonda...	119	3	98	65	117	4	78	61	34	1	23	18	15	...	6	9
Marathwara...	135	23	121	158	133	13	102	141	39	2	42	54	14	1	13	22
Aurangabad	124	38	151	326	134	20	119	290	23	7	54	151	14	1	12	46
Bhir	158	23	140	247	151	16	123	245	60	3	56	87	21	2	17	37
Nander	144	20	46	147	153	7	40	141	33	22	22	32	11	3	7	10
Parbhani	188	26	184	105	191	13	116	83	20	4	20	23	4	...	7	13
Gulbarga	106	20	78	105	110	13	59	82	41	7	36	25	13	5	13	9
Osmanabad	144	14	117	122	133	10	88	93	91	5	80	64	23	3	21	28
Raichur	68	10	45	86	50	7	42	32	21	2	35	19	14	4	11	11
Bidar	179	28	149	96	77	14	127	82	38	5	36	30	11	1	11	13

Note.—After deducting 76 males and 5 females inmates of the Lunatic Asylum attached to the Central Jail, Hyderabad City, born outside the City, the corrected proportion for that locality under insanes for males and females is 53 and 28, respectively.

SUBSIDIARY TABLE II—Distribution of the Infirm by age per 10,000 of each sex.

Age	Insane.								Deaf-Mute.							
	Male.				Female.				Male.				Female.			
	1911	1901	1891	1881	1911	1901	1891	1881	1911	1901	1891	1881	1911	1901	1891	1881
1	2	3	4	5	6	7	8	9	10	11	12	13	14	15	16	17
Total	10,000	10,000	10,000	10,000	10,000	10,000	10,000	10,000	10,000	10,000	10,000	10,000	10,000	10,000	10,000	10,000
0—5	207	293	310	336	267	316	550	318	448	246	359	228	521	302	463	443
5—10	788	251	852	1,046	760	737	987	1,070	1,420	1,010	1,086	922	1,506	995	1,300	802
10—15	1,157	628	1,152	974	1,254	1,158	1,188	1,236	1,487	1,231	1,221	885	1,559	1,041	1,062	865
15—20	866	544	1,036	1,630	1,318	632	1,371	1,605	995	1,059	953	1,098	1,138	1,086	991	992
20—25	1,047	920	1,289	1,854	1,115	1,579	1,298	1,745	1,305	961	1,075	1,644	1,116	1,041	1,027	1,442
25—30	1,248	878	1,104		987	737	969		1,118	1,034	983		979	1,176	962	
30—35	1,157	1,590	1,278	1,755	1,106	2,421	987	1,465	1,015	1,133	964	1,453	769	1,131	926	1,547
35—40	731	1,046	678		533	105	292		511	690	535		500	407	480	
40—45	970	2,134	784	1,152	859	1,268	750	1,121	746	837	748	1,318	790	905	780	1,350
45—50	524	544	290		355	105	384		250	345	389		295	362	374	
50—55	614	460	610	887	721	526	548	930	349	296	601	1,526	874	498	468	1,575
55—60	207	84	185		118	...	91		75	148	220		69	181	166	
60 and over ...	484	623	532	364	612	421	585	510	281	1,010	866	928	384	815	1,056	984

Age.	Blind.								Leper.							
	Male.				Female.				Male.				Female.			
	1911	1901	1891	1881	1911	1901	1891	1881	1911	1901	1891	1881	1911	1901	1891	1881
1	18	19	20	21	22	23	24	25	26	27	28	29	30	31	32	33
Total	10,000	10,000	10,000	10,000	10,000	10,000	10,000	10,000	10,000	10,000	10,000	10,000	10,000	10,000	10,000	10,000
0—5	570	594	536	436	440	371	496	425	11	127	44	99	40	213	84	218
5—10	801	1,048	1,022	817	608	948	846	714	65	381	58	317	121	...	322	482
10—15	871	1,013	995	767	602	825	670	585	208	254	204	463	442	745	602	619
15—20	677	885	689	961	499	742	564	940	322	382	465	883	482	851	868	1,250
20—25	813	873	866	1,531	715	763	738	1,417	550	763	692	2,159	853	638	714	1,983
25—30	816	943	885		664	722	759		891	932	838		884	638	981	
30—35	830	873	852	1,325	923	928	780	1,369	1,184	1,314	1,263	2,300	1,446	1,170	1,205	1,939
35—40	511	629	529		502	495	545		985	1,017	904		813	213	756	
40—45	755	710	713	1,357	844	1,093	935	1,338	1,713	1,356	1,720	1,993	1,496	1,277	1,401	1,588
45—50	450	267	422		386	309	337		865	1,144	1,041		653	1,170	686	
50—55	780	722	710	1,596	925	660	876	1,811	1,455	890	1,299	1,214	1,305	745	980	1,158
55—60	263	186	233		228	309	263		427	169	328		281	688	322	
60 and over ...	1,863	1,257	1,548	1,210	2,664	1,835	2,191	1,401	1,329	1,271	1,144	572	1,084	1,702	1,079	768

SUBSIDIARY TABLE III.—Number afflicted per 100,000 Persons of each age-period, and number of Females afflicted per 1,000 Males.

Age.	Number afflicted per 100,000.								Number of females afflicted per 1,000 males.			
	Insane.		Deaf-Mute.		Blind.		Leper.		Insane.	Deaf-Mute.	Blind.	Leper.
	Male.	Female.	Male.	Female.	Male.	Female.	Male.	Female.				
1	2	3	4	5	6	7	8	9	10	11	12	13
Total	23	15	87	29	122	121	41	15	655	752	962	361
0-5	8	3	12	10	51	35	...	...	542	533	574	429
5-10	14	9	42	34	77	58	2	1	613	556	578	600
10-15	23	20	49	47	94	76	7	7	585	559	601	560
15-20	27	26	51	43	115	79	18	10	502	537	585	650
20-25	30	18	61	34	126	91	23	14	589	608	542	641
25-30	31	17	45	31	107	89	39	15	659	603	561	737
30-35	31	18	44	24	118	131	56	24	619	637	483	715
35-40	28	17	32	29	105	123	67	25	677	576	514	771
40-45	30	19	37	32	124	144	94	34	633	556	482	748
45-50	32	19	25	30	147	166	94	35	692	529	548	786
50-55	27	22	25	21	183	222	114	39	565	553	467	756
55-60	32	15	19	17	219	242	119	37	727	594	545	809
60 and over	20	15	19	18	409	528	97	91	547	493	421	778

SUBSIDIARY TABLE IV.—Number afflicted per 100,000 Persons of each selected Caste, Tribe or Race; and number of Females afflicted per 1,000 Males.

Caste.	Number afflicted per 100,000.								Number of females afflicted per 1,000 males.			
	Insane.		Deaf-Mute.		Blind.		Leper.		Insane.	Deaf-Mute.	Blind.	Leper.
	Male.	Female.	Male.	Female.	Male.	Female.	Male.	Female.				
1	2	3	4	5	6	7	8	9	10	11	12	13
HINDU.												
1. Brahman ...	50	17	37	35	152	123	26	11	828	918	778	423
2. Dhangar ...	9	7	22	19	128	132	31	9	783	818	1,026	303
3. Golla	26	21	48	29	145	160	32	14	758	647	1,079	427
4. Goundla... ...	34	23	36	45	142	112	42	10	660	1,193	752	227
5. Kapu	37	24	41	33	116	91	32	11	621	766	755	324
6. Koli	16	5	40	37	116	187	46	11	833	907	1,160	228
7. Kamati	57	25	67	48	264	202	70	19	415	675	734	268
8. Lingayath ...	15	9	33	26	83	78	20	8	586	782	912	372
9. Madiga, Mang ...	23	19	36	27	109	106	57	23	787	735	951	396
10. Mahar, Mala ...	17	17	27	23	121	126	55	18	1,082	994	1,023	321
11. Maratha... ...	7	4	24	20	137	160	34	12	593	815	1,160	267
12. Mannur	24	15	33	33	128	132	65	18	607	974	1,014	367
13. Mutrasi	30	19	42	38	104	134	75	20	585	842	1,252	250
14. Sale	22	21	40	27	103	87	44	13	897	652	807	298
15. Telaga	23	26	53	31	130	127	49	25	1,074	561	958	491
MUSALMAN.												
16. Pathan	34	16	22	20	74	84	22	8	417	813	1,019	313
17. Sayyed	26	25	27	22	70	73	29	8	885	741	957	241
18. Shaikh	34	14	37	22	94	86	36	12	406	590	887	333
CHRISTIAN.												
19. Indian-Christian.	17	13	38	22	123	130	34	9	750	536	1,000	250
ANIMIST.												
20. Gond	6	11	29	23	66	84	19	13	1,750	778	1,268	667
21. Lambada ...	22	8	29	28	70	49	22	15	118	818	593	588

Chapter XI.

CASTE.

217. Caste. The Basis of the Hindu Society.

Hindu Society rests upon caste. Orthodox Hinduism is best known amongst its votaries as *Varshrama Dharma*, which may be roughly rendered into English as the social polity based on the caste system. Nor is the influence of caste confined to Hindus. Though Mahomedanism inculcates the principle of brotherhood amongst its followers and has, in practice, succeeded in giving effect to it more than any other religion in India, even it has fallen under the spell of caste. There are Mahomedan castes as well as Hindu castes, although of course, the former are not so rigidly closed as the latter.

218. Origin of Caste.

The question of the origin and development of the caste system has been so much discussed that it is impossible to say anything new on it. The only purpose of this paragraph is to call attention to the comprehensive treatment of the whole subject by the learned authors of the *Vedic Index* published last year. Their article on "Varna" is the latest authoritative pronouncement on the origin and history of caste, and, on the whole, it is the most satisfactory yet made upon it. Drs. Macdonnell and Keith incline to Risley's view that the ultimate source of caste was the distinction between Aryan and non-Aryan. While dissenting from Senart's theory which places the greatest stress on the Aryan constitution of the family, they allow that the development of caste might have been helped by the family traditions of some *gentes* or Gotras. In like manner, while dismissing Nesfield's opinion, that occupation was the one ground of caste, as hardly worth serious criticism as an ultimate explanation of caste, they regard it as perfectly certain that gilds of workers tended to become castes. They conclude :—

> "There is no probabilty in the view of Senart or of Risley that the names of the old classes were later superimposed artificially on a system of castes that were different from them in origin. We cannot say that the castes existed before the classes, and that the classes were borrowed by India from Iran, as Risley maintains, ignoring the early Brahmanic evidence for the four Varnas, and treating the transfer as late. Nor can we say with Senart that the castes and classes are of independent origin. If there had been no Varna, caste might never have arisen ; both colour and class are needed for a plausible account of the rise of caste."*

In other words, once the conception of hereditary castes as the natural basis of society, got hold of the Indian mind, all social divisions, and groupings, however caused, tended to run to caste. Differences of occupation, differences of locality, and differences of dialect, all became starting-points of new castes.

219. Multiplicity of Modern Castes.

The question of the origin of the castes, however, is only of antiquarian interest at the present day. The four original castes of Manu have increased to several hundreds, though many of the latter claim to be branches of one of the first three castes. Whatever might have been the case in the remote past, the general impression among foreign observers, *viz.*, that Indian society is divided, so to speak, into a number of horizontal strata, each representing a caste, is, as Sir Henry Maine pointed out many years ago, an entire mistake.

* Vedic Index of Names and Subjects, by Macdonnell and Keith (John Murray, 1912), Vol. II, pp. 268, 269 and 270.

" The real India " he wrote,

"contains one priestly caste, which in a certain, though a very limited sense, is the highest of all, and there are, besides, some princely houses and a certain number of tribes, village-communities, and guilds, which still in our day advance a claim, considered by many good authorities extremely doubtful to belong to the second or third of the castes recognised by Brahminical writers. But otherwise, caste is merely a name for trade or occupation, and the sole tangible effect of the Brahminical theory is that it creates a religious sanction for what is really a primitive and natural distinction of classes. The true view of India is that, as a whole, it is divided into a vast number of independent, self-acting, organised social groups trading, manufacturing, cultivating."*

These observations are especially true of Southern India where the second and third castes of Manu never existed, and where the Aryan scheme of caste was loosely superimposed on the Dravidian classes. A glance at any of the Tables, relating to this Chapter, shows that Sir Henry Maine's observations are true of the Hindu castes in this State. Except the Brahmin and the Rajput, there are few other castes which can be referred to any of the first three castes of Manu.

220. Statistics.

An index of castes and tribes in this State, prepared for the present Census, contains the names of 240 groups. Imperial Table XIII, which is the principal Table for this Chapter, gives the number and distribution of 72 castes and tribes, the rest being grouped as " others " under each main religion.

In the Census of 1901 the various castes and races were classified into 26 groups, the Hindu castes, according to social precedence, and the others each under a separate group, and the minor religions all in a single group. Each group contained several castes, numerous sub-castes, many territorial or occupational names and not a few vague names. In the present Census, only those castes that contributed one per mille to the total population of the State are shown in Table XIII under their respective religions and all the minor castes have been grouped under one denomination, " Others ". Imperial Table XIV gives particulars regarding the civil condition of selected tribes and castes and Imperial Table IX of their literacy. Two subsidiary Tables, appended to this chapter, indicate respectively the traditional occupations and the variations in number since the Census of 1881, of the several castes. It may be mentioned here that during the decade, an Ethnographic Survey of the State has been conducted under the supervision of Dr. Syed Sirajal Hassan, LL.D., and the mass of informamation collected, awaits publication.

221. Accuracy of the Returns.

In spite of taking the necessary precautions, it was found that certain sub-castes or titular, occupational and territorial names were shown in the caste column of the Census schedules. Other errors such as the recording of some vague word, the misrecording of a word unfamiliar to the enumerator and mistakes in the course of transference of entries from schedules to slips were not uncommon. Similarity of caste names, such as Gandla (oil presser) and Goundla (liquor seller), Jad (a weaver) and Jat (cultivator employed in the British Army), Cachi (a vegetable grower) and Cutchi (a trader from Cutch), Kurma (a shepherd), Kurmi (a cultivator) and Mala (a menial) and Mali (a gardener) also caused confusion. The true castes had to be sifted out and classified under the proper group. An index of all the castes found in the State numbering 240 and showing the sub-caste of each main caste was prepared beforehand. This greatly facilitated the classification. The above may be said to be unintentional errors. There are intentional errors also which affected the returns to a certain extent. These were, (1) the return of some higher caste, by persons belonging to an inferior caste than the one returned, and (2) the return of an old Varna name, such as Sudra for the caste name. In the first case it was impossible for the Census Office to trace out the real caste, but in the second case the occupation of the person helped to find out the caste. The different kinds of unintentional and intentional

* Village communities in the East and West, 4th edition, (John Murray), pp. 56, 57.

errors which were detected during the course of tabulation and compilation were of course corrected. The number of those errors that were not detected must be too small to affect the caste returns and, therefore, the figures for the various castes can be accepted as a fairly accurate record of their numerical strength.

222. Caste and Traditional Occupations.

From what has been said above it is clear that while the system of caste did not originate in differences of occupation, differences of occupation have come to be associated with different castes in course of time. The traditional occupations under which the several castes are grouped in Subsidiary Table I, are no longer exclusively followed by a few castes, but so far as the majority of them are concerned, they are still their principal occupations. The Brahman has always allowed himself a wide choice of occupation. "The Greek authorities and the evidence of the Jatakas" observe the learned authors of the *Vedic Index*, "concur in showing it to have been the general rule that each caste was confined to its own occupations, but that the Brahmanas did engage in many professions beside that of simple priest. The Jatakas recognize the Brahmins as engaged in all sorts of occupations, as merchants, traders, agriculturists, and so forth,"* In the Mahabharata, as in the Maratha period of Indian history, Brahmins have led armies. The office of Chief Minister to the Ruler has in most Hindu States devolved on persons of the Brahman caste. Members of this caste have also been more forward than others in taking advantage of Western education, and, as a consequence, they occupy a proportionately large share of offices in the public services. There are, besides, at the present day Brahman lawyers and Brahman doctors. Very few Brahmans follow the traditional occupation of priest which is no longer a remunerative one. Similarly, though to a less extent, the other literate castes of Hindus also. show an increasing tendency to take to occupations other than those which have been traditionally associated with their caste. As regards the masses, except where the introduction of modern appliances of conservancy, railways and factories, have provided them with new, more regular and better paid occupations, or where the introduction of law and order has made certain traditional occupations impossible, they still make a living in much the same way as their forefathers. The sweeper caste tends to disappear with the introduction of mechanical processes for the removal and disposal of refuse. The extension of railways and Tramway has an immediate effect on the traditional carriers by pack animals, as soal, incidentally, on the castes which regarded highway robbery as their traditional occupation. The application of steam and of electric power to the weaving, oil pressing and other industries has likewise the effect of breaking down the occupational basis of the castes which follow these as their hereditary trades. It is not the weaver caste but the agriculturists who furnish the largest contingent of our mill-hands. The Lambada and Wanjara, traditional carriers by pack animals, do not become railway porters and pointsmen. When once the caste occupation is gone, its members are at liberty to turn their hand to any other and, as a rule, it is seldom that they show a preference for an occupation which may be regarded as being nearest to their old traditional one.

223. Variations in occupational groups.

The occupational groups are in some.respects more reliable than individual castes, as a means of gauging the evolution of Indian society. Each occupational group consists of several castes, some of which, at any rate, seem to be interchangeable. Some are merely a Sanskritised periphrasis intended to mask the lowly position of some old caste, *e.g.*, Panchamas for Pariahs. The variations in the number returning each separate caste are, therefore, often apt to be the result of changing fashions in nomenclature. This point will be further referred to in a subsequent paragraph. Occupations, unlike names, or not easy to change, and as pointed out above so far as the mass of the people is concerned, the traditional

* Vedic Index Vol. II, p. 260.

occupations, still retain their sway. It is, however, necessary to direct attention to a prevailing tendency, in this context. Occupations representing a more primitive stage of society than the agricultural, tend to die out as a consequence of the settlement on land of the castes or tribes which originally followed them. The old village industries, too, are becoming extinct, and this is another cause of the increasing pressure on land. These movements will not be represented by a statement which groups the several castes by their traditional rather than by their actual occupations. Still it may be expected that some indication of these tendencies will be discernible in the variations in numbers of the occupational groups during a reasonably long period of time. In the marginal table are included the occupational groups each of which number more than one million persons. These three groups, representing the pastoral and agricultural industries, and village organization, claim more than 40 per cent. of the population. Only Hindu castes are included in the groups, the non-Hindus and the Lingayaths, being regarded as having no traditional occupation. These latter aggregate 161 in 1,000 of the population, so that the occupational groups cover only 839 persons in a thousand. Of these, 400 or nearly 50 per cent. are agriculturists, village functionaries and graziers and dairy men. In 1891, the agricultural group numbered 4,897,994 but it included some castes which at the present Census has been assigned to other groups, and also some others, which are not found in the schedules. Some of the castes included among graziers at this Census, were separately grouped as shepherds in 1891. In 1901, occupational groups were not used. In these circumstances, a comparison of the statistics with those obtained at preceding Censuses, is of little value, even if it can be instituted.

Occupational group.	Total number.	Number per mille.
Cultivators	3,367,750	252
Village watchmen and menials	2,282,941	170
Graziers and Dairymen. ...	1,113,388	83

The marginal table contains particulars of the groups which number 10 and more than 10 in 1,000 of the population. They are all occupations which may be expected to prevail in a predominantly rural and agricultural population. The presence of gold and silversmiths in this table where the more useful arts of the carpenter and the blacksmith are conspicuous by their absence, is no doubt to be accounted for by the fact that several places in the State, especially in Marathwara, were once the head-quarters of thriving Kingdoms. The Kings and Chiefs liberally patronised the art of the gold and silversmith, and the present exponents of it are the descendants of those who ministered to the splendour of bygone royalty. These groups together account for 253 in 1,000 of the population, leaving about 170 for the minor trades. Tailors, carpenters, masons, blacksmiths, brass-smiths, oil-pressers, leatherworkers and basket makers are the principal trades of the rest of the population.

Occupational group.	Total number.	Number per mille.
Weavers, Carders, Dyers ...	472,954	35
Hunters and Fowers	468,876	35
Toddy drawers and Distillers..	406,321	31
Carriers by pack animals ...	316,083	24
Priest	291,112	22
Washermen	242,224	15
Traders and Padlers	223,380	17
Gold and Silver smiths ...	205,747	16
Fishermen, Boatmen, &c. ...	177,004	13
Potters	151,986	11
Landholders	145,424	11
Earth Workers...	131,799	10
Forest and hill tribes ...	136,887	10

224. Variations in Castes.

Subsidiary Table II shows the strength of the principal castes in the past 4 Censuses and the percentage of variation. The variations in columns 6 and 7 in the majority of cases strike one as extraordinary, but before considering the causes of variations it is desirable to explain how the figures have been arrived at.

In the Census of 1901, castes were classified into (26) groups according to the social status of their people. Thus in the Velama group several distinct castes such as Nayars, Jat, Kayath, Balija, Manne, etc., were lumped together. In the caste Velama, not only castes but diverse sub-castes were also entered. For example the marginally noted divisions of Vysias appear as castes. There are also certain names in the caste column such as Komral, Kaikoli, Mothe, Chafri, Bhatgar, and Metaiwad which cannot be correctly placed under any. It was, therefore, a difficult task to decide what all names in column 1 of the table of 1901 should be grouped together to represent the strength in 1901 of a certain caste. Discretion was, therefore, to be used and all that was possible to secure correct strength of castes has been done and the figures in columns 3, 6 and 7 are the result. The variations should, therefore, be ascribed more to the difficulty of the correct classification of the caste figures of 1901 than to real increase or decrease in the number of caste people.

Komati.
Arwa Komati.
Yegana „
Gouri „
Neti „
Vani „
Vani Dekshavanth.
„ Rasavanth.
„ Selavanth.
Doubbula Vani.

225. Castes which show a decrease in numbers.

In the chapter on Religion, the probable cause of variations in the numbers of the several religious communities of the State, have been discussed. It is convenient to recall here that Hindus have increased during the decade by 17·7, Musalmans by 19·4, the Christians by 136·1 and the Animists by 337·14 per cent. It would be interesting to discuss the variation in strength of the principal castes of each religion from Census to Census, but this is impossible owing to the widely different caste designations and groupings adopted at each of the preceding Censuses. One example brings this out very clearly. Of the fifty and odd castes of which particulars are furnished in Subsidiary Table II, four show an actual decrease in numbers at the present Census. Three of them, namely, the Brahman, the Kumbhar and the Lohar are Hindu castes, while the fourth the Lambada is classed as Animists. To take the Brahman, first, it has to be noted that in 1901, this caste showed an abnormal increase of over 146 per cent., while from 1881 to 1891, it increased only by a little over 3 per cent. The net result in thirty years is that this caste has apparently remained stationary as regards its numbers. The sudden and large increase in 1901 and the equally sudden and if somewhat smaller decrease in 1911, may suggest that a large number of persons of this caste came into this State at about the time of the last Census, and left it before the present Census was taken. The Superintendent at the 1901 Census was inclined to think that the increase in the numbers of certain castes, including the Brahmin, was so great that it was not possible to believe that both the figures (of 1891 and 1901) represented the strength of the same castes ten years previously and then*. The only other alternative is that some caste (or castes) was included in the Brahmin in 1901, which was not reckoned as such in 1891 and at the present Census. This is what did happen. In 1901 over 300,000 Telagas were reckoned as Brahmins, which explains the large increase of the latter at that Census. The classification of the Telagas as a separate caste has brought about an apparent large decrease of Brahmins and an increase of Telagas, at the present Census. Even otherwise, the Brahmans are in a considerably smaller proportion to the total population in 1911 than they were at any previous Census. They number only 20 persons in 1,000 as against 24 in 1891. The Kumbhar caste shows a decrease of about 23 per cent. This caste also exhibited an abnormal increase in

Variation per cent.

Caste.	1901-1911.	1881-1911.
Brahman	— 60·8	+ 0·4
Kumbhar	— 22·2	+ 76·4
Lohar	— 5·2	+ 25·6
Lambada	— 18·4	+ 55·5

* Hyderabad Census Report, 1901, p. 220.

1901. The Kumbhars, as their name implies, are potters. They are a Maratha caste, the corresponding Telugu caste being known as Kummara. The latter has incrased by 20·8 per cent. That the large increase of 1901, accompanied by the decrease of 1911, occurred in the Maratha caste, rather supports the theory that there was a temporary influx of persons of the caste in the famine of 1900. In 1901, the Kumbhar was given as a sub-caste of the Kummara, and it may be that the increase under the latter and the decrease under the former at the present Census, are due to many Kumbhars returning themselves or being classed as Kummaras. The third and only other Hindu caste which shows an actual decrease is the Lohar. The decrease which is only 5·4 per cent. seems to be due to natural causes. This caste is about equally distributed between Telingana and Marathwara. The Lohars figure as one of many sub-castes of Ausalas in the 1901 Report, and the apparent decrease at the present Census may be merely a matter of names. The Animist caste of Lambadas shows a decrease of 18·4 per cent. This probably represents the proportion which has returned itself as Hindu.

226. Castes which show a small increase.

The castes shown in the marginal table show a rate of increase less than that of the Hindu population as a whole. The Kolis have just made good the loss they suffered in 1901, which amounted to 12·3 per cent. of their population. The Komatis increased by 5·6 per cent. This is the first Census which records an increase against this caste. Both in 1901 and 1891, they showed a decrease of population. In thirty years, they have gained only by 3·4 per cent. Attention has been called in previous chapters to the peculiar social and pathological condition of this caste. It is evident that it is a decadent one. The rate of increase of the Lingayaths has been decreasing steadily during the last thirty years. Between 1881 and and 1891, it was 21·8 between 1891 and 1901, 13·6; and in the last decade, it is 9·6 per cent. Another caste which shows a smaller increase than at the last Census is the Mangala. Members of this caste are barbers, musicians and torch-bearers. This is a Telingana caste. The barber caste of Marathwara is the Nahvi (Warik) which increased by 27·7 per cent. It is worthy of note that while the Mangala showed an increase of 23·3 per cent. at the 1901 Census, the Nahvis had decreased by 24·5 per cent. and the small increase in the former and the large one in the latter at the present Census may be due to the name Nahvi, having become more popular than that of Mangala. It is also probable that several Mangalas returned themselves as belonging to one of the other castes which are more distinctly associated with the practice of music than with the handling of the razor. The profession of barber is looked down upon in this country, and nobody who can lay a possible claim to some other trade, is likely to proclaim himself as addicted to it. The rate of increase of the Marathas, the largest single caste in the State, at the present Census is about the same as at the last Census, and the nominal increase shown in the table since 1881, is due to the fall in their numbers at the 1891 Census, due probably to a large proportion of them being classed as Kunbis. The Satanis increased by 98·9 at the 1901 Census. Their relatively small increase now may be simply a reaction from the high increase ten years ago. The Sonar caste shows an increase of only 1·2 per cent. The members of this caste are gold and silver smiths. There are both Maratha and Telugu Sonars. The Panchal, also gold and silver smiths, increased by 25·2 per cent. It seems probable that a certain proportion of Sonars, especially in Telingana, returned themselves as Panchals. The latter word

Variation per cent.

Caste.	1901 1911.	1881-1911.
Koli	+ 12·2	+ 24·7
Komati	+ 5·6	+ 3·4
Lingayat	+ 9·6	+ 51·6
Mangala	+ 7·7	+ 56·6
Maratha	+ 11·7	+ 1·5
Satavi	+ 14·6	+115·5
Sonar	+ 1·2	+ 37·7
Teli	+ 8·3	+ 13·4
Uppara	+ 3·7	+ 58·9

sounds more classical and the tendency now-a-days is for some castes to give themselves some high-sounding name. The best-known example is that of the Pariah who is usually spoken of as the Panchama or the man of the fifth caste. The Teli and the Uppara are the only other Hindu castes which have increased by less than 10 per cent. The Teli is the oil-presser of Marathwara as the Gundla is of Telingana. The caste showed a large decrease in 1901, and might be expected to show a larger increase than 8·3 per cent. at the present. The Uppara or the earth-workers caste showed an increase of only 3·7 per cent., but this is a caste with many *aliases*, and it is also probable that members of it who rise in the world or acquire skill in some other trade declare themselves as belonging to other castes. Of the Musalman castes, the Moghul shows an increase of only 4·4 per cent. The Pathans and Shaikhs have increased by about 16 per cent., which is less than the rate of the whole Musalman community in the State.

227. Castes which show very high increases.

The Telaga caste shows an increase of 513·7 per cent. At the preceding Censuses it has consistently shown a decrease of population, 16·1 per cent. in 1881-1891 and 76·5 in 1891-1901. As compared with its numbers in 1881, that at the present Census is only 21·1 per cent. more, which is by no means an abnormal rate of growth. The Telagas, as the name indicates, is a Telugu caste, and only a small proportion of them is found in the Marathwara districts. There is a caste Telugu in that of 1891, but it is said of it that it is a mere linguistic group and represents no distinct caste. There is no caste of that name to be found in the 1901 Report, owing to the Telugus having been included among Brahmins. The result was an abnormal addition to the Brahmin caste at that Census. The classification of the Telagas as a separate caste, explains the very large proportion of increase of that caste, and partly, also the considerable decrease of Brahmins at the present Census. The marginal Table gives the names of Hindu castes which show rates of increase exceeding 50 per cent. One common feature of the statistics of all the castes, is that they all showed decreases, some of them very heavy ones, in the Census of 1901. The Madiga is, next to the Maratha, the largest Hindu caste in these Dominions. It is a Telugu caste corresponding to the Mang of Marathwara. Its members are engaged as village menials, and their traditional occupations are basket-making and leather working. They also supply the place of musicians for the low castes. In the case of this as well as of the other castes which show increases much in excess of the general average for the Hindus and for the State, the explanation seems to be that several castes which were found at the Census of 1901 and are not found at the present one, have for some reason or other returned themselves or been grouped together under these names. Of Musalman castes the Syeds have increased by 42·6 per cent. The high increase of the Indian Christian population is due, of course, to the success of missionary endeavours at conversion.

Madiga	+ 95·9	+ 74·2
Wanjari...	+ 81·1	+ 29·5
Mala	+ 68·5	+ 21·5
Wakligar	+ 68·2	+ 6·1
Golla	+ 65·7	+ 48·3
Darzi	+ 60·0	+ 31·1
Kurma	+ 59·9	+ 18·3
Sutar	+ 51·5	+ 20·9

SUBSIDIARY TABLE I.—Castes classified according to their traditional occupation.

Group and Caste.	Strength.	Number per mille of the population of the State.
1	2	3
Hunters and Fowlers	468,876	35
1. Bedar	208,096	16
2. Mutrasi	260,770	19
Priests and Devotees	291,112	22
1. Brahman	261,241	20
2. Gosain	29,871	2
Temple Servants	45,405	3
1. Satani	27,883	2
2. Others (Gurav)	17,522	1
Musicians, Singers, Dancers, Mimics and Jugglers ...	10,381	1
1. Others (Bogam)	10,381	1
Traders and Pedlars	223,380	17
1. Komati	223,380	17
Carriers by pack Animals ...	316,083	24
1. Lambada	142,044	11
2. Wanjari	174,039	13
Barbers	135,488	10
1. Mangala	76,514	6
2. Nahvi (Warik)	58,974	4
Washermen	242,224	18
1. Chakala	175,626	13
2. Dhobi	66,598	5
Weavers, Carders and Dyers.	472,954	35
1. Devang or Koshti	71,400	5
2. Rangari	22,508	2
3. Sale	343,130	25
Landholders	145,424	11
1. Rajput	61,687	5
2. Velama	83,737	6
Cultivators (including growers of special products) ...	3,367,750	252
1. Hatkar	67,934	5
2. Kapu	648,254	48
3. Koli	266,840	20
4. Kurmi	23,078	2
5. Mali	107,097	8
6. Maratha	1,538,874	115
7. Munnar	228,354	17
8. Telaga	458,622	34
9. Wakligar	38,497	3
Forest and Hill Tribes ...	136,887	10
1. Gond	124,341	9
2. Others	12,546	1
Graziers and dairymen ...	1,113,388	83
1. Dhangar	488,609	37
2. Golla	460,760	34
3. Kurma	144,688	11
4. Others (Gouli)	19,331	1
Fishermen, Boatmen and Palkibearers	177,004	13
1. Bhoi...	177,004	13
Ladaf	30,721	2
Others (Momin)	5,195	......
Tailors	47,947	4
1. Darzi or Simpi	47,947	4
Carpenters...	69,205	5
1. Sutar	69,205	5
Masons	57,000	4
1. Uppara	57,000	4
Potters	151,986	11
1. Kumbhar	72,504	5
2. Kummara	79,482	6
Blacksmiths	47,844	4
1. Lohar	47,844	4
Gold and Silversmiths ...	205,747	16
1. Panchal	117,710	9
2. Sunar	88,037	7
Brass and Coppersmiths ...	14,522	1
1. Others (Kasar)	14,522	1
Oil Pressers	69,959	5
1. Teli	56,944	4
2. Others (Gandla)	13,015	1
Toddy Drawers and Distillers	406,321	31
1. Gondla	306,071	23
2. Idiga	24,911	2
3. Kalal	75,339	6
Leather Workers	90,882	7
1. Chambhar	70,618	5
2. Others	20,264	2
Basket Workers and Mat makers	26,511	2
1. Burud	24,498	2
2. Others (Erkala)	2,018	......
Earth, Salt, etc., Workers, Quarriers	131,799	10
1. Waddar	131,799	10
Village Watchmen and Menials	2,282,941	170
1. Madiga	804,893	60
2. Mahar	689,643	52
3. Mala	448,046	33
4. Mang	340,959	25
Others	2,158,613	161
1. Shaik	985,019	74
2. Lingayet	757,611	57
3. Sayyed	189,574	14
4. Pathan	135,148	10
5. Indian Christian	45,908	3
6. Moghal	33,411	3
7. Others (Dasari)	11,942	1

SUBSIDIARY TABLE II.—Variation in Caste, Tribe, &c., since 1881.

Caste, Tribe or Race.	Persons.				Percentage of variation —Increase + Decrease —			Percentage of net variation 1881-1911.
	1911.	1901.	1891.	1881.	1901 to 1911.	1891 to 1901.	1881 to 1891.	
1	2	3	4	5	6	7	8	9
Hindu.								
Bedar	208,096	157,072	162,391	129,217	+ 32·5	— 3·8	+ 25·7	+ 61·4
Bhoi	177,004	142,179	134,282	93,478	+ 24·4	+ 5·9	+ 43·7	+ 89·4
Brahman	261,241	666,856	270,482	261,120	— 60·8	+146·6	+ 3·2	+ ·04
Chakala	175,626	142,832	140,494	113,124	+ 23·3	+ 1·8	+ 24·2	+ 55·3
Chambhar	70,618	53,834	53,692	44,111	+ 31·2	+ ·8	+ 21·7	+ 60·1
Darsi or Simpi	47,947	36,315	36,778	30,991	+ 32·0	— 1·3	+ 18·7	+ 54·7
Dewang or Koshti	71,400	44,687	72,687	54,467	+ 60·0	— 38·6	— 33·5	+ 31·1
Dhangar	488,609	396,674	364,043	359,767	+ 23·1	+ 9·0	+ 1·2	+ 35·8
Dhobi	66,598	49,843	53,503	48,988	+ 34·3	— 6·8	— 9·3	+ 36·1
Golla	460,760	278,140	338,358	310,597	+ 65·7	— 17·8	+ 9·0	+ 48·3
Gosain	29,871	21,067	27,142	21,395	+ 41·8	— 22·4	+ 26·9	+ 39·6
Goundla	306,071	229,156	235,662	215,900	+ 33·6	— 2·8	+ 9·2	+ 41·8
Hatkar	67,934	46,118	48,466	41,128	+ 47·3	— 4·8	+ 17·8	+ 65·2
Kalal	75,339	56,600	49,165	23,700	+ 33·1	+ 15·1	+107·4	+214·9
Kapu	648,254	521,230	603,489	598,847	+ 24·4	— 13·6	+ 0·8	+ 8·3
Koli	266,840	236,884	270,188	213,966	+ 12·2	— 12·3	+ 26·3	+ 24·7
Komati...	223,380	211,628	212,865	216,080	+ 5·6	— 0·6	— 1·5	+ 3·4
Kumbhar	72,504	93,211	46,799	41,111	— 22·2	+ 99·1	+ 13·8	+ 76·4
Kummara	79,482	65,806	60,212	49,724	+ 20 8	+ 9·3	+ 21·1	+ 59·8
Kurma	144,688	90,510	97,543	122,268	+ 59·9	— 7·2	— 20·2	+ 18·3
Lingayat	757,611	691,394	608,457	499,655	+ 9·6	+ 13·6	+ 21·8	+ 51·6
Lohar	47,844	50,479	44,857	38,079	— 5·2	+ 12·5	+ 17·8	+ 25·6
Madiga...	804,393	410,636	664,556	461,822	+ 95·9	— 38·2	+ 43·9	+ 74·2
Mahar	689,543	583,031	501,241	438,302	+ 18·3	+ 16·3	+ 14·4	+ 57·3
Mala	448,046	265,829	395,574	368,704	+ 68·5	— 32·8	+ 7·3	+ 21·5
Mali	107,097	86,215	99,983	83,806	+ 24·2	— 13·8	+ 19·3	+ 27·8
Mang	340,959	261,829	265,450	259,474	+ 30·2	— 1·4	+ 2·3	+ 31·4
Mangala	76,514	71,039	57,614	48,872	+ 7·7	+ 23·3	+ 17·9	+ 56·6
Maratha	1,538,874	1,377,305	1,233,930	1,516,207	+ 11·7	+ 11·6	— 18·6	+ 1·5
Munnur	228,354	175,358	121,983	187,458	+ 30·2	+ 43·8	— 34·9	+ 21·8
Mutrasi	260,770	200,119	182,560	164,282	+ 30·3	+ 9·6	+ 11·1	+ 58·7
Nahvi (Warik)	58,974	46,198	61,161	53,341	+ 27·7	— 24·5	+ 14·7	+ 10·6
Panchal	117,710	94,002	108,863	94,777	+ 25·2	— 13·6	+ 14·9	+ 24·2
Rajput	61,637	48,737	51,959	49,848	+ 26·5	— 6·2	+ 4·2	+ 23·7
Sale	343,130	284,535	243,378	219,790	+ 20·6	+ 16·9	+ 10·7	+ 56·1
Satani	27,883	24,323	12,226	12,950	+ 14·6	+ 98·9	— 5·6	+115·3
Sunar	88,037	86,978	66,766	63,916	+ 1·2	+ 30·3	+ 4·5	+ 37·7
Sutar	69,205	45,687	62,549	57,382	+ 51·5	— 27·0	+ 9·3	+ 20·9
Telaga	458,622	74,738	317,765	378,717	+513·7	— 76·5	— 16·1	+ 21·1
Teli	56,944	52,594	64,362	50,233	+ 8·3	— 18·3	+ 28·1	+ 13·4
Uppara	57,900	54,982	50,238	37,026	+ 3·7	+ 9·5	+ 35·7	+ 59·9
Velama	83,787	71,561	65,735	63,101	+ 17·1	+ 8·9	+ 4·2	+ 32·8
Waddari	131,799	100,570	64,912	54,883	+ 31·1	+ 54·8	+ 18·5	+140·4
Wakligar	38,497	22,892	37,359	36,229	+ 68·2	— 38·7	+ 2·9	+ 6·1
Wanjari	174,039	96,081	139,844	134,408	+ 81·1	— 31·3	+ 4·0	+ 29·5
Musalman.								
Ladaf	30,721	18,798	......	......	+ 63·4	...	......	+ 63·4
Mogha	33,411	32,008	21,764	15,423	+ 4·4	+ 47·1	+ 41·1	+116·6
Pathan	135,148	117,153	122,999	61,437	+ 15·4	— 4·6	+100·2	+120·0
Sayyed	189,574	132,921	113,287	89,909	+ 42·6	+ 17·3	+ 26·0	+110·9
Shaikh	985,019	850,906	856,123	484,155	+ 15·8	— 0·6	+ 76·8	+103·5
Christian.								
Indian Christian	45,908	15,357	12,563	6,386	+198·9	+ 22·2	+101·5	+636·2
Animist.								
Gond	124,841	107,585	98,806	88,711	+ 15·6	+ 8·9	+ 11·	+ 40·2
Lambada	142,044	174,159	161,399	91,324	— 18·4	+ 7·9	+ 16·7	+ 55·5

Chapter XII.

OCCUPATION.

228. Table XV, Parts A to E, and Table XVI, contain the statistical material for this Chapter. The scheme of classification adopted at this Census, is based on the one drawn up by Monsieur Bertillon and recommended by the International Statistical Institute for general adoption so as to render possible comparison of the occupation statistics of different countries. The number of "groups" in the new scheme is 170. The necessity to preserve throughout the scheme the distinction between industry and trade, made further reduction in the number of groups impossible. Persons who make any article are in all cases classed under "Industry," whether they sell the articles made by them to middlemen or direct to the consumer, while persons who sell only and do not make are classified under "Trade." The following notes are provided in explanation of the general principles underlying the system of classification :—

A person is classified in Table XV-A according to his principal occupation ; the number of persons in each group who are partly dependent on agriculture is given, but otherwise subsidiary occupations are not dealt with in this part of the Table, but in parts B and C. Only those Government servants are shown in Sub-Class VII who are engaged in the general administration, including the administration of Justice. Members of the medical, irrigation, opium, post office and other similar services are classed under the special heads provided for these occupations. What is looked to is the actual occupation and not the source from which the salary comes or the ultimate object which it serves. This leads to a point of difference between Table XV-E, based on the special industrial schedule and the general occupation table. In the former the industry is looked to and not the actual occupation of individual employes—a carpenter in a brewery, for instance, is merged in the general head of brewery employes. For the latter on the other hand only persons directly concerned with the industry and trade, including clerks and menials, are classed under it, and not those with distinctive occupations of their own. Persons temporarily out of employ are shown under the occupation previously followed by them. Many countries sub-divide each occupation according to age and status (employer, superior staff or workman). This is done in Table XV-E, which is compiled from the industrial schedules, but not in the general occupation table.

Subsidiary tables, appended to this Chapter, contain particulars relating to (1) the general distribution of the population according to occupation, (2) the same by Natural Divisions, (3) the distribution of the agricultural, industrial, commercial and professional population in Natural Divisions and Districts, (4) the distribution of persons following occupations combined with agriculture where the latter is the subsidiary, and (5) where it is the principal occupation, (6) the occupations of females, (7) variations in the number following selected occupations since 1901, (8) occupations of selected castes, and (9) distribution by religion and occupation of the population.

229. The four main classes under which all the 170 occupational groups are distributed : are (A) Production of Raw Materials, (B) Preparation and Supply of substances, (C) Public Administration and Liberal Arts and (D) Miscellaneous. Each of these classes is divided into sub-classes, and these again are sub-divided into orders. There are 12 sub-classes in all and 55 orders comprising the 170 group. Sub-table I shows that 6,287 persons in every 10,000 of the population find support in occupations coming under the important class *A* Production of raw materials. This and class *B* Preparation and Supply of material substances, account for 8,635 out of 10,000 persons. Public Administration and the liberal arts, class *C* have only 559 persons depending on them, while class *D*, Miscellaneous, which includes beggars, criminals, lunatics, and prostitutes, covers the occupations, or want of them, of 806, in 10,000 of the population.

230. Production of Raw Materials.

This class has two sub-classes, the first comprising the occupations which consist of the exploitation of the surface of the earth in one form or another, and the second, covering those connected with the extraction of minerals. Sub-class I has two orders: (1) Pasture and Agriculture and (2) Fishing and Hunting. There are only 81 persons in 10,000 of the population who support themselves, or are supported by fishing and hunting.

231. Fishing and Hunting.

Hunting	29,620
Fishing	78,269

The actual number of persons concerned either as workers or dependents in each of these two occupations, is given in the margin. Subsidiary Table VII shows that while the fishing population has increased since 1901 by 135 per cent., the number of persons who follow hunting as their principal occupation has increased by over 2,650 per cent. It is, of course, impossible that this enormous increase can be due to natural causes. More accurate enumeration probably accounts for a large part of the increase. The Bhoi is the principal fishermen caste in the State, and Table XVI shows that a considerable number of them, especially, females earn a livelihood as field-labourers and wood-cutters. This is also the case with the Mutrasis who form the principal hunting caste among the Hindu population of these Dominions. Fishing and hunting are not occupations peculiarly suitable to women, and although a certain number of them is returned as actual workers in them, it is not surprising that a larger number belonging to these castes, should turn their hands to field labour. A single Bhil is entered in the column of "Agents and Managers of landed estates." There is a stage in the evolution of the hunter and the fisherman into a cultivator, when he continues to follow his traditional occupations as subsidiary ones.

232. Pasture.

Hunting and fishing belong to the most primitive stage of human industry. The next stage in the order of evolution is the pastoral. The total number of persons who follow pastoral occupations in these Dominions is, including dependents, 597,728 or 447 in 10,000 of the population. This is the third largest Order in point of numbers, the first being ordinary cultivation, and the second, industries of dress and toilet. The number of persons following the several special kinds of this occupation are given in the margin. Of these four groups, cattle and buffalo breeders show a decrease of about 33 per cent. and breeders of horses, mules, camels and asses one of over 80 per cent. Sheep, goat and pig breeders, on the other hand, have increased by 475 and herdsmen by 108 per cent. Sheep and goat-breeding is chiefly carried on in Marathwara, Gulbarga and Raichur, being the principal districts for this occupation, but the largest number of herdsmen and shepherds are found in Telingana, especially in Warangal and Nalgonda. Pastoral occupations, however, are essentially nomadic, and the presence of a large number of persons following them in a particular district at the date of the Census, may be due to seasonal conditions. The breeding of horses and camels may be said to be practically disappearing as a distinct occupation in the State. How far the decrease in the number of cattle and buffalo breeders is due to the extension of cultivation during the decade, is a point deserving careful investigation by the Administration. The Dhangar and the Golla are the two principal live-stock raising castes in the State and a considerable proportion of them, as shown in Subsidiary Table VIII, have become field-labourers and cultivators. The females of these castes especially, have practically deserted the traditional occupation. It is interesting to note that, according to Subsidiary Table IV, while 161 in 1,000 persons engaged in fishing

Cattle and buffalo breeders	42,480
Sheep, goat and pig breeders	109,789
Breeders of other animals (horses, mules, camels, asses, &c.)	418
Herdsmen, Shepherds, Goat herds	445,158

and hunting are partial agriculturists, only 64 in 1,000, persons following pastoral occupations are of the latter class. In both cases, the proportion of partial agriculturists is larger in Marathwara than in Telingana. There are 18 persons in the State grouped together as engaged in the raising of small animals such as birds, bees and silkworms.

233. Agriculture.

Agriculturists are divided for the purpose of the Census under three heads, namely, (*a*) Ordinary cultivators, (*b*) Growers of special products and market-gardening, and (*c*) Forestry. Ordinary cultivators are, again, sub-divided into (1) Rent-receivers, (2) Cultivators, (3) Agents and Managers, and (4) Farm-servants and Field-labourers. The total number of persons depending on ordinary cultivation in any of the above capacities, or as dependents, is 7,619,505 or 5697 per 10,000 of the population. The number of persons under each of the four heads, and the variations in them during the decade are shown in the marginal table. The extraordinary increase in the number of rent receivers, if it at all represents an actual tendency means that the land is going out of the hands of the cultivators into those of rent-takers. The relatively small increase in the number of the latter, and the large increase of 172 per cent. in that of farm servants and field labourers, also point to the same result. The ranks of the latter are swollen not only by peasant proprietors who are ousted from their holdings but also by accessions from the more primitive occupations of the hunting and pastoral stage, as also from that of indigenous artisans thrown out of employ by their handiwork being superseded in popular favour by cheaper imported articles. The decrease in the number of agents and managers probably indicates that land is passing out of the hands not only of cultivators, but also out of those of the hereditary landed proprietors who managed their estates through agents and managers. The two great lessons which these statistics convey are, first, that the pressure on the land is increasing from various causes, and, secondly, that the ownership and the profits thereof are being increasingly appropriated by mere rent-receivers.

Variation in Groups engaged in Ordinary Cultivation. I (a)

Group.	Number.	Variation per cent.
Rent receivers...	731,803	+ 1,748·8
Ordinary cultivators	4,064,950	+ 17·0
Agents, Managers, &c. ...	34,540	— 45·1
Farm-servants and Field-labourers	2,788,212	+ 172·8

234. There has been a decrease of 95·7 per cent. in the number of growers of special products and market-gardening. There were 91 persons in the Census of 1901, who were returned as engaged in tea, coffee, cinchona and indigo plantations, but these have altogether disappeared at the present Census. The number returned as fruit, flower, vegetable, betel-vine and arecanut growers this time is but 5 per cent. of what it was in 1901. Here, again, the tendency is for the cultivator of what may be called special produce to merge into ordinary cultivation. The third sub-head under Agriculture, namely, forestry, consists of two classes. The first is composed of the employés of the Forest Department, in all 869, and the second, of wood-cutters and other exploiters of forest produce The latter number 40,905, representing an increase of 697·8 per cent. since 1901.

235. (a) Extraction of Minerals.

There are 3 Orders under this head, namely, Mines, Quarries of hard rocks, and Salt, etc. There are no salt workers at this Census. The number of persons engaged in quarrying of hard rocks is 3,149 and this is the first time that they appear in our schedules. The only important Order in this Sub-class is Mines. From an insignificant 139 at the Census of 1901, workers in mines have increased to 15,325 (11,550 coal mines in Warangal and 2,896 employed in gold-mining in Raichur).

236. Preparation and Supply of Material Substances.

This is the second main class in the occupational scheme adopted at this Census. It consists of three great Sub-classes, (1) Industry, (2) Transport, and (3) Trade. Orders 6 to 9 comprising 12 groups come under the first Sub-class. Orders 20 to 23 which cover 21 occupational groups, belong to the Sub-class of Transport, and Orders 35 to 41 are assigned to Trade. The number of workers under Industry have increased 11·2 per cent., that under Transport by 93·7 per cent., and that under Trade 37·5 per cent. since 1901. These percentages afford a rough measure of gauging the effect of improvements in the means of communication and facilities of transport on Trade and Industry. Trade, it is obvious, has responded more readily to the improved facilities of Transport than Industry, as the latter term is used in this connection. The reason is plain. Many of the commodities which find their way to outside markets are agricultural raw produce. The industry immediately benefited by the expansion of roads and railways is the agricultural industry.

237. Textiles.

The proportion of persons who follow an industrial occupation is 1,400 in 10,000 of the population. 387 of these are assigned to Textiles. Of the Textiles, cotton is the most considerable, and employs about three-fourths of the total number of persons supported by textile industries. While the woollen industries have lost ground during the decade, judged by the number of persons supported by them in 1901 and at the present Census, the position of those which have cotton for their raw material has been strengthened. The marginal table compares the variations under the different textiles during the decade. While the cotton ginning, cleaning and pressing industry employs over 60 per cent. more workers than in 1901, the increase in the number of those engaged in spinning and weaving is 7 per cent. This confirms what has been said in the preceding paragraph. Additional facilities of transport have the immediate effect, not of creating industries (for which several other conditions are required) but of stimulating trade, especially the export trade, in raw material. The expansion of the area under cotton cultivation during the decade, as pointed out in a preceding chapter, has been phenomenal. The cotton grown has to be prepared for transport, and hence the large increase in the number of persons employed in the processes of ginning, cleaning and pressing. The depression of the woollen industries is due to the fact that the indigenous methods are too slow and costly to withstand the competition of machine-made goods. The increase in the number of silk-weavers is evidently due to the more prosperous seasons during the decade. In a time of famine, the silk-weavers' produce is not much in demand. Jute spinning, pressing and weaving appears for the first time at this Census among industries giving employment to His Highness' subjects. The number of persons supported by processes of Jute industry is 1,098. More than 75 per cent. of those engaged in Jute industries are found in the Parbhani District. Rope, twine and string-making gives occupation for about 29,000 persons. In 1901, less than 1,000 were returned as following these occupations. There is a large decrease, of nearly 100 per cent., under persons whose occupations have hair, camel and horse-hair, and bristles for raw material. The dyeing, bleaching and other cognate industries are in a more flourishing state than in 1901, judging from the number of persons who returned them as their occupations.

Industry.	Variations per cent.
Cotton ginning, cleaning and pressing ...	+ 62·9
Cotton spinning, sizing and weaving ...	+ 7·8
Wool carders, spinning, etc.	— 22·5
Silk spinners and weavers	+ 146·2

238. Dress and Toilet.

It is noteworthy that in a community mainly of agriculturists, the proportion of persons who find employment in industries, connected with dress and toilet, should be so high as 480 per 10,000 of the population. As might be expected there has been a large increase of tailors, milliners, dressmakers, darners and embroiders on linen since 1901 when famine conditions were just disappearing. There is a considerable disparity between the number of persons supported by industries of dress and toilet in Telingana and in Marathwara. In the former division 71 in 10,000 persons depend on them for a livelihood, whereas the corresponding proportion in the latter is only 27.

239. Other Principal Industries.

The other principal industrial occupations and the proportion of persons following them are indicated in the marginal Table. The wood industry includes basket-making. Of about 120,000 persons engaged in "food industries" nearly 80,000 are toddy drawers. The next largest class under this group is the butchers, numbering 21,192. Of the rest, rice pounders (7,308), bakers and biscuit makers (2,869), grain-parchers (2,082) and sweetmeat makers (1,652) are the more important. There is a decrease of 17 per cent. in the number of persons engaged in food industries, as a whole, the only classes showing a large increase being bakers and biscuit-makers, and makers of sugar, molasses and gur. Practically all the bakers are inhabitants of the city, and the sugar makers were all enumerated in Medak. Ceramics is represented principally by potters and earthen pipe and bowl makers. A decrease of over 80 per cent. in the number of plinth-makers and well-sinkers and an increase of about 39 per cent. in that of stone and marble workers, are the chief factors in the net increase of 15 per cent. under building industries. Of nearly 100,000 persons following industries of luxury over 93,000 are goldsmiths. About 50 newspaper editors, managers and other journalists are included among those who labour at industries of luxury. Under metal, the making of iron implements and of brass, copper and bell metal utensils are the principal occupations. The unreality of much of this classification is strikingly brought home by the fact that only 9 persons in the whole State owned to being plough and agricultural implement makers, and all the nine were inhabitants of Hyderabad City. In 1901, over 10,000 persons were placed in this category.

Industry.	Number in 10,000 persons.
Wood	110
Food industries	89
Building industries	83
Ceramics	78
Industries of luxury	73
Metals	67

240. Transport.

The industries connected with Transport include four groups :—Transport by water, by road, by rail and the Post office, telegraph and telephone. The increase in the number of persons supported by these industries, taken all together, is more than 90 per cent. The largest increases are in the number of labourers employed in making roads and railways. The decrease in the number of palki-bearers and drivers of pack animals tells its own story.

241. Trade.

This sub-class, as a whole, shows an increase of 37·5 per cent. in the number of persons supported by it over that in 1901. The piece-goods and hides-trades show a large increase in the number of persons depending on them, and this, no doubt, represents a prevailing tendency. The increase in the number of vendors of wine, liquors and aerated waters is also probably a correct representation of fact. But it is not easy to reconcile a decrease of over 50 per cent. in the number of sellers of sweetmeats, sugar, gur and molasses with the increase of 99 per cent. in that of the makers of these articles. The fact is that the scheme of classification which has been adopted presupposes a division of labour and specialisation of trade enterprise which do not exist in Hyderabad or, for the matter of that, in any other part of India. The producer here is often also the trader. Trade and industry are not sufficiently differentiated in rural India, which is the largest part of the country. Another anomaly of the same kind is presented by the increase of about 40 per cent. in the number of stone and marble workers, masons and bricklayers, and the decrease of 44 per cent. in that of persons engaged in the trade in stones. bricks, plaster and so on. Trade in wood (not firewood) supports 27 per cent. more persons than in 1901, though the number of sawyers, carpenters, turners and joiners is 12 per cent. less than in that year. The number of individuals suported by trade in fuel has increased by about 950 per cent. The increase of 478 per cent. in the number of dealers in sheep, goats and pigs closely corresponds to the increase (475·4 per cent.) in that of breeders of these animals. Furniture industries as well as the trade in furniture show a decided set-back in the decade, for which it is not easy to find a satisfactory explanation. The number of fish dealers increased by over 1,000 per cent., although the number of persons supported by fishing increased only by 134 per cent. The ratio of dealers to fishers is 1 to 3, and the presumption that an import trade (by rail) in fish might have sprung to account for the large increase in the number of dealers, is rather made difficult by the fact that more than 50 per cent. of the dealers, are found in Mahbubnagar, the larger part of which is not served by any railway, and in Karimnagar which lies wholly out of the track of either of the railways which traverse the State. Nizamabad which has the second largest fishing, population in the State has comparatively few dealers in fish. The increase of about 50 per cent. in the population supported by trade in readymade clothes and shoes is a sign of the times.

242. Administration and the Professions.

Sub-classes VI, VII and VIII relate to the public force, the public administration, and the professions and the liberal arts. The most noteworthy feature of the statistics of the military population, is the decrease of 75 per cent. in the Imperial Army. In 1901, this numbered 22,227, whereas in 1911 the number fell to 5,554. The Army of the State, on the other hand, shows an increase of nearly 50 per cent. The Police Force numbers over 3,000 per cent. more than in 1901, and the number of village watchmen has been augmented by 56 per cent. The increase of the former evidently represents the results of the administrative measures adopted to strengthen the Police Force. It is difficult to attribute the increase of village watchmen to a policy of conserving and developing the indigenous village system in the face of the decrease of over 20 per cent. exhibited in the number of village officials and servants other than watchmen in the next sub-class. The decrease of 31·8 per cent. in the number of persons supported by the public administration is evidently a measure of the endeavours that are being made to introduce economy and efficiency in the administrative system. The professional classes in the State show an increase of over 80 per cent. over the figure for 1901. Religion leads with an increase of 146 per cent. The increase in the number of priests and ministers is nearly 950 per cent. It is interesting to note that 8,075 females are returned as actual workers under this head. This number is equivalent to 54 per cent. of the number of male priests and ministers. The number of persons depending in some way or other on the profession of law shows a decrease of 1·7 per cent. The decrease, however, is chiefly in the class of lawyers' clerks, petition writers and other camp-followers, so to speak, of the legal profession. The regular profession itself shows an increase in numbers to the extent of 12·9 per cent. There is a gratifying increase of over 60 per cent. under medicine. Medical practitioners have increased by 50·4 per cent. and midwives, nurses, vaccinators, compounders and masseurs by over 106 per cent. The school master is abroad in His Highness' Dominions as elsewhere, as is evidenced by an increase not far short of 150 per cent. in the number of persons connected with Public Instruction during the decade. In the order of letters, arts and sciences, musicians and dancers increased by over 41. per cent., while authors, photographers, astronomers and astrologers decreased by 12 per cent.

243. Persons living on their Income.

The returns show 28,377 persons in this sub-class as against 51,757 in 1901. No less than 22,852 of this class were enumerated in Hyderabad City.

The income here referred to is income derived from sources other than agricultural land. It is probable that the decrease in this head, amounting to 45·1 per cent. during the decade, explains to some extent the large increase in the number of rent receivers under the head of Agriculture. It may be also due to a reduction in the number of pensioners of the State during the decade. Outside the City of Hyderabad, a leisured class is practically non-existent in these Dominions.

244. Domestic Service.

The increase under this head is 7·7 per cent. Cooks and water-carriers, and other indoor servants increased by over 9 per cent., but there was a decrease of about 22 per cent. in the number of grooms and dog-boys.

245. Insufficiently Described Occupations.

The number of persons whose business was not definitely specified, was considerably less at the present Census than in 1901.

246. Unproductive Class.

This includes inmates of jails, asylums and hospitals, as well as beggars, vagrants and prostitutes. There was a total decrease in this group of about 30 per cent. The largest decrease was among inmates of jails, asylums and hospitals. Beggars, vagrants, procurers, prostitutes, receivers of stolen goods and cattle poisoners, show a decrease of nearly 30 per cent.

247. Distribution of the population of Natural Divisions and Districts by occupations.

The foregoing paragraphs are mainly based on the materials contained in Subsidiary Tables I and VII. Subsidiary Table II gives particulars of the distribution of occupation in the two Natural Divisions and Subsidiary Table III furnishes similar but more general information for the districts.

248. It is clear from Sub-table II, that Marathwara is the predominantly agricultural division of the State. It has 665 in every 10,000 of its population depending on agriculture while Telingana's proportion is 511 . There are only two other sub-classes in which Marathwara's proportions exceed that of Telingana, and they are public administration and the professions and liberal arts. In every other group, Telingana is ahead and in many, far ahead, of Marathwara, and this is excluding the city, for which separate figures are worked out in Sub-table II. In respect of some of the industries, and of all the sub-classes commencing from transport, the city has, as might be expected, a very much higher ratio of its population following them than either of the Natural Divisions. It has, as noticed above, practically a monopoly of persons living on their income. It has by far the largest proportion of persons engaged in domestic service. In fact, one person in every five residing in the city is a domestic servant of some kind or other. Even of persons following insufficiently described occupations, the city has a far larger proportion than Telingana or Marathwara. It has also the highest proportion of persons belonging to the unproductive or disreputable group in the occupational scheme. The four districts in which the proportion of agricultural population to the total population exceeds 700 per 1,000 are named in the margin. All four are Marathwara districts. The four districts which have less than 500 in 1,000 as the ratio of agricultural to total population are all in Telingana. Karimnagar in Telingana and Gulbarga in Marathwara have the largest proportion of industrial to total population amongst districts. The former has 239 and the latter 222 in 1,000 persons, following industrial avocations. The only district in Marathwara which has a commercial population exceeding 100 persons in 1,000 is Parbhani. In Telingana, on the other hand, there is only one district, Adilabad, which has a commercial population of less than 100 in 1,000. The districts which show the highest proportions in this respect are

Districts.	Ratio of agricultural to 1,000 of total population.
Osmanabad	778
Bhir	744
Aurangabad	714
Nander	710
Nalgonda	498
Atrafbalda	481
Karimnagar	466
Medak	422

Districts.	Commercial per 1,000 of total population.
Hyderabad City	179
Medak	151
Mahabubnagar	128
Atrafibalda	125
Karimnagar	124

given in the marginal table. The distribution of the commercial and industrial population, as indicated by the Census schedules is their distribution on a particular date at a particular time of the year. Seasonal industries, the time for which was past or had not come at the time, are left out and the impression produced by the statistics is thus inconclusive. The City has, of course, the largest proportion of persons following professions.

249. Workers and Dependants.

In all the principal tables, workers in any industry are distinguished from dependants. Agriculture and industries support about the same percentage of workers and dependants, namely, 54 and 46 respectively. Commerce supports 48 dependants and the professions, 53 for every 100 persons maintained from their proceeds. Thus, professions are the most remunerative of occupations in the State, judging by the proportion of non-workers supported by them. Of course, within each of the main groups there are striking differences in the ratio of workers to dependants. And also, the same occupation does not support the same number of dependants in the several districts. Thus, in agriculture there are as many as 58 dependants to 42 workers in Raichur, while in Mahbubnagar the proportions are 64 workers and 36 dependants in every 100 of the agricultural population. Osmanabad has 57 dependants to 43 workers in industries as against Nizamabad's ratio of 61 workers and 39 dependants. The labour of 42 persons in commercial concerns in Aurangabad produces enough to support 58 dependants in addition to themselves, whereas in Atrafibalda 59 active workers in commerce can support only 41 dependants. Professions, again, support 63 dependants to every 37 workers in the Capital City, whereas in Atrafibalda, in the very environs of the city, 64 professional men have only 36 dependants. The dependant class is as a rule larger, in most occupations, in the city than in the rural areas, as a glance at columns 8 and 9 of Subsidiary Table I shows. The exceptions to this rule are readily explained by the nature of the occupations concerned. The occupations which support the largest number of dependants to workers, are shown in the marginal table. The presence of the Post Office in this category (and at the top of it too), is rather strange. The most arduous "occupation," judging from the proportion of active workers to dependants, is that of inmates of jails, asylums and hospitals. There are only 3 dependants to 97 workers in this class. Persons who returned some general term which does not indicate a definite occupation, have also to be equally busy.

Occupation.	Percentage of dependants.
Post Office, Telegraph and Telephone Services	64
Brokerage, Commission and export.	63
Law	62
Army	61
Persons living on their income ...	61

250. Women's Occupations.

Some further light is thrown on the subject-matter of the foregoing paragraph by the particulars furnished in Subsidiary Table VI of the occupations of females. The occupations in which women preponderate are stated in the marginal table. Most of the occupations in this table are recognised as women's occupations by custom and tradition. Most of them are connected with small or light articles produced in or near the homestead, or are such as make but a slight demand on physical strength. Rice pounding is, no doubt, a heavy occupation, but like drawing water from deep wells or fetching it from

Occupation.	Number of females per 1,000 males.
Rice pounders, huskers, &c.	1,30,857
Midwives, vaccinators, &c.	3,807
Sellers of milk, butter, eggs, &c. ...	2,831
Fish dealers	1,452
Dealers in hay, grass, &c.	1,398
Trade in pottery	1,283
Grain parchers...	1,243
Cotton ginning, cleaningadpsisren g	1,233
Manufacturers of tobacco	1,198
Sellers of sweetmeat, &c.	1,192
Farm servants and field labourers ...	1,184
Unspecified	1,055
Cardamom, betel leaf, &c., sellers ...	1,030
Toy, kite makers and taxidermists ...	1,029
Dealers in precious stones, &c. ...	1,026
Indefinite occupations.	1,012

distant tanks, it has for centuries been specially assigned to women. And, performed as it usually is by a group of neighbours and to the accompaniment of rural songs, it is perhaps less taxing than it seems to be. Cotton ginning, pressing and cleaning as a predominantly female occupation is, of course, a modern development. The preponderance of females among dealers in precious stones, is worthy of note. As regards other occupations, there is hardly one in which females do not figure as active workers, though they do not occupy the same position of predominance as in those referred to above. In many occupations connected with the cultivation of land and the breeding of animals, women workers take an important place. In industries, they naturally take a less prominent part, though in some, as in basket-making, manufacture of soaps and perfumery, tailoring and millinery, in industries concerned with refuse matter, and, curiously enough, among persons employed in the construction and maintenance of bridges, they are not far behind men. Reference has already been made to the large proportion of women returned as priests and ministers. Indian women of most castes have a keen commercial instinct, and they carry on a good deal of domestic trade and money-lending unknown to their husbands or other male relatives.

251. Occupation of Females by Caste.

Several tests have been proposed to gauge social precedence among castes. An infallible one is whether a caste does or does not permit its women to serve as field-labourers. Of the more than fifty castes for which particulars are furnished in Subsidiary Table VIII, 8 Hindu, and 3 Musalman castes eschew field labour as fit occupation for their women. These are the Brahman, the Komati, the Lingayat, the Lohar, the Panchal, the Rajput, the Satani and the Sutar among Hindus, and the Moghal, the Pathan and the Sayyad among Musalmans. Agriculture has always been recognised as a noble occupation, and the proudest Brahman or Sayyad has no objection to his females appearing as cultivators. Females of the Lingayat, the Mali, the Maratha and the Wanjari castes, appear in the capacity of rent receivers, a fact which shows that women in these castes are accorded larger rights of property and all that they imply in respect of their position in the home and in the family.

252. Traditional and Actual Occupation of Castes.

Imperial Table XVI gives particulars of the occupation of certain selected castes. Subsidiary Table VIII which is abstracted from it, is interesting as showing to what extent the selected castes follow their traditional occupations and how far they have diverged from it. It is evident that there is a great and growing change in some castes in this respect. The traditional occupation of the Bhois is fishing, but only 402 per 1,000 of the castes now follow it. Others have become field-labourers, cultivators and domestic servants. The Brahmin is by tradition a priest, but only 329 of the caste come under arts and professions which include law and medicine as well as religion. The Chakalas are a caste of washermen, and a considerable proportion of them are still washermen, as 800 in 1,000 of the castes are returned as following industries. The same is the case with the Dewangs, who are weavers, the Goundlas and the Kalals who are toddy sellers, the Komatis, who are traders, the Panchals who are artisans, and several others. It is not necessary to say more here in view of the observations contained in the last chapter on this point.

253. Mixed and Partial Occupations.

It has been observed above that the principle of the division of labour is very imperfectly carried out in the economic scheme of Indian society. Not only is the line between industry and commerce very faintly drawn, but industries themselves are often mixed up. The cultivator fills up his slack season by working at almost any industry which does not take him far away from his land. Certain other industries are followed in combination with cognate industries or trades. Some others still have without any apparent reason come to be traditionally associated with some others. A good illustration of this is the combination of the functions of a barber with those of a musician, which is very common in this country. Imperial Tables XV B and C give statistical information regarding the subsidiary occupations of agriculturists and certain other occupations which are followed in combination with others. Subsidiary Tables IV and V give particulars of occupations pursued in combination with agriculture either as a principal or subsidiary occupation. The rent receivers have naturally the largest proportions of persons following subsidiary occupations among the agricultural classes, the occupations most largely followed being those of agricultural labourers and rent payers. Only 56 in 10,000 cultivators are rent receivers. Administration and the professions furnish the principal subsidiary occupations of rent receivers, while the cultivators find an outlet for their surplus energies as petty tradesmen, as cattle breeders and milkmen, as weavers, blacksmiths, washermen, carpenters and so on. They may have preferences but they do not seem to have any exclusions in respect of subsidiary occupations. Farm servants and field-labourers are glad to eke out their earnings by turning their hand to cooly work, mill labour, rice pounding, weaving and any other village industry. Agriculture is followed as a subsidiary occupation by any class which has made money enough to require investment, as also by the fishing and hunting tribes which are glad to get a chance of adding to their precarious earnings by working on the fields. Public administration claims the largest proportion of persons who have agriculture as a subsidiary occupation. The mixed occupations for which statistics are given in Imperial Table XV C present a quaint combination. Thus, figures are given showing how many fishermen are palanquin-bearers and how many of the latter are fishermen, how many agricultural labourers are shoe-makers ; shepherds ; basket-weavers; cattle-breeders ; milk-sellers ; grain-dealers ; money-lenders ; barbers ; musicians ; and *vice versa*.

254. Religion and Occupation.

Subsidiary Table IX is of interest as showing the distribution of the population following each of the principal occupations by religion, and that of each religion by occupation. Except the Jain and the Parsi, who are pre-eminently traders, all religions have by far the largest proportion of their followers associated with agriculture as their principal occupation. The Hindu has the largest proportion of his co-religionists in agriculture and industry, the Jain in trade and agriculture, the Musalman in agriculture and domestic service, the Christian in agriculture, the Parsi in trade, agriculture and insufficiently described occupations, the Animist in agriculture, and " others " in agriculture, public administration, domestic service and the public force. The Hindu, of course, occupies numerically the first place in every occupation, with the Musalman a close second and in the public force, and in the public administration, among persons living on their income and in domestic service.

255. Industries in the State.

Imperial Table XV E contains statistics of factories, mills and other places of manufacture in the State, in which at least 20 persons were employed on the day of the Census. It is divided into four parts, Part I furnishes information regarding the number, race, sex and age of workers in each factory, distinguishing between factories in which mechanical power is employed and those in which it is not, Part II contains the district figures without these details, and Parts III and IV are designed to show the caste and nationality of owners and managers respectively. The last column in Part I contains remarks showing the state of each industry at the time of the Census. There are in all 121 factories in the State, of which 75 were worked by mechanical power, chiefly steam. The total number of persons employed in all the factories is 24,317 (19,461 males and 4,856 females). Europeans and Anglo-Indians are to be found only in the ranks of Managers and skilled workmen. The number of them employed in direction, supervision and clerical work is 113 (including 10 females). The number of Europeans and Anglo-Indian skilled workmen in the factories in the State is 230; over 50 per cent. of the former (actual number 57) are employed in the colliery and gold mines in these Dominions. 34 are engaged in

Railway workshops. This number includes the 10 females shown as engaged in direction, supervision and clerical work. Only 5 Indian women are employed in this grade, and all of them in cotton mills. The number and distribution of Indian males in superior employ in the several industries is given in the marginal Table. Only the principal industries are shown therein. 74 out of the 86 employed in metal industries are employes of the mint, and 138 of those engaged in construction and means of transport are connected with railway workshops. Turning to the skilled workmen class, we find that the number of Indian females (there are no European and Anglo-Indian females) in this class is 248, textile industries alone accounting for 234 of them. The number of males in this class is 7,378 distributed as shown in the margin. Only the principal industries are shown in the table.

Direction, Supervision and Clerical Work.

Industry.	Number of employés.
Textile industries	557
Mines	348
Constructions and means of transport.	145
Metal industries	86
Food industries	83
Leather and other industries	54
Industries connected with chemical products.	34

Skilled Workmen, Indian.

Industry.	Factory.
Mines	2,600
Textiles	1,739
Railway workshops	1,516
Granite dressing work	565

256. Female and child labour.

The unskilled labourers employed in all the factories of the State are distributed by age and sex, thus: Adult labourers, male 9,595, female 3,750; child labourers, male 810, female 843. The age of 14 is taken as the dividing line between children and adults for the purpose of this classification. The mines and the textile industries between them absorb over two-thirds of the adult male, and practically all the adult and child female, labourers. Male children are most in demand in textile industries. The marginal table shows the distribution of male, female and child labour in these two great industries, and in railway workshops. The mints employ 1,392 men and 30 boys.

Factory.	Men.	Women.	Boys.	Girls.
Mines	4,919	1,742	39	605
Textiles	1,736	1,748	494	192
Railway	1,377	51	12	...

257. Distribution of Factories by Districts.

Hyderabad City contains 24 factories, representing almost all industries in the State. The only electric works in these Dominions is also situated in it. Warangal is the colliery district of the State. Medak has a granite dressing works. There is a silk mill in Nizamabad. Nalgonda owns several rice mills. Aurangabad is the principal centre of the Cotton mills industry. There are several Cotton ginning factories in Parbhani. Gulburga possesses quarries of Shahabad stone, and cotton and silk mills and ginning factories. A trial exploitation was made in this district for gold, hence the entries in the Table containing a list of industries in the State. But the results were not encouraging and the Company has gone into liquidation. On the other hand, the Hutty gold mine in the Raichur district is a paying concern and is doing very well. There is every prospect of further development of this mine, when the new railway is built from Hyderabad *via* Raichur to Lingsugar. This will enable the mine to get coal fuel at a reasonable cost, and as soon as the Railway is opened it is expected that several other gold mines will be worked in this district. Raichur has also ginning and weaving factories, and is, besides, the site of a Railway and carriage works. Mussalmans head the list of factory owners and Managers, Parsis come second, and are followed in order by Komatis, Marwaris, Brahmans and Gujarati Banias. Mussalmans take the lead in leather industries and Parsis in the textiles.

SUBSIDIARY TABLE I.—General Distribution by Occupations.

Class, Sub-class and Order.	No. per 10,000 of total population.		Percentage in each Class, Sub-class and Order of		Percentage of actual workers employed.		Percentage of dependents to actual workers.	
	Persons supported.	Actual workers.	Actual workers.	Dependents.	In City.	In rural areas.	In City.	In rural areas.
1	2	3	4	5	6	7	8	9
A—Production of raw materials	6,287	3,436	55	45	1	99	122	83
I.—Exploitation of the surface of the earth.	*6,273*	*3,427*	*55*	*45*	*1*	*99*	*123*	*83*
1. Pasture and Agriculture	6,192	3,384	55	45	1	99	124	83
(a) Ordinary cultivation	5,697	3,100	54	46	1	99	128	84
(b) Growers of special products and market gardening	17	10	59	41	17	83	71	69
(c) Forestry	31	15	47	53	8	92	125	113
(d) Raising of farm stock...	447	259	58	42	1	99	143	72
(e) Raising of small animals	...	...	61	39	...	100	...	64
2. Fishing and hunting	81	43	53	47	1	99	121	87
II.—Extraction of minerals	*14*	*9*	*68*	*32*	*3*	*97*	*32*	*48*
3. Mines	12	8	69	31	3	97	17	46
4. Quarries of hard rocks	2	1	62	38	6	94	67	60
5. Salt, etc.	...	...	...	...	...	...	...	...
B—Preparation and supply of material substances	2,348	1,236	53	47	4	96	110	89
III.—Industry	*1,400*	*743*	*53*	*47*	*3*	*97*	*101*	*88*
6. Textiles	387	210	54	46	1	99	127	84
7. Hides, skins and hard materials from the animal kingdom	12	6	54	46	2	98	125	85
8. Wood	110	57	51	49	2	98	127	94
9. Metals	67	31	47	53	3	97	110	113
10. Ceramics	78	42	54	46	2	98	124	84
11. Chemical products, properly so called and analogous	14	8	53	47	2	98	94	87
12. Food industries	89	47	53	47	9	91	116	86
13. Industries of dress and toilet	480	262	54	46	3	97	87	84
14. Furniture industries	...	...	49	51	82	18	109	74
15. Building industries	83	43	52	48	5	95	80	92
16. Construction of means of transport	2	1	64	36	77	23	50	77
17. Production and transmission of physical forces (heat, light, Electricity, motive power, etc.)	...	54	54	46	100	...	86	...
18. Industries of luxury and those pertaining to literature and the arts and sciences ...	73	33	46	54	6	94	111	120
19. Industries concerned with refuse matter ...	58	3	55	45	39	61	95	75
IV.—Transport	*100*	*53*	*53*	*47*	*15*	*85*	*75*	*93*
20. Transport by water	2	1	57	43	...	100	67	77
21. Do. road	83	45	54	46	12	88	76	87
22. Do. rail	14	7	46	54	38	62	62	152
23. Post Office, Telegraph and Telephone Services	1	...	36	64	69	31	198	122

SUBSIDIARY TABLE I.—General Distribution by Occupations—*continued.*

Class, Sub-class and Order.	No. per 10,000 of total population.		Percentage in each Class, Sub-class and Order of		Percentage of actual workers employed.		Percentage of dependents to actual workers.	
	Persons supported.	Actual workers.	Actual workers.	Dependents.	In City.	In rural areas.	In City.	In rural areas.
1	2	3	4	5	6	7	8	9
V.—Trade ...	*848*	*440*	*51*	*49*	*5*	*95*	*131*	*91*
24. Banks, establishments of credit, exchange and insurance ...	16	7	44	56	9	91	151	127
25. Brokerage, commission and export ...	3	1	37	63	69	31	204	96
26. Trade in textiles ...	61	31	52	48	3	97	129	93
27. Trade in skins, leather and furs ...	11	6	55	45	4	96	87	83
28. Trade in wood ...	6	4	54	46	·11	89	43	90
29. Trade in metals ...	1	...	44	56	47	53	215	53
30. Trade in pottery ...	8	4	51	49	6	94	90	97
31. Trade in Chemical product... ...	2	1	45	55	54	46	163	73
32. Hotels, cafes, restaurants, etc. ...	181	101	50	50	2	98	116	78
33. Other trade in food stuffs ...	293	151	51	49	6	94	137	92
34. Trade in clothing and toilet articles ...	13	6	49	51	7	93	168	101
35. Trade in furniture ...	6	3	53	47	9	91	88	89
36. Trade in building materials ...	1	1	46	54	27	73	102	123
37. Trade in means of transport ...	12	6	49	51	2	98	253	101
38. Trade in fuel ...	19	10	52	48	9	91	118	90
39. Trade in articles of luxury and those pertaining to letters and the arts and sciences ...	35	18	53	47	7	93	111	87
40. Trade in refuse matter ...	...	...	...	...	...	...	...	...
41. Trade of other sorts ...	181	90	50	50	5	95	123	100
C.—Public Administration and Liberal arts ...	**559**	**249**	**45**	**55**	**15**	**85**	**169**	**116**
VI.—Public Force ...	*123*	*51*	*42*	*58*	*33*	*67*	*180*	*120*
42. Army ...	51	20	39	61	71	29	168	135
43. Navy ...	...	...	...	...	...	...	...	...
44. Police ...	72	31	44	56	1	99	238	117
VII.—Public Administration ...	*259*	*117*	*45*	*55*	*9*	*91*	*129*	*120*
45. Public Administration ...	259	117	45	55	9	91	129	120
VIII.—Profession and liberal arts ...	*156*	*73*	*47*	*53*	*8*	*92*	*189*	*108*
46. Religion... ...	76	32	43	57	7	93	176	132
47. Law ...	5	2	38	62	31	69	187	157
48. Medicine ...	23	13	56	44	9	91	167	70
49. Instruction ...	17	8	44	56	18	82	182	116
50. Letters and arts and sciences ...	35	13	52	48	4	96	286	84
IX.—Persons living on their income ...	*21*	*8*	*39*	*61*	*80*	*20*	*161*	*151*
51. Persons living principally on their income.	21	8	39	61	80	20	161	151
D.—Miscellaneous ...	**806**	**441**	**55**	**45**	**13**	**87**	**165**	**79**
X.—Domestic service ...	*315*	*162*	*51*	*49*	*24*	*76*	*111*	*89*
52. Domestic service ...	315	162	51	49	24	76	111	89
XI.—Insufficiently described occupations ...	*284*	*166*	*58*	*42*	*7*	*93*	*93*	*70*
53. General terms which do not indicate a definite occupation ...	284	166	97	3	7	93	93	70
XII.—Unproductive ...	*207*	*113*	*55*	*45*	*6*	*94*	*9*	*82*
54. Inmates of jails, asylums and hospitals ...	3	2	97	3	23	77	10	1
55. Beggars, vagrants, and prostitutes... ...	204	111	54	46	6	94	102	83

SUBSIDIARY TABLE II.—Distribtiuon by occupation in Natural Divisions.

Sub-classes and selected orders.	No. per mille of the total population supported in Natural Division.		
	Hyderabad City.	Telingana.	Marathwara.
1	2	3	4
I.—Exploitation of the surface of the earth ...	97	578	714
(a) Agriculture (order 1) (groups 1-6)	75	511	665
(b) Pasture (order 1) (groups 9-12)	13	50	42
(c) Fishing and hunting (order 2)	2	11	6
(d) Others (order 1) (groups 7, 8 and 13)	7	6	1
II.—Extraction of minerals...	1	2	1
III.—Industry	131	185	99
(a) Textile industries (order 6)	14	53	27
(b) Wood industries (order 8)	8	12	11
(c) Metal industries (order 9)	4	9	5
(d) Food industries (order 12)	26	14	3
(e) Industries of dress and the toilet (order 13)... ...	39	71	27
(f) Other industries (orders 7, 10, 11, 14 to 19) ...	40	26	26
IV.—Transport	37	10	8
V.—Trade	142	107	60
(a) Trade in food-stuffs (order 32 and 33)	75	66	26
(b) Trade in textiles (order 26)	6	7	5
(c) Other trades (orders 24, 25, 27 to 31 & 34 to 41) ...	61	34	27
VI.—Public force	126	8	8
VII.—Public administration...	54	17	32
VIII.—Professions and liberal arts	49	13	15
IX.—Persons living on their income	46	... ...	......
X.—Domestic service	219	27	22
XI.—Insufficiently described occupation	62	32	22
XII.—Unproductive	36	21	19

SUBSIDIARY TABLE III—Distribution of the Agricultural, Industrial, Commercial and Professional Population in Natural Divisions and Districts.

District and Natural Division.	Agricultural. Population supported by Agriculture.	Proportion of agricultural population per 1,000 of district population.	Percentage on agricultural population of. Actual workers.	Dependents.	Industry (including mines). Population supported by industry.	Proportion of industrial population per 1,000 of district population.	Percentage on industrial population of. Actual workers.	Dependents.
1	2	3	4	5	6	7	8	9
State	**7,642,309**	**571**	**54**	**46**	**1,891,207**	**141**	**54**	**46**
Telingana	**3,219,019**	**479**	**60**	**40**	**1,228,433**	**183**	**55**	**45**
Hyderabad City	37,413	75	45	55	66,127	132	50	50
Atrafibalda	250,201	481	58	42	99,068	190	55	45
Warangal	485,225	536	59	41	161,576	178	56	44
Karimnagar	527,009	466	60	40	270,806	239	54	46
Adilabad	417,450	673	54	46	69,365	112	52	48
Medak	290,282	422	61	39	135,543	197	54	46
Nizamabad	297,094	528	57	43	100,756	177	61	39
Mahbubnagar	399,801	535	64	36	126,004	169	55	45
Nalgonda	514,544	498	66	34	199,188	191	58	42
Marathwara...	**4,423,290**	**665**	**50**	**50**	**662,774**	**100**	**50**	**50**
Aurangabad	621,293	714	50	50	77,805	89	45	55
Bhir	462,954	744	58	42	49,036	79	57	43
Nander	500,478	710	55	45	61,817	88	52	48
Parbhani...	465,111	597	53	47	75,294	97	50	50
Gulbarga...	679,891	591	48	52	140,135	222	52	48
Osmanabad	491,506	773	53	47	43,062	83	43	57
Raichur	605,097	607	42	58	110,418	111	48	52
Bidar	596,960	671	47	53	95,212	107	49	51

District and Natural Division.	Commerce. Population supported by commerce.	Proportion of commercial population per 1,000 of district population.	Percentage on commercial population of Actual workers.	Dependents.	Professions. Population supported by profession.	Proportion of professional population per 1,000 of district population.	Percentage on professional population of Actual workers.	Dependents.
1	10	11	12	13	14	15	16	17
State	**1,268,319**	**95**	**52**	**48**	**209,039**	**16**	**47**	**53**
Telingana	**815,179**	**121**	**54**	**46**	**107,709**	**16**	**47**	**53**
Hyderabad City	89,458	179	46	54	24,508	49	37	63
Atrafibalda	64,867	125	59	41	7,877	15	64	36
Warangal	101,639	112	53	47	15,528	17	50	50
Karimnagar	139,994	124	54	46	12,310	11	49	51
Adilabad	41,978	68	55	45	5,576	9	42	58
Medak	108,470	151	53	47	10,650	16	46	54
Nizamabad	64,590	114	54	46	5,540	10	48	52
Mahbubnagar	95,819	128	56	44	10,111	14	47	53
Nalgonda	113,394	109	58	42	15,614	15	53	47
Marathwara	**453,140**	**68**	**48**	**52**	**101,330**	**15**	**46**	**54**
Aurangabad	44,575	51	42	58	12,853	15	37	63
Bhir	24,860	40	52	48	7,085	11	49	51
Nander	40,768	58	48	52	18,013	26	61	39
Parbhani	79,442	102	46	54	13,866	18	46	54
Gulbarga	109,044	95	48	52	17,825	15	39	61
Osmanabad	26,608	42	46	54	9,432	15	44	56
Raichur	68,641	69	52	48	14,188	14	45	55
Bidar	59,002	66	47	53	8,068	9	43	57

SUBSIDIARY TABLE IV.—Occupations combined with Agriculture (where agriculture is the subsidiary occupation).

Occupation.	Number per mille of actual workers who are partially agriculturists.		
	State.	Telingana.	Marathwara.
1	2	3	4
I.—Exploitation of the surface of the earth ...	26	35	18
(a) Agriculture (order 1 to 6)	21	30	11
(b) Pasture (order 1,9-12)	64	62	68
(c) Fishing and hunting (order 2)	161	110	255
(d) Others (order 1-7-8-13)	130	145	11
II.—Extraction of minerals	11	......	36
III.—Industry	86	80	98
(a) Textile (order 6)	64	55	83
(b) Wood industries (order 8)	90	87	94
(c) Metal „ („ 9)	110	109	111
(d) Food „ („ 12)	99	98	109
(e) Industries of dress (order 13)	98	86	118
(f) Others (7, 10-11 and 14 to 19)	93	89	97
IV.—Transport	61	56	69
V.—Trade	86	83	93
(a) Trade (orders 32 and 33)	90	88	96
(b) Trade (order 26)	92	62	141
(c) Other trades (24, 25, 27 to 31 and 34 to 41) ...	80	78	82
VI.—Public force...	74	59	103
VII.—Public administration	133	120	142
VIII.—Professions and liberal arts...	99	94	104
IX.—Persons living on their income	20	11	69
X.—Domestic service	50	33	81
XI.—Insufficiently described occupation	60	66	49
XII.—Unproductive	54	46	65

SUBSIDIARY TABLE V.—Occupations combined with Agriculture (where agriculture is the principal occupation).

Landlords (Rent receivers).		Cultivators (Rent payers).		Farm servants and field labourers.	
Subsidiary occupation.	Number per 10,000 who follow it.	Subsidiary occupation.	Number per 10,000 who follow it.	Subsidiary occupation.	Number per 10,000 who follow it.
1	2	3	4	5	6
All subsidiary occupations.	876	....	838	....	224
Rent payers	249	Rent receivers	56	Rent receivers	34
Agricultural labourers ...	263	Agricultural labourers ...	104	Rent payers	38
Government employés of all kinds.	45	General labourers ...	17	General labourers ...	45
Money lenders and grain dealers.	34	Government employés of all kinds.	14	Village watchmen ...	5
Other traders of all kinds	59	Money lenders and grain dealers.	14	Cattle breeders and milkmen.	20
Priests	19	Other traders of all kinds	25	Mill hands	6
Clerks of all kinds (not Government.)	20	Fishermen and boatmen.	9	Fishermen and boatmen.	4
School masters	15	Cattle breeders and milkmen.	20	Rice pounders	14
Lawyers	6	Village watchmen ...	6	Traders of all kinds ...	11
Estate agents and managers.	6	Weavers	9	Oil pressers	3
Medical practitioners ...	15	Barbers	7	Weavers	8
Artisans	40	Oil pressers	6	Potters	5
Others	105	Washermen	11	Leather workers... ...	6
		Potters	9	Washermen	8
		Blacksmiths and carpenters	8	Blacksmiths and carpenters.	8
		Others	18	Others	19

SUBSIDIARY TABLE VI.—Occupation of Females by Sub-Classes and Selected Orders and Groups (1911).

Group Number.	OCCUPATION.	Number of Actual Workers.		Number of females per 1,000 males.
		Males.	Females.	
1-15	I.—Exploitation of the surface of the earth	*2,721,445*	*1,862,451*	*684*
1-13	1. *Pasture and agriculture*	*2,670,018*	*1,856,165*	*695*
1-4	(*a*) Ordinary cultivation	2,408,868	1,737,615	721
1	Income from rent of agricultural land	234,108	113,407	484
2	Ordinary cultivators	1,367,676	727,383	532
4	Farm servants and field labourers	790,731	896,825	1,134
5 & 6	(*b*) Growers of special products and market gardening	8,137	5,349	657
6	Fruit, flower, vegetable, betel vine, areca-nut, etc., growers	8,137	5,349	657
7 & 8	(*c*) Forestry	12,248	7,285	595
8	Wood-cutters, firewood, lac, catechu, rubber, etc., collectors and charcoal burners	11,897	7,285	612
9-12	(*d*) Raising or farm stock	240,754	105,916	440
9	Cattle and buffalo breeders and keepers	13,153	10,446	794
10	Sheep, goat and pig breeders	38,398	19,916	520
12	Herdsmen, shepherds, goat-herds, etc.	188,979	75,552	400
14 & 15	2. *Fishing and hunting*	*51,427*	*6,286*	*122*
14	Fishing	37,954	5,520	145
15	Hunting	13,473	766	57
16-20	II.—Extraction of minerals	*9,734*	*2,780*	*286*
16-17	3. *Mines*	*8,224*	*2,328*	*283*
16	Coal mines and petroleum wells	6,577	1,996	303
21-93	III.—Industry	*676,082*	*318,086*	*470*
21-31	6. *Textiles*	*174,159*	*106,746*	*613*
21	Cotton ginning, cleaning and pressing	16,737	20,636	1,233
22	Cotton spinning, sizing and weaving	107,226	60,586	565
24	Rope, twine, and string	9,468	6,575	694
26	Wool carders and spinners, weavers of woollen blankets, carpets, etc.	31,486	14,515	461
27	Silk spinners and weavers	652	374	574
30	Dyeing, bleaching, printing, preparation and sponging of textiles	7,134	4,015	563
32-35	7. *Hides, skins, and hard materials from the animal kingdom*	*6,634*	*1,921*	*290*
33	Tanners, curriers, leather dressers, dyers, etc.	2,067	1,064	514
36 & 37	8. *Wood*	*55,611*	*19,837*	*357*
36	Sawyers, carpenters, turners, joiners, etc.	36,290	3,955	109
37	Basket markes and other industries of woody material including leaves	19,321	15,882	822
38 & 44	9. *Metals*	*30,665*	*10,956*	*357*
41	Other workers in iron and makers of tools principally or exclusively of iron	24,296	9,652	397
42	Workers in brass, copper and bell metal	5,284	1,253	237
45-49	10. *Ceramics*	*37,591*	*18,566*	*494*
47	Potters and earthen pipe and bowl makers	37,046	18,460	498
50-55	11. *Chemical products properly so called, and analogous*	*7,568*	*2,704*	*357*
53	Manufacture and refining of vegetable and mineral oils	7,110	2,534	356
55	Others (soap, candles, lac, cutch, perfumes and miscellaneous drugs)	177	166	938
56-66	12. *Food industries*	*49,288*	*13,892*	*282*
56	Rice pounders, huskers, and flour grinders	28	3,664	130,857
58	Grain purchers, etc.	642	798	1,243
59	Butchers	7,258	2,803	386
60	Fish curers	8	5	625
63	Sweat makers, preparers of jam and condiments, etc.	506	385	761
65	Toddy drawers	38,858	5,233	135
66	Manufactures of tobacco, opium and ganja	565	677	1,198
67-73	13. *Industries of dress and the toilet*	*234,466*	*115,228*	*491*
68	Tailors, milliners, dress makers and darners, embroiderers on linen	20,022	16,848	841
69	Shoe, boot and sandal makers	101,423	41,983	414
70	Other industries pertaining to dress gloves, socks, gaiters, belts, buttonss, umbrellas, canes, etc.	373	302	810
71	Washing, cleaning and dyeing	75,606	51,071	675
72	Barbers, hair dressers and wig makers	36,672	5,018	137

SUBSIDIARY TABLE VI.—OCCUPATION OF FEMALES BY SUB-CLASSES AND SELECTED ORDERS AND GROUPS (1911)—*contd.*

Group Number.	OCCUPATION.	Number of Actual Workers. Males.	Number of Actual Workers. Females.	Number of females per 1,000 males.
74-79	*15. Building industries* ...	*41,344*	*16,678*	*403*
78	Stone and marble workers, masons, bricklayers ...	37,021	15,798	427
84-92	*18. Industries of luxury and those pertaining to literature and the arts and sciences* ...	*34,780*	*9,831*	*283*
89	Workers in precious stones and metals, enamellers, imitation jewellery scavengers, makers, gilders, etc. ...	33,079	9,452	286
91	Toy, kite, cage, fishing tackle, etc., makers, taxidermists, etc. ...	84	85	1,029
93	*19. Industries concerned with refuse matter* ...	*1,976*	*1,699*	*860*
93	Sweepers, scavengers, dust and sweeping contractors ...	1,976	1,699	860
94-105	IV.—TRANSPORT ...	*51,561*	*18,866*	*366*
98-102	*21. Transport by road* ...	*41,919*	*18,004*	*429*
98	Persons employed on the construction and maintenance of roads and bridges ...	15,891	13,208	831
99	Cart owners and drivers, coachmen, stable-boys, tramway, mail carriage, etc., managers, employes (excluding private servants) ...	21,226	3,666	172
101	Pack elephant, camel, mule, ass and bullock owners and drivers.	449	257	572
103-104	*22. Transport by rail* ...	*7,861*	*698*	*89*
103	Railway employes of all kinds other than construction coolies.	6,323	210	33
106-138	V. TRADE. ...	*357,289*	*230,646*	*646*
	24. Banks, establishments of credit, exchange and insurance ...	*7,313*	*2,382*	*326*
106	Bank managers, money lenders, exchange and insurance agents, money changers and brokers and their employes ...	7,313	2,382	326
107	*25. Brokerage commission and export* ...	*794*	*532*	*670*
107	Brokers, commission agents, commercial travellers, warehouse owners and employes ...	794	532	670
108	*26. Trade in textiles* ...	*32,680*	*9,108*	*279*
108	Trade in piece-goods, wool, cotton, silk, hair and other textiles.	32,680	9,108	279
109	*27. Trade in skins, leather and furs* ...	*6,165*	*2,163*	*351*
109	Trade in skins, leather, furs, feathers (horn), etc. ...	6,165	2,163	351
110	*28. Trade in wood* ...	*2,593*	*2,005*	*773*
110	Trade in wood (not firewood), cork, bark, etc. ...	2,593	2,005	773
112	*30. Trade in pottery* ...	*2,503*	*3,211*	*1,283*
112	Trade in pottery ...	2,503	3,211	1,283
113	*31. Trade in chemical products* ...	*713*	*394*	*553*
113	Trade in chemical products (drugs, dyes, paints, petroleum, explosives, etc.) ...	713	394	553
114&115	*32. Hotels, cafes, restaurants, etc.* ...	*69,324*	*65,721*	*948*
114	Vendors of wine, liquors, aerated waters, etc. ...	69,248	65,656	948
115	Owners, managers of hotels, cook, shops, sarais, etc., and their employes ...	76	65	855
116-124	*33. Other trades in food stuffs* ...	*115,556*	*85,551*	*740*
116	Fish dealers ...	5,318	7,722	1,452
117	Grocers and sellers of vegetables, oil, salt and other condiments	32,155	21,919	683
118	Sellers of milk, butter, ghee, poultry, eggs, etc....	2,193	6,209	2,831
119	Sellers of sweetmeats, sugar, gur and molasses ...	990	1,188	1,192
120	Cardamon, betel leaf, vegetables, fruit and arecanut sellers ...	27,214	28,019	1,030
121	Grain and pulse dealers ...	37,380	14,815	396
122	Tobacco, opium, ganja, etc., sellers...	1,354	690	510
123	Dealers in sheep, goats and pigs ...	7,664	3,189	416
124	Dealers in hay, grass and fodder ...	1,288	1,800	1,398
125	*34. Trade in clothing and toilet articles* ...	*4,688*	*3,395*	*724*
125	Trade in ready made clothing and other articles of dress and the toilet, hats, umbrellas, socks, ready made shoes, perfumes, etc. ...	4,688	3,395	724
126& 127	*35. Trade in furniture* ...	*2,960*	*1,099*	*371*
126	Trade in furniture, carpets, curtains and bedding ...	2,206	1,027	466

SUBSIDIARY TABLE VI.—Occupation of Females by Sub-Classes and Selected Orders and Groups (1911)—*concld.*

Group Number.	OCCUPATION.	Number of Actual Workers — Males.	Number of Actual Workers — Females.	Number of females per 1,000 males.
129	*37. Trade in means of transport*	*5,838*	*1,814*	*311*
129	Dealers and hirers of elephants, camels, horses, cattle, asses, mules, etc., sellers (not makers) of carriages saddlery, etc.	5,838	1,814	311
130	*38. Trade in fuel*	*7,063*	*6,379*	*903*
130	Dealers in firewood, charcoal, coal, cowdung, etc.	7,063	6,379	903
131-133	*39. Trade in articles of luxury and those pertaining to letters and the arts and sciences*	*12,453*	*12,069*	*969*
131	Dealers in precious stones, jewellery (real and imitation), clocks, optical, instruments, etc.	2,008	2,061	1,026
132	Dealers in common bangles, bead necklaces, fans, small articles, toys, hunting and fishing tackle, flowers, etc.	10,151	9,960	981
135& 138	*41. Trade of other sorts*	*85,825*	*34,645*	*404*
136	Shop keepers otherwise unspecified	85,082	34,311	403
137	Conjurors, acrobats, fortune-tellers, reciters, exhibitors of curiosities and wild animals	743	305	410
139-143	VI.—Public force	*68,271*	*278*	*4*
139& 140	*42. Army*	*26,328*	*278*	*11*
140	Army (Native States)	23,392	278	12
144-147	VII.—Public Administration	*149,366*	*7,343*	*49*
144-147	*45. Public administration*	*149,366*	*7,343*	*49*
147	Village officials and servants other than watchmen	84,278	6,523	77
148-160	VIII.—Professions and liberal arts	*71,038*	*26,305*	*371*
148-151	*46. Religion*	*30,137*	*12,953*	*430*
148	Priests, ministers, etc.	14,931	8,075	541
149	Religions, mendicants, inmates of monasteries, etc.	11,507	4,261	370
154-155	*48. Medicine*	*13,383*	*3,880*	*290*
154	Medical practitioners of all kinds, including dentists, occulists, and veterinary surgeons	12,651	1,093	86
155	Midwives, vaccinators, compounders, nurses, masseurs, etc.	732	2,787	3807
156	*49. Instruction*	*8,360*	*1,995*	*239*
156	Professors and teachers of all kinds and clerks and servants connected with education	8,360	1,995	239
157-160	*50. Letters and arts and sciences*	*16,665*	*7,501*	*450.*
159	Others (authors) photographers, artists, sculptures, astronomers, meteo rologists, botanists, astrologers, etc.	5,031	1,463	291
160	Music composers and masters, players on all kinds of musical instruments (not military) singers, actors and dancers	11,215	6,038	538
161	IX.—Persons living on their income	*8,651*	*2,289*	*265*
161	*51. Persons living principally on their income*	*8,650*	*2,289*	*265*
161	Proprietors (other than of agricultural land) fund and scholarship holders and pensioners	8,650	2,289	265
162-163	X.—Domestic service	*140,971*	*75,814*	*538*
162&163	*52. Domestic service*	*140,971*	*75,814*	*538*
162	Cooks, water carriers, door-keepers, clerks and other employes in unspecified offices, warehouses and shops	133,663	75,580	565
163	Private grooms, coachmen, dog boys, etc.	7,308	234	32
164-167	XI.—Insufficientey described occupations	*110,010*	*111,369*	*1,012*
164-165	*53. General terms which do not indicate a definite occupation.*	*110,010*	*111,369*	*1,012*
164	Manufacturers, business men, and contractors otherwise unspecified	2,080	992	477
167	Labourers and workmen otherwise unspecified	103,555	110,296	1,065
168-169	XII.—Unproductive	*336,361*	*253,042*	*752*
169	*55. Beggars, vagrants, prostitutes*	*82,182*	*65,728*	*800*
169	Beggars, vagrants, procurers, prostitutes, receivers of stolen goods, cattle poisoners	82,182	65,728	800

SUBSIDIARY TABE VII.—Selected Occupations (1911 and 1901).

Group Number.	Occupation.	Population supported in 1911.	Population supported in 1901.	Percentage of variation.
	Grand Total ...	13,374,676	11,141,142	+ 20·0
	I.—EXPLOITATION OF THE SURFACE OF THE EARTH	*8,389,718*	*5,471,452*	+ *53·3*
	1. Pasture and Agriculture	*8,281,829*	*5,436,981*	+ *52·3*
	(a) Ordinary cultivation	7,619,505	4,599,741	+ 65·6
1	Income from rent of agricultural land	731,803	39,581	+ 1,748·8
2	Ordinary cultivators	4,064,950	3,473,561	+ 17·0
3	Agents, managers of landed estates (not planters), clerks, rent collectors, etc.	34,540	62,956	— 45·1
4	Farm servants and field labourers	2,788,212	1,028,643	+ 172·8
	(b) Growers of special products and market gardening ...	22,804	532,175	— 95·7
5	Tea, coffee, chinchona and indigo plantations	......	91	......
6	Fruit, flower, vegetable, betel vine, arecanut, etc., growers.	22,804	532,084	— 95·7
	(c) Forestry	41,774	6,103	+ 584·4
8	Woodcutters, firewood, lac, catechu, rubber, etc., collectors and charcoal burners...	40,905	5,127	+ 697·8
	(d) Raising of farm stock	597,728	298,962	+ 99·9
9	Cattle and buffalo breeders and keepers	42,418	64,055	— 33·7
10	Sheep, goat, pig breeders	109,739	19,070	+ 475·4
11	Breeders of other animals (horses, mules, camels, asses, etc.)	413	2,654	— 84·4
12	Herdsmen, shepherds, etc.	445,158	213,183	+ 108·8
	(e) Raising of small animals	18	......	......
	2. Fishing and hunting	*107,889*	*34,471*	+ *212·9*
14	Fishing	78,269	33,897	+ 134·3
15	Hunting	29,620	1,074	+ 2,657·9
	II.—EXTRACTION OF MINERALS	*18,474*	*384*	+ *4,712·5*
	3. Mines	*15,325*	*139*	+ *10,925·1*
	4. Quarries of hard rocks	*3,149*	......	......
	5. Salt, etc.	......	*245*	......
	III.—INDUSTRY	*1,872,733*	*1,682,751*	+ *11·2*
	6. Textiles	*517,750*	*462,721*	+ *11·8*
21	Cotton ginning, cleaning and pressing	69,943	42,932	+ 62·9
22	Cotton spinning, sizing and weaving...	302,745	280,604	+ 7·8
23	Jute spinning, pressing and weaving...	1,098	......	......
24	Rope, twine and string	28,954	994	+ 2,812·8
26	Wool carders and spinners, weavers of woollen blankets, carpets, etc.	89,095	114,991	— 22·5
27	Silk spinners and weavers	1,901	772	+ 146·2
28	Hair, camel and horsehair, bristles work, brush makers, etc.	77	9,071	— 99·1
29	Persons occupied with feathers	204	250	— 18·4
30	Dyeing bleaching, printing preparation and sponging of textiles	22,810	12,776	+ 74·6
	7. Hides, skins and hard materials from the animal kingdom	*15,930*	*7,959*	+ *100·1*
32	Tanner, curriers, leather dressers, dyers, etc.	7,061	5,010	+ 40·9
33	Makers of the leather articles, such as trunks, waterbags, etc.	7,946	1,499	+ 430·0
34	Furriers	462	619	+ 25·3
35	Bone, ivory, horn, shells, etc., workers	461	831	— 44·5
	8. Wood	*146,747*	*130,392*	+ *12·5*
36	Sawyers, carpenters, turners, joiners, etc.	87,903	100,935	— 12·9
37	Basket-makers and other industries of woody material including leaves	58,844	29,457	+ 99·7
	9. Metal	*88,772*	*94,465*	— *6·0*
39	Plough and agricultural implement makers	9	10,115	— 0·9
41	Other workers in iron and makers of implements and tools principally or exclusively of iron	73,586	60,391	+ 21·8
42	Workers in brass, copper and bell metal	12,925	19,168	— 32·5
	10. Ceramics	*103,514*	*83,154*	+ *24·4*
47	Potters and earthen pipe and bowl makers	102,373	78,838	+ 29·8
	11. Chemical products properly so-called, and analogous.	*19,211*	*25,166*	— *23·6*
53	Manufacture and refining of vegetable and mineral oils ...	18,091	14,928	+ 21·1

SUBSIDIARY TABLE VII.—Selected Occupations (1911 and 1901)—*contd.*

Group Number.	Occupation.	Population supported in 1911.	Population supported in 1901.	Percentage of variation.
	12. Food industries	*119,245*	*144,502*	− 17·4
56	Rice pounders, huskers, and flour grinders	7,308	9,542	− 23·4
57	Bakers and biscuit makers	2,869	1,030	+ 178·5
58	Grain parchers, etc.	2,082	7,851	− 17·6
59	Butchers	21,192	28,748	− 26·3
60	Fish curers	13	......	......
62	Makers of sugar, molasses and gur	249	125	+ 99·3
63	Sweetmeat makers, preparers of jams and condiments, etc.	1,652	1,410	+ 17·1
64	Brewers and distillers	443	5,841	− 92·4
65	Toddy drawers	79,852	88,702	− 9·9
	13. Industries of dress and the toilet	*642,448*	*530,308*	+ 21·1
68	Tailor milliners, dressmakers and darners, embroiderers on linen	70,859	38,434	+ 84·3
69	Shoe, boots and sandal makers	269,048	234,674	+ 14·6
71	Washing, cleaning and dyeing	214,921	149,082	+ 44·1
72	Barbers, hair dresser and wig makers	85,880	85,986	− 0·1
	14. Furniture industries	*255*	*1,483*	− 82·8
	15. Building industres	*111,174*	*95,966*	+ 15·8
77	Excavators, plinth builders, and well sinkers	2,149	17,153	− 87·4
78	Stone and marble workers, masons, bricklayers	101,530	73,847	+ 38·4
	16. Construction of means of transport	*2,910*	*1,246*	+ *133·5*
	17. Production and transmissions of physical forces (heat light, electricity, motive power, etc.)	*78*	*202*	− 61·3
	18. Industries of luxury and those pretaining to literature and the arts and sciences	*97,951*	*96,387*	+ 1·6
89	Workers in precious stones and metals, enamellers, imitation jewellery makers, gilders, etc.	93,489	83,718	+ 11·6
90	Makers of bangles, rosaries, bead and other necklaces, spangles, lingams and sacred threads	2,871	2,249	+ 27·6
	19. Industries concerned with refuse matter	*6,728*	*8,800*	− 25·5
93	Sweepers, scavengers, dust and sweeping contractors	6,728	8,800	− 23·5
	IV.—TRANSPORT	*133,951*	*69,129*	+ *93·7*
	20. Transport by water	*2,667*	*2,718*	+ *1·8*
95	Ship owners and their employès, ship brokers, ships' officers, engineers, mariners and firemen	......	.....	......
96	Persons employed on the maintenance of streams, rivers and canals (including construction)	2,336	2,273	+ 2·7
97	Boat owners, boatmen and towmen	331	438	− 24·4
	21. Transport by road	*111,476*	*52,168*	+ *113·6*
98	Persons employed on the construction and maintenance of roads and bridges	51,879	2,864	+ 1,711·4
99	Cart owners and drivers, coachmen, stable boys, tramway mail carriage, etc., managers and employès (excluding, private servants)	47,907	28,135	+ 70·2
100	Palki, etc., bearers and owners	1,674	11,106	− 84·9
101	Pack elephant, camel, mule, ass, bullock owners and drivers	1,335	1,865	− 28·4
102	Porters and messengers	8,681	8,198	+ 5·8
	22. Transport by rail	*18,609*	*10,537*	+ *76·6*
103	Railway employès of all kinds other than construction coolies	13,794	10,262	+ 34·4
104	Labourers employed on railway construction	4,815	275	+ 1,650·9
	23. Post office, telegraph and telephone service	*1,199*	*3,706*	− *67·6*
105	Post office, telegraph and telephone service	1,199	3,706	− 67·6
	V.—TRADE	*1,134,368*	*824,485*	+ *37·5*
	24. Banks, establishments of credit exchange and insurance	*22,223*	*36,232*	− *38·6*
106	Bank managers, money lenders, exchange and insurance agents, money changers and brokers and their employès	22,223	36,232	− 38·6
	25. Brokerage, commission and export	*3,588*	*3,001*	+ *19·5*
107	Brokers, commission agents, commercial travellers, warehouse owners and employès	3,588	3,001	+ 19·5

SUBSIDIARY TABLE VII.—SELECTED OCCUPATIONS (1911 AND 1901)—*concld.*

Group Number.	Occupation.	Population supported in 1911.	Population supported in 1901.	Percentage of variation.
	26. Trade in textiles	*81,139*	*28,648*	*+ 183·2*
108	Trade in piece-goods, wool, cotton, silk, hair, and other textiles	81,139	28,648	+ 183·2
	27. Trade in skins, leather and furs	*15,218*	*5,454*	*+ 179·0*
109	Trade in skins, leather, furs, feathers, horn, etc.	15,218	5,454	+ 179·0
	28. Trade in wood	*8,511*	*6,662*	*+ 27·7*
110	Trade in wood (not fire wood), cork, bark, etc.	8,511	6,662	+ 27·7
	29. Trade in metals	*959*	*1,150*	*— 16·6*
	30. Trade in pottery	*11,228*	*7,427*	*+ 51·1*
112	Trade in pottery	11,228	7,427	+ 51·1
	31. Trade in chemical products	*2,454*	*13,351*	*— 81·6*
113	Trade in chemical products (drugs, dyes, paints, petroleum, explosives, etc.)	2,454	13,351	— 81·6
	32. Hotels, cafes, restaurants, etc.	*241,975*	*129,571*	*+ 86·7*
114	Venders of wine, liquors, aerated waters, etc.	241,714	129,125	+ 87·1
115	Owners and managers of hotels, cookshops, sarais, etc., and their employés	261	446	— 41·4
	33. Other trade in food stuffs	*391,941*	*192,789*	*+ 103·3*
116	Fish dealers	24,960	2,032	+ 1,128·3
117	Grocers and sellers of vegetable oil, salt and other condiments	112,156	58,486	+ 91·9
118	Sellers of milk, butter, ghee, poultry, eggs, etc.	17,040	14,977	+ 13·7
119	Sellers of sweetmeats, sugar, gur, molasses	4,656	9,699	— 51·9
120	Cardamom, betel-leaf, vegetables, fruit and arecanut sellers	97,564	55,322	+ 76·3
121	Grain and pulse dealers	106,171	40,554	+ 161·8
122	Tobacco, opium, ganja, etc., sellers	4,615	2,972	+ 55·2
123	Dealers in sheep, goats and pigs	19,400	3,356	+ 478·0
124	Dealers in hay, grass and fodder	5,379	5,441	— 1·1
	34. Trade in clothing and toilet articles	*16,622*	*11,141*	*+ 49·1*
125	Trade in ready-made clothing and other articles of dress and the toilet hats, umbrellas, socks, ready-made shoes, perfumes, etc.	16,622	11,141	+ 49·1
	35. Trade in furniture	*7,670*	*20,606*	*— 62·7*
127	Hardware, cooking utensils, porcelain, crockery, glassware, bottle, articles for gardening, the cellar, etc.	1,553	15,477	— 89·9
	36. Trade in building materials	*1,260*	*2,253*	*— 44·1*
128	Trade in building materials (stones, bricks, plaster, cement, sand, tiles, thatch, etc.	1,260	2,253	— 44·1
	37. Trade in means of transport	*15,597*	*14,565*	*+ 7·0*
129	Dealers and hirers of elephants, camels, horses, cattle, asses, mules, etc., sellers (not makers) of carriages, saddlers, etc.	15,597	14,565	+ 7·0
	38. Trade in fuel	*25,880*	*2,437*	*+ 961·9*
130	Dealers in firewood, charcoal, coal, cowdung, etc.	25,880	2,437	+ 961·9
	39. Trade in articles of luxury and those pertaining to letters and the arts and sciences	*46,316*	*45,630*	*— 1·5*
131	Dealers in precious stones, jewellery (real and imitation), clocks, optical instruments, etc.	7,265	4,794	+ 51·5
132	Dealers in common bangles, beads, necklaces, fans, small articles, toys, hunting and fishing tackle, flowers, etc.	38,144	38,710	— 1·4
	40. Trade in refuse matter	......	......	......
	41. Trade of other sorts	*241,787*	*303,568*	*— 20·3*
135	Shopkeepers otherwise unspecified	239,765	276,102	— 19·0
138	Other trades (including farmers of pounds, tolls and markets	......	798	......
	VI.—PUBLIC FORCE	*164,398*	*104,312*	*+ 57·6*
	42. Army	*68,750*	*64,468*	*+ 6·6*
139	Army (Imperial)	5,554	22,227	— 75·0
140	Army (Native States)	63,196	42,241	+ 49·5

SUBSIDIARY TABLE VII.—Selected Occupations (1911 and 1901). *contd.*

Group Number.	Occupation.	Population supported in 1911.	Population supported in 1901.	Percentage of variation.
	43. Navy	......	......	......
	44. Police	*95,648*	*39,844*	+ *140·0*
142	Police	35,135	1,074	+ 3,171·4
143	Village Watchmen	60,513	38,770	+ 56·0
	VII.—PUBLIC ADMINISTRATION.	*346,184*	*508,037*	— *31·8*
	45. Public Administration	*346,184*	*508,037*	— *31·8*
144	Service of the State	4,567	12,967	— 64·7
145	Service of Native and Foreign States	130,881	156,971	— 16·6
146	Municipal and other local (not village) service	8,926	84,043	— 89·3
147	Village officials, and servants other than watchmen ..	201,860	254,056	— 20·5
	VIII.—PROFESSIONS AND LIBERAL ARTS. ...	*209,039*	*115,798*	+ *80·5*
	46. Religion	*101,187*	*41,128*	+ *146·0*
148	Priests, ministers, etc....	57,809	5,543	+ 942·9
149	Religious mendicants, inmates of monasteries, etc. ...	33,743	25,637	+ 31·6
150	Catechists, readers, church and mission service ...	2,217	3,032	— 26·8
151	Temple, burial or burning ground service, pilgrim conductors and circumcisers	7,418	6,916	+ 7·2
	47. Law	*6,863*	*6,984*	— *1·7*
152	Lawyers of all kinds, including kazis, law agents and mukhtiars.	6,835	6,052	+ 12·9
153	Lawyers' clerks, petition writers, etc.	28	932	— 96·9
	48. Medicine	*30,973*	*19,288*	+ *60·5*
154	Medical practitioners of all kinds, including dentists, occulists, and veterinary surgeons....	23,760	15,790	+ 50·4
155	Midwives, vaccinators, compounders, nurses, masseurs, etc.	7,213	3,498	+ 106·2
	49. Instruction	*23,574*	*9,856*	+ *139·1*
156	Professors and teachers of all kinds, and clerks, and servants connected with education	23,574	9,856	+ 139·1
	50. Letters and arts and sciences	*46,442*	*38,542*	+ *20·4*
159	Others (authors, photographers, artists, sculptors, astronomers, meteorologists, botanists, astrologers, etc.) ...	11,502	13,072	— 12·0
160	Music composers and masters, players on all kinds of musical instruments (not military) singers, actors and dancers....	33,774	23,934	+ 41·1
	IX.—PERSONS LIVING ON THEIR INCOME ...	*28,377*	*51,757*	— *45·1*
	51. Persons living principally on their income	*28,377*	*51,757*	— *45·1*
161	Proprietors (other than of agricultural land), fund and scholarship holders and pensioners.	28,377	51,757	— 45·1
	X.—DOMESTIC SERVICE...	*421,147*	*390,882*	+ *7·7*
	52. Domestic service	*421,147*	*390,882*	+ *7·7*
162	Cooks, water carriers, door-keepers, watchmen and other indoor servants.	406,181	371,738	+ 9·2
163	Private grooms, coachmen, dog boys, etc.	14,966	19,144	— 21·8
	XI.—INSUFFICIENTLY DESCRIBED OCCUPATIONS...	*380,148*	*1,524,628*	— *75·0*
	53. General terms which do not indicate a definite occupation.	*380,148*	*1,524,628*	— *75·0*
164	Manufacturers, business men and contractors, otherwise unspecified	6,828	9,652	— 29·2
165	Cashiers, accountants, book-keepers, clerks and their employes in unspecified offices, warehouses and shops.	8,073	101,804	— 92·0
167	Labourers and workmen otherwise unspecified	364,157	1,413,825	— 74·2
	XII.—UNPRODUCTIVE	*276,139*	*396,781*	— *30·4*
	54. Inmates of jails, asylums and hospitals	*3,428*	*9,077*	— *62·2*
168	Inmates of jails, asylums and hospitals	3,428	9,077	— 62.2
	55. Beggars, vagrants and prostitutes	*272,711*	*387,704*	— *29.6*
169	Beggars, vagrants, procurers, prostitutes, receivers of stolen goods, cattle-poisoners	272,711	387,704	— 29.6

SUBSIDIARY TABLE VIII.—Occupations of Selected Castes.

Caste and Occupation.	Number per 1,000 workers engaged on each occupation.	Number of female workers per 100 males.
Bhoi.		
Fishing and hunting ...	402	66
Field labourers	251	222
Cultivators	132	41
Domestic service	56	28
Others	159	60
Brahman.		
Arts and Professions ...	329	......
Cultivators	161	33
Public Administration ...	110	......
Others...	400	36
Chakala.		
Industries	800	85
Cultivators	80	44
Field labourers	63	140
Others...	57	53
Chambhar.		
Industries	480	38
Field labourers	235	154
Cultivators	68	68
Others...	217	59
Dewang or Koshti.		
Industries	603	42
Field labourers	131	171
Cultivators	105	56
Others...	161	69
Dhanger.		
Raisers of live-stock ...	447	38
Field labourers	234	142
Cultivators	171	54
Others	148	79
Dhobi.		
Industries	599	81
Field labourers	220	118
Cultivators	90	56
Others	91	86
Golla.		
Raisers of live-stock ...	479	49
Field labourers	256	287
Cultivators	210	76
Others	55	44
Goundla.		
Trade	723	61
Cultivators	129	46
Field labourers	112	176
Others	36	86
Hatkar.		
Cultivators	585	53
Field labourers	245	89
Others	170	61
Kalal.		
Trade	629	51
Cultivators	121	55
Field labourers	116	111
Others	134	56
Kapu.		
Cultivators	713	63
Field labourers	169	251
Raisers of live-stock ...	31	16
Public administration ...	9	......
Others...	78	56
Koli.		
Cultivators	560	87
Field labourers	251	161
Raisers of live-stock ...	33	81
Others...	156	59
Komati.		
Trade	827	44
Cultivators	101	73
Others	72	65
Kummara, Kumbhar.		
Industries	664	61
Field labourers	131	238
Cultivators	112	62
Others	93	59
Kurma.		
Raisers of live-stock ...	627	62
Field labourers	162	267
Cultivators	115	66
Others...	96	79
Lingayet.		
Trade	799	50
Cultivators	86	48
Income from rent of land ...	21	53
Persons living on their income	27	74
Others...	67	59
Lohar.		
Industries	594	26
Cultivators	110	71
Others	296	115
Madiga, Mang.		
Domestic service	419	41
Field labourers	365	181
Cultivators	113	67
Industries	13	42
Others	90	84
Mahar, Mala.		
Domestic service	400	56
Field labourers	333	184
Cultivators	129	56
Industries	10	89
Others	128	72
Mali.		
Cultivators	533	58
Field labourers	259	121
Income from rent of land ...	51	48
Others	157	55
Mangala.		
Industries	555	29
Cultivators	121	75
Field labourers	216	508
Others	108	88
Maratha.		
Cultivators	570	58
Field labourers	228	123
Income from rent of land...	50	26
Raisers of live stock ...	33	12
Domestic service	22	82
Others	97	72
Munnur.		
Cultivators	586	64
Field labourers	213	197
Domestic service ...	32	40
Labourers unspecified ...	25	188
Others	144	38
Mutrasi.		
Fishing and hunting ...	306	50
Field labourers	292	184
Cultivators	239	57
Trade	41	123
Others	122	59
Nahavi (Warik).		
Industries	528	20

SUBSIDIARY TABLE VIII.—OCCUPATIONS OF SELECTED CASTES—*contd.*

Caste and Occupation.	Number per 1,000 workers engaged on each occupation.	Number of female workers per 100 males.
Nahvi (Warik)—*contd.*		
Field labourers	199	249
Cultivators	128	70
Others	145	91
Panchal.		
Industries	775	29
Cultivators	120	95
Others	105	38
Rajput.		
Public force	477	40
Cultivators	163	51
Trade	67	51
Others	293	49
Sale.		
Industries	736	63
Field labourers	131	248
Cultivators	71	61
Others...	62	93
Satani.		
Arts and Professions ...	577	70
Cultivators	114	40
Others...	309	55
Sunar.		
Industries	723	22
Cultivators	87	69
Field labourers	95	321
Others...	95	66
Sutar.		
Industries	764	45
Cultivators	129	126
Others...	107	81
Telaga.		
Cultivators	504	60
Field labourers	263	181
Trade	54	36
Public Administration ...	11	......
Others...	168	52
Teli.		
Industries	589	54
Cultivators	108	51
Field labourers	102	108
Trade	78	77
Others	123	50
Uppara.		
Industries	512	76
Field labourers	186	165
Cultivators	134	55
Others	168	78
Velama.		
Cultivators	722	53
Field labourers	162	150
Others	116	53
Waddar.		
Industries	626	62
Field labourers	138	168
Extraction of minerals ...	41	76
Others	195	93
Wanjari.		
Cultivators	592	59
Field labourers	200	99
Income from rent of land ...	45	22
Others	163	164
Moghal.		
Domestic service	202	114
Cultivators	153	42
Public Administration ...	97	......
Public force	86	......
Others...	462	39
Pathan.		
Domestic service	159	49
Public force	112	......
Cultivators	135	48
Trade	103	23
Others	491	43
Sayyed.		
Domestic service	192	35
Cultivators	151	32
Public Administration ...	76	......
Public force	69	......
Others	512	41
Shaik.		
Cultivators	164	33
Domestic service	137	46
Field labourers	134	94
Public Administration ...	68	......
Public force	68	......
Others	429	31
Anglo-Indian.		
Public Administration ...	210	1
Arts and Professions ...	142	143
Others	648	19
Armenian.		
Contractors	1,000	......
European.		
Public force	470	......
Others...	530	6
Indian Christian.		
Field labourers	316	131
Domestic service	166	89
Cultivators	149	108
Trade	69	29
Raisers of live-stock ...	52	6
Others	248	37
Bhil.		
Fishing and hunting ...	270	28
Field labourers	153	201
Cultivators	76	31
Others	501	94
Erkala.		
Industries	184	54
Cultivators	167	43
Others	649	58
Gond.		
Cultivators	575	57
Field labourers	325	176
Raisers of live-stock ...	42	30
Others	58	84
Lambada.		
Cultivators	445	48
Field labourers	242	192
Transport	137	62
Raisers of live-stock ...	74	20
Others	102	84

SUBSIDIARY TABLE IX.—Distribution by Religion and occupation of 10,000 persons.

Order and selected groups.	Distribution by occupation of 10,000 persons following each religion.						
	Hindu.	Jain.	Musalman.	Christian.	Parsi.	Animist.	Others.
1	2	3	4	5	6	7	8
I—Exploitation of the surface of the earth	*6,399*	*3,310*	*4,823*	*5,334*	*1,413*	*8,650*	*2,779*
(a) Agriculture (Order 1, groups 1-6) ..	5,719	3,259	4,750	5,183	1,893	8,065	2,750
(b) Pasture (Order 1, groups 9-12) ...	508	44	82	57	...	67	25
(c) Fishing and hunting (Order 2) ...	89	...	23	21	...	56	...
(d) Others (Order 1, groups 7, 8 and 13.).	23	7	18	70	20	442	4
II.—Extraction of Minerals	*15*	...	*8*	*71*	...	...	...
III.—Industry	*1,515*	*854*	*741*	*754*	*615*	*94*	*286*
(a) Textile Industries (Order 6)	896	423	400	223	353	9	8
(b) Wood Industries (Order 8)	121	4	25	117	7	54	28
(c) Metal Industries (Order 9)	71	28	35	14	26	...	139
(d) Food Industries (Order 12)	89	56	111	20	137	5	...
(e) Industries of dress and the toilet (Order 13)	541	311	87	210	...	5	83
(f) Other Industries (Orders 7, 10, 11, 14 to 19)	297	32	83	170	92	21	28
IV.—Transport	*88*	*24*	*158*	*726*	*798*	*175*	*271*
V.—Trade	*870*	*4,167*	*738*	*330*	*4,120*	*356*	*330*
(a) Trade in food stuffs (Orders 32 and 33)	511	1,095	250	78	1,151	104	105
(b) Trade in textiles (Order 26)	58	730	86	57	26	7	32
(c) Other trades (Orders 24, 25, 27 to 31, 34 to 41)	301	2,342	402	195	2,913	245	193
VI.—Public Force	*80*	*1*	*485*	*604*	*105*	*4*	*1,252*
VII.—Public Administration	*214*	*107*	*670*	*412*	*903*	*29*	*2,078*
VIII.—Professions and Liberal Arts ...	*145*	*278*	*256*	*748*	*451*	*3*	*801*
IX.—Persons living on their income ...	*14*	...	*84*	*67*	*216*	...	*159*
X.—Domestic service...	*191*	*661*	*1,379*	*358*	*366*	*146*	*1,299*
XI.—Insufficiently described occupations	*275*	*259*	*326*	*508*	*1,007*	*417*	*254*
XII.—Unproductive	*194*	*339*	*332*	*88*	*6*	*126*	*491*

Order and selected groups.	Distribution by religion of 10,000 persons or each occupation.						
	Hindu.	Jain.	Musalman.	Christian.	Parsi.	Animist.	Others.
1	9	10	11	12	13	14	15
I.—Exploitation of the surface of the earth	*8,867*	*8*	*794*	*34*	...	*295*	*2*
(a) Agriculture (Order 1, groups 1-6) ...	8,792	9	858	37	...	302	2
(b) Pasture (Order 1 groups 9-12) ...	9,886	2	75	5	...	33	..
(c) Fishing and hunting (Order 2) ...	9,551	...	290	11	...	148	...
(d) Other (Order 1, groups 7, 8 and 13)...	6,296	4	591	90	1	3,018	...
II.—Extraction of Minerals	*9,189*	...	*597*	*208*	...	*6*	...
III.—Industry	*9,407*	*10*	*546*	*22*	...	*14*	*1*
(a) Textile Industries (Order 6)	8,888	17	1,066	23	1	5	...
(b) Wood Industries (Order 8)	9,620	1	228	44	...	106	1
(c) Metal Industries (Order 9)	9,427	7	550	8	...	...	8
(d) Food Industries (Order 12)	8,679	10	1,289	9	2	11	...
(e) Industries of dress and the toilet (Order 13)	9,782	10	188	18	...	2	..
(f) Other Industries (Orders 7, 10, 11, 14 to 19)	9,636	2	319	26	...	17	...
IV.—Transport	*7,676*	*4*	*1,634*	*294*	*9*	*373*	*10*
V.—Trade	*8,911*	*77*	*899*	*16*	*6*	*90*	*1*
(a) Trade in food stuffs (Orders 32 and 33)	9,361	545	36	7	3	47	1
(b) Trade in textiles (Order 26)	8,284	189	1,464	38	...	23	2
(c) Other trades (Orders 24, 25, 27 to 31, 34 to 41)	8,353	113	1,324	25	11	2	167
VI.—Public Force	*5,680*	...	*4,075*	*200*	*1*	*6*	*38*
VII.—Public Administration	*7,201*	*6*	*2,671*	*64*	*4*	*24*	*30*
VIII.—Professions and Liberal Arts ...	*8,062*	*28*	*1,690*	*194*	*3*	*4*	*19*
IX.—Persons living on their income ...	*5,761*	...	*4,070*	*129*	*12*	...	*28*
X.—Domestic service	*5,285*	*33*	*4,521*	*46*	*1*	*99*	*15*
XI.—Insufficiently described occupations	*8,407*	*14*	*1,186*	*73*	*4*	*313*	*3*
XII.—Unproductive	*8,154*	*26*	*1,661*	*17*	...	*133*	*9*